LEARNING-FOCUSED LEADERSHIP IN ACTION

In an educational context where school and district performance is of increasing focus, it's essential for leaders at all levels of the educational system to focus on improving student performance. This volume zeros in on a promising set of strategies and practices for all leaders to motivate, support, and sustain learning in contemporary schools. *Learning-Focused Leadership in Action* explores what it means for educational leadership to be "learning-focused," what this looks like in practice at both the school and district levels, and how such leadership changes can be set in motion. Drawing on extensive case study research in schools and districts that are making progress on learning improvement, this volume explores how leaders at all levels of the educational system can productively seek to improve the quality of learning opportunities and student performance, no matter how challenging the circumstances.

Michael S. Knapp is Professor of Educational Leadership, Policy, & Organization Studies and Director of the Center for the Study of Teaching & Policy at the University of Washington, Seattle, USA.

Meredith I. Honig is Associate Professor of Educational Leadership, Policy, & Organization Studies, Adjunct Associate Professor of Public Affairs, and Partner at the Center of Educational Leadership at the University of Washington, Seattle, USA.

Margaret L. Plecki is Associate Professor of Educational Leadership, Policy, & Organization Studies and Co-Director of the Center for the Study of Teaching & Policy at the University of Washington, Seattle, USA.

Bradley S. Portin is Director and Professor of the Education Program at the University of Washington, Bothell, USA.

Michael A. Copland is Deputy Superintendent, Bellingham Public Schools, Bellingham, Washington, USA.

LEARNING-FOCUSED LEADERSHIP IN ACTION

Improving Instruction in Schools and Districts

Michael S. Knapp, Meredith I. Honig,
Margaret L. Plecki, Bradley S. Portin,
and Michael A. Copland

Routledge
Taylor & Francis Group

NEW YORK AND LONDON

First published 2014
by Routledge
711 Third Avenue, New York, NY 10017

and by Routledge
2 Park Square, Milton Park, Abingdon, Oxon OX14 4RN

Routledge is an imprint of the Taylor & Francis Group, an informa business

Library of Congress Cataloging-in-Publication Data

Knapp, Michael S. (Michael Sturgis), 1946-
    Learning-focused leadership in action : improving instruction in schools and districts / by Michael S. Knapp, Meredith I. Honig, Margaret L. Plecki, Bradley S. Portin, and Michael A. Copland.
        pages cm
    Includes bibliographical references and index.
    1. Educational leadership.   2. Education—Aims and objectives.   3. Urban schools.   I. Honig, Meredith I., 1971–   II. Plecki, Margaret L.   III. Portin, Bradley S.   IV. Copland, Michael A.   V. Title.
LB2831.6.K53   2014
371.2—dc23   2013040680

ISBN: 978-0-415-71621-5 (hbk)
ISBN: 978-0-415-71623-9 (pbk)
ISBN: 978-1-315-88001-3 (ebk)

Typeset in Bembo
by Apex CoVantage, LLC

CONTENTS

FIGURES

TABLES

PREFACE

This volume was born over a decade ago, at a time when the quality and impact of leadership in schools and systems came once again into focus in national reform conversations. Significant philanthropic investment accompanied this wave of concern, prominently the set of investments made by The Wallace Foundation to support experimentation, developmental work, and related research on educational leadership. As part of its early investment strategy, several of us were asked by The Foundation to create a grounded framework linking leadership and learning. The results of our efforts, entitled *Leading for Learning: Reflective Tools for School and District Leaders* (Knapp, Copland, & Talbert, 2003) offered such a framework, a detailed sketch of a rich and intriguing territory that we have subsequently referred to as "learning-focused leadership." But it was only a framework, and it left unanswered many questions about what such an idea would mean in everyday practice.

Then, as now, educational reformers, system leaders, educational practitioners, and others were preoccupied with school and district performance, and generally assumed that leaders at all levels of the educational system were essential to improving performance—and growing evidence since that time bears out that assumption. But precisely how leaders are to pursue this goal remains elusive. This volume zeroes in on a promising set of strategies and practices that embody leaders' persistent, public embrace of learning and learning improvement—as both the goals and means for adults working within the system as well as for the young people the system seeks to serve, to achieve a better educational experience and result.

In a phrase or two, the volume answers these questions: What does it mean for educational leadership to be "learning-focused"? What does it look like in practice, at both the school and district levels? What changes in leadership practice and system design does such an approach entail, and how could such changes be set in motion? Our answers derive from our own recent case study research in various parts of the United States, through an extended national investigation (also funded by The Wallace Foundation) that allowed us to dig much deeper into this territory. Concentrating on schools and districts that were making progress in learning improvement, the volume offers images of how leaders at all levels of the educational system can productively seek to improve the quality of learning opportunities and ensuing results across an educational system.

The coordinated set of investigations on which this volume is based explored the practice of a variety of educational leaders involved in contemporary efforts to improve teaching and learning, among them school principals, teacher leaders, and instructional coaches, to name a few at the school level, and joined by the principal's supervisors, staff developers, district-based coaching staff, and even assistant superintendents who oversee efforts to improve instruction, at the district central office level. As our argument will make clear, many others—especially at the central office level—are also implicated in this learning-focused work. In short, the investigations on which this volume draws take the reader into the actual mechanisms of leadership practice and show how they are trying to guide the improvement of teaching and learning we are all searching for.

Reformers, practicing leaders, and other interested audiences will find in these "images of possibility" ways to think about the work of learning improvement, and also practical examples of how it is being done under the most challenging circumstances. Specifically, the volume is likely to appeal to educators at various levels of the educational system: school leaders (and not just principals); district-level and regionally based educators who are responsible directly or indirectly for improving the quality of learning opportunities and the results that accrue; and others located at state and national levels who take seriously the role that leaders may play in the improvement equation. Add to that a variety of other players who interface with the school system: leadership developers in universities, non-profit organizations, and other kinds of reform support organizations; staff of professional associations who seek to support the work of school and district leaders; and scholars whose research, teaching, and service aims at leadership, administration, reform, and related policy matters.

In our own work as university-based leadership developers, we have found continuing opportunities to apply the ideas presented here to the challenges of preparing the next generation of school and district-level leaders. A focus on learning and learning improvement permeates our work, and we draw continuously from the experiences and framing ideas assembled in this volume. Above all, we are reminded how much we, too, are learning in this process. Leadership is fundamentally about learning.

ACKNOWLEDGMENTS

The findings and thinking presented in this book reflect the contributions of many individuals and groups, and we owe them a great deal. First, we are especially thankful to The Wallace Foundation, our sponsors in this research and the earlier framework building which created a foundation for it, and, in particular, to Lucas Held, Kim Jinnett, Richard Laine, Mary Mattis, Lee Mitgang, Edward Pauly, Jessica Schwartz, and Jody Spiro, among other program staff, all of whom offered active support, encouragement, and constructive criticism. They set a high bar for our work and embodied the best of "engaged philanthropy" in support of educational improvement. They also invited us into this work as part of a wide-ranging "Leadership Issues" exploration process drawing together hundreds of leading practitioners, reformers, and scholars—our repeated interactions with this group helped build the foundation for our work and set the research in motion.

The research team we assembled (actually three overlapping research teams) had many members, and their collective efforts to assemble ideas, design the investigations, carry out the fieldwork, and make sense of what we found were the lifeblood of our learning about learning-focused leadership in action. Each chapter in this volume acknowledges those members of the team whose analysis and writing directly contributed in some way to the chapter's contents and argument (Lydia Rainey, Juli Lorton, Morena Newton, Felice Russell, Sue Feldman, Chad Lochmiller, and Tino Castañeda); however, many others played important roles in building the base of information on which our insights draw: Chris Alejano, Scott Dareff, Chrysan Gallucci, Jennifer Harris, Brenda Hood, Robin LaSota, Elizabeth Matson, Liza Pappas, Bethany Rogers, Judy Swanson, and Ling Yeh. And we all owe a great deal to Sylvia Soholt, for help designing and communicating what we learned, and to Angie Windus, for her patient and persistent efforts to keep this multiyear effort organized, logistically sound, and well accounted for.

Finally, the insights we developed and reported here reflect, most of all, the continuing efforts, often against significant odds, of hundreds of educators—teachers, instructional coaches and staff developers, instructional specialists, parent coordinators, principals and assistant principals, teacher leaders in a variety of old and new roles, central office coordinators and directors, assistant superintendents and superintendents, business officers, and human resource staff—in the seven school districts and 27 schools that generously served as case study sites for a year and half, in one or more of the three investigations we undertook. You spoke with us (more than 600 of you, across the three study strand investigations) and shared experiences, accomplishments, and conflicts; and you let us watch you work. To all of you, our deepest admiration for all that you have been able to accomplish in the service of improving the educational experiences and outcomes for a diverse population of young people. Thanks so much for letting us—and others—learn from you.

—Michael S. Knapp
Center for the Study of Teaching and Policy
University of Washington

1

INTRODUCTION

The Evolution of Learning-Focused Leadership in Scholarship and Practice

Michael S. Knapp

Picture the challenges facing a new school principal, committed to making education work for the students in his charge, in a context that puts substantial obstacles in front of the school. This account describes the principal's own reflections years afterward on the struggles he faced in working with his staff to improve instruction:

> ... Early on, [the new principal] tried to address the isolation and lack of teamwork among teachers. He tried to focus staff meetings on instruction, published a school newsletter that was largely about teaching, and revised the schedule so the teachers teaching the same grade level had the same preparation time, and, later, a weekly 90-minute team meeting. [But as the principal later reflected] "Morale never seemed to get out of the basement. Staff meetings gravitated to student discipline problems." In team meetings, "there was a strong tendency for the agendas to be dominated by field trips, war stories about troubled students, and other management issues, with little attention to using student work and data to fine-tune teaching." Almost inevitably, teacher pessimism was a significant barrier. "Discouraged by the visible results of poverty and having never seen an urban school that produces very high student achievement, many teachers found it hard to believe that it could be done. They regarded themselves as hardworking martyrs in a hopeless cause. . . ." (Payne, 2008, citing material from Marshall, 2003)

The staff in question were hardworking, largely veteran professionals, caught up in a cycle of demoralization and ineffective practice that their circumstances had fostered for many years. Above all, the school was unable to focus on the core matters of teaching and learning. One committed, energetic principal walking in the door was not about to change these circumstances. Though describing events that transpired more than a decade ago, this account speaks for many contemporary schools and many well-meaning school leaders, as they struggle to improve the quality of education for young people in schools located in a variety of urban and exurban settings.

Now add to the scenario the heightened expectations of high-stakes accountability, along with calls for educational practice that is data-based, the prospect of diminished resources, and an increasingly diverse population of students, many of whom enter school speaking a first language other than English. We visited a setting like this in the course of the research reported in this volume and asked a new third-grade teacher, barely two months into her first year of teaching in a challenging inner city elementary school, to talk about where she and others in the school were focusing their efforts at learning improvement. Without hesitation, she answered as follows:

> Okay, the priorities for learning. I believe that, well, first of all, in terms of subject, I believe reading, writing, and math are the utmost importance for the school. I believe that [the leadership team] speaks about differentiating our instruction to reach all kinds of learners, no matter what level they are at and no matter how they learn, what modality they learn by. We really want to collect data, make sure that everything is assessment-based so that we can see where they stand and what progress, if any, they are making. That is pretty much what I have been told by the school, which I think is exactly what we need to do. . . .[1]

Her answer communicates a wholly different image of the working ethos of the school she is in. Instead of demoralization, she communicates hope, clarity of purpose, and confidence. Her words express a sense of school-wide commitment and direction. It is clear that a leadership team has consistently communicated to her a productive way to think about her work and that of others in the school. This teacher's emerging view of the work ahead attends to the differences among school children and to a finely tuned way of teaching them, based in evidence about their progress. In short, she owns the goal of learning improvement and, despite her inexperience, she has a beginning sense of how to get there. Her response and other things we learned about this school give further clues about the sources of her view of her responsibilities, among them:

- *The school's leadership team placed priority on knowing the students as individuals*—as both learners and members of a cultural community.
- *A school-wide learning improvement "agenda" was in place*—a set of improvement goals generated and communicated by a leadership *team*, led by the principal and including assistant principals and several teacher leaders.

- *Regular instructional support was available to all teachers, especially novices*, offered by administrative leaders and several others in the school who had assumed newly reconfigured roles that offer instructional leadership.
- *The school had devised its own system for tracking students' progress, and for making regular adjustments in their learning experiences*, based on measures of their progress, that incorporated district tracking measures and other data the school found useful.
- *School staff shared responsibility for student progress*, reflected in a set of agreements as well as unspoken norms among school staff, to assume such responsibility and to accept that all will be answerable for their efforts to accomplish this goal.

Digging a little deeper takes one beyond this school's leadership, norms, and data systems to the larger district and state system in which the school sits. Several features of that environment further explain what has happened at this school:

- *The district central office had placed priority on assisting school principals in becoming strong instructional leaders*, while also helping the principal attend to other aspects of the management of the school.
- *The district reform plan granted the principal significant discretion (and some additional discretionary resources)* to define and deploy staff in ways that optimally support instruction, and to access resources for professional development. The principal had made use of this discretion to configure her leadership team and engage several external partners to help address particular instructional improvement issues.
- *Clear system-wide improvement expectations communicated from both the district and state* had set direction and lent urgency to the school's efforts on behalf of its students, an urgency this principal accepts and leverages in her dealings with her staff.

This school's scenario differs from the first image of demoralized school staff unable or unwilling to engage questions of improving teaching and learning. Not surprisingly, the second school showed clear evidence of student learning growth, where the first did not.

The second scenario raises numerous questions about what is at work and how it got to be that way. While many things are involved, at the root of them is the exercise of leadership—by many people at different levels of the system—that brings focus, resources, and effort to the task of learning improvement. At first glance, it is tempting to conclude that the committed, energetic principal of the second school is the primary explanation for the difference in the two schools, but to do so would miss the point (after all, the first school had one such leader as well). Such an assumption would miss, among other things, the fact that others inside the school share in the leadership work, some more visibly than others. And it would miss leadership at other levels of the system that empowers and guides the work of educators in the school. Finally, it would miss the distinction that all these leaders are *themselves* supported and led in ways that focus *their* leadership energy and attention productively on the improvement of teaching and learning.

Context for Our Learning About Learning-Focused Leadership

Research is beginning to probe the kind of leadership revealed in the second scenario. The chapters in this volume summarize what the authors learned from a multi-strand investigation, the *Study of Leadership for Learning Improvement*, which adds to the understanding of this realm of educational leadership (Knapp, Copland, Honig, Plecki, & Portin, 2010). Together, the three study strands in our research shed light on the questions:

- What makes the leadership of districts and schools most likely to contribute to learning improvement?
- To what extent, and how, do different leadership activities, structures, and practices focus others on a coherent improvement agenda and mobilize efforts in pursuit of it?
- Who or what supports leaders who are working to improve the quality of teaching and learning? What does that "leadership support" entail?

In approaching these questions, our research was guided by what we refer to as "learning-focused leadership," an overarching set of ideas related to what others have described as "learning-centered leadership" (Murphy, Elliott, Goldring, & Porter, 2006), "student-centered leadership" (Robinson, 2011), "leadership for learning" (e.g., Hallinger, 2011; Resnick & Glennan, 2002; Stoll, Fink, & Earl, 2002; Swaffield & MacBeath, 2009), and "leading for learning" (e.g., Breidenstein, Fahey, Glickman, & Hensley, 2012).[2] Our particular take on this way of characterizing leadership work, discussed more fully later in this chapter, focuses attention on *powerful, equitable learning* among students and professionals, and within the system as a whole. And, as we will argue in this book, both are connected to the idea of *leadership support*, that is, the existence of a system that provides assistance, resources, and guidance for learning-focused leadership work (Knapp, Copland, Plecki, & Portin, 2006; Portin, Knapp, Plecki, & Copland, 2008). As such, we assume leaders *need* support, at the same time that they provide it to others.

"Leadership" we define as the *shared work and commitments that shape the direction of a school or district and their learning improvement agendas, and that engage effort and energy in pursuit of those agendas.* In this respect we intentionally broaden the focus from the work done by individuals in particular roles (such as school principals or instructional coaches) to the collective work that groups of individuals and teams do. And as part of this conception we are careful to distinguish *leadership* from "leaders," "roles," or "positions," though the latter are instrumental in achieving the former, and as such figure prominently in our research. In short, we locate leadership in the relationships among people occupying various positions, though the positions people hold and the actions they take in those positions matter.

Across all, we pay special attention to what is variously referred to as "instructional leadership," broadly defined to include intentional efforts at all levels of an educational system to guide, direct, or support teachers as they seek to increase their repertoire of skills, gain professional knowledge, and ultimately improve their students' success. We, thus, subsume within this term much more than conventional images of instructional leadership that concentrate on individuals providing assistance, feedback, or guidance directly to teachers, as in the school principal engaged in "clinical supervision" or the teacher leader or instructional coach offering nonsupervisory "literacy coaching" (see Neumerski, 2013 for a review of research related to these roles). Rather, we are concerned about the full range of activities, carried out by various educators (including principals, coaches, and others) that offer teachers ideas, assistance, or moral support specifically directed at instruction, and that motivate or even compel teachers to try to improve. We further assume that instructional leadership is *inherently distributed* among different staff in the school building and across levels of the system—that is, more than one kind of individual or unit are intentionally seeking to influence teachers' work, whether or not they recognize and coordinate their respective efforts. These aspects of our thinking are located in several rich streams of scholarly work, as we explain more fully later in the chapter.

To explore the way these ideas show up in practice, the *Study of Leadership for Learning Improvement* took a close look at different facets of learning-focused leadership in large, complex school systems that were located in medium to large urban and exurban areas. The three study strands all relied heavily on qualitative inquiry strategies conducted over a year and a half (the 2007–08 school year, and the beginning of the following year) through repeated visits to seven districts and to a combined set of 27 schools within them, varying somewhat by the three investigations (not all districts or schools were visited for each investigation—see Methodological Appendix for a more detailed description of study methods and designs). The research teams for the three study strands accumulated hundreds of interviews, many observations of leadership events, and numerous archival sources that shed light on the leadership issues under investigation. The study strands investigated learning-focused leadership and how it is supported from these vantage points:

- *The development and exercise of distributed instructional leadership within the school.* This study strand profiled the activities of the full range of staff in the school engaged in leadership aimed at teaching and learning, both those in administrative positions (principals, assistant principals) and others exercising teacher leadership, either formally or informally, while also detailing the central role that principals play in this distributed leadership work (Portin et al., 2009).[3]

- *The transformation of central office work practices and the district-school relationship to develop and sustain instructional leadership capacity.* This study strand concentrated on the daily work of administrators throughout the central office as they transformed their work practices to help build principals' capacity for instructional leadership (Honig, Copland, Rainey, Lorton, & Newton, 2010).[4]
- *The investment of staffing and other resources in support of equitable learning improvement.* This study strand examined decisions made by district- and school-level leaders concerning the improvement of teaching and learning, and the dynamics of doing so when increasing equity was a goal (Plecki, Knapp, Castañeda, Halverson, LaSota, & Lochmiller, 2009).[5]

The three study strands examined these matters within districts and schools where leaders were engaged in proactive attempts to address learning-focused leadership issues. All three study strands focused on the same two district sites (Atlanta Public Schools and the New York City/Empowerment Schools Organization)[6] and selected schools within them. Each study strand added to these sites one or two others that offered useful contrasts related to the focus of investigation—Springfield, MA, and Norwalk-La Mirada, CA (for school leadership analyses), Oakland, CA (for central office transformation analyses), and Portland, OR and Eugene, OR (for resource investment analyses). Together, the study sites offered a wide range of contexts, all of which were making learning improvement a high priority, displaying promising practices and structures, and showing some evidence of progress (locally defined) in educating a diverse, impoverished urban population.

Despite the differences in the samples and in our approaches to studying them, the three study strands offer complementary insights into the exercise of learning-focused leadership and how it is guided and supported. Two sets of themes emerged from the study findings. The first concerns the practice of learning-focused leadership and what it means to bring it to bear in a more compelling way on instructional improvement. The second concerns the ways in which learning-focused leaders are themselves supported. And, as suggested schematically in Figure 1.1, leadership support is integrally connected to the practice of learning-focused leadership, and vice versa.

While the three-strand investigation offers the most detailed and systematically explored source for our learning, we note several others prior to and subsequent to the study that have also informed our thinking in important ways. For one thing, we all regularly teach in leadership preparation programs—all of us have been architects and core faculty of an Ed.D. program aimed at preparing leaders for school systems (e.g., superintendent, assistant superintendent, and other roles), and three of us have participated regularly in a principal preparation program as well (Ginsberg, Knapp, & Farrington, 2012; Jackson & Kelley, 2002). These efforts to develop a new generation of educational leaders have confronted us continually with questions about how leaders learn to lead and what precisely

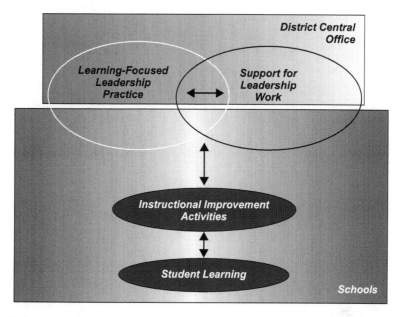

FIGURE 1.1 Learning-Focused Leadership Practice and Leadership Support Aimed at Instructional Improvement

they need to learn. And in this context we have continually tried out the ideas emerging from our scholarship. Furthermore, especially since the conclusion of the three-strand investigation, a number of us have done regular consulting work with school districts, a superintendent network, Foundation-supported reforming district networks, and even states, helping them address the issues and practices that learning-focused leadership entails. Finally, our relationship with The Wallace Foundation leadership initiatives over the years has brought us regularly into contact with a large number and variety of educational leaders, reformers, and participants in leadership development. All of these sources have offered us a way to continually test and refine our thinking about learning-focused leadership.

The remaining chapters in this book unfold what we learned from the three investigations and from these other sources regarding the two themes of the nature of learning-focused leadership practice and leadership support. But first let us locate our thinking and investigation in a longer stream of thought and activity by educators, reformers, and scholars, who have been hard at work for a long time on the problems we are tackling.

Leadership for Learning: Growth of an Idea

The questions about what educational leaders contribute to the ultimate outcomes of schooling—students' learning—have been with us forever, and necessarily so.

Why else put people in charge of a school or school system than to help the organization achieve its most central aim, that of educating young people effectively? But the nature of that linkage—between leaders, the leadership they exercise, and the results of the schooling enterprise—are elusive, and have generated decades of investigation meant to demonstrate what effective leadership is, enhance its presence in the system, and prepare people for it. While this body of research, now voluminous, has much to say about effective leadership, especially for individuals occupying particular roles like school principal, it has struggled with the fact that leadership effects are almost entirely indirect, though still potentially powerful.

The challenge is both conceptual (what exactly is the leadership work that can produce, directly or indirectly, the improvements in learning we desire? Who does it?) and empirical (what is the evidence that this sort of leadership does accomplish its goal?). Earlier generations of scholarship have met this challenge part way, and offered a cumulative line of insight into the nature of leadership in "effective schools" (Levine & Lezotte, 1990; Lezotte, 1994), and more specifically "instructional leadership," construed as a set of actions by the school principal that would set the stage for and guide better instruction in the school (e.g., Hallinger, 2005; Hallinger & Heck, 1996; Hallinger & Murphy, 1985). Other work has charted various leadership stances, styles, and qualities, providing us with a rich vocabulary for imagining how leaders engage others and through what means they seek to work their effects—for example, as captured in research on transformative, moral, and participative models of leadership as well as those that approach leadership in more managerial and contingent terms (Leithwood & Duke, 1999).

A Recent Decade of Work on Leadership for Learning

Building on this base, various scholars (ourselves included) have been at work over the past decade and more, in an attempt to carry the conversation about "effective leadership" further, to the point that the leadership at different levels of the educational system is more clearly described and linked to each other and with demonstrable learning outcomes. The connecting thread through all this work has been an explicit attempt to show how "leadership" (variously defined) and "learning" (also conceived in multiple ways) are connected to one another—and most of all, how leadership prompts, promotes, and enhances learning of both young people and adult professionals.

The decade of work has been accompanied by a rhetorical flourish, in which the phrase "leadership for learning" or a close synonym has been used so frequently, and in so many ways, that it has almost ceased to have specific or useful meaning. Numerous books, chapters, articles, research reports, and other documents bear that phrase or some equivalent in their titles, across a spectrum of meanings and purposes. On one end of the continuum is work that offers detailed practical advice to the practicing, school-based leader (e.g., DuFour, 2002;

Glickman, 2002) and on the other end, an organizational view of educational systems and what it will take to enhance their capacity to support ambitious learning (Schlechty, 2009). These efforts have produced work with very similar titles, though with different tag lines, signaling their particular focus—e.g., *Leading for Learning: How to Transform Schools into Learning Organizations* (Schlechty, 2009) and *Leading for Powerful Learning: A Guide for Instructional Leaders* (Breidenstein et al., 2012); *The Learning Leader: How to Focus School Improvement for Better Results* (Reeves, 2006) and *Leaders of Learning: How District, School, and Classroom Leaders Improve Student Achievement* (DuFour & Marzano, 2011); and *Connecting Leadership with Learning: A Framework for Reflection, Planning, and Action* (Copland & Knapp, 2006) and *Connecting Leadership and Learning: Principles for Practice* (MacBeath & Dempster, 2009). And by now, the body of literature is not only voluminous but also worldwide, with a growing body of international work (e.g., O'Donoghue & Clarke, 2010; Robertson & Timperley, 2012) and the recent appearance of several international handbooks of leadership for learning, the later one featuring 66 chapters from authors in over thirty countries (MacBeath & Cheng, 2008; Townsend & MacBeath, 2011).

What is missing from this body of work to date are systematic attempts to develop the conceptual footing of this generative idea and at the same time explore it empirically, *at multiple levels* (e.g., both school and district level), *across roles* (not just within the province of a single position, however central), *with a focus on actual practice* (not just role definitions, structures, policies, or the "infrastructure" of leadership), and *with a close eye to how leaders' actions and interactions produce learning*—for both young learners and adults. There are clear steps in this direction, among them, a recent national study that looked quantitatively and qualitatively at the links between leadership and student achievement at school, district, and state levels (Leithwood & Louis, 2012) and efforts to synthesize evidence across decades of research (primarily quantitative) on school leadership, mainly focused on the principal, to develop a "research-based model of leadership for learning" that identifies leadership dimensions and means that have demonstrable impacts on student learning outcomes (Hallinger, 2011).

To respond to this need, other serious scholarly work has proceeded, aggressively driven by certain forces and conditions in the United States. Among the catalysts for this work are the reform policy context and its push toward performance and greater accountability, substantial philanthropic investments in the improvement of leadership and leadership development (such as those by The Wallace Foundation, which supported our work), and growing concerns over the quality of leadership preparation (e.g., Levine, 2005). Prompted by and informing these conditions, several intellectual currents in the relevant fields have helped to build a stronger base for understanding leadership for learning.

Anchoring all of this work have been vigorous attempts to demonstrate in convincing ways that leadership contributes to student learning outcomes, as well as to identify what it contributes, how much, and how it does so. Building on earlier syntheses (Leithwood, Louis, Anderson, & Wahlstrom, 2004), recent empirical work demonstrates convincing linkages between leadership exercised at multiple levels of the educational system and student achievement and engagement (Leithwood & Louis, 2012). Especially at the school level, where the evidence base is the strongest, certain practices appear strongly and positively linked to student achievement (Supovitz, Sirinides, & May, 2010; Hallinger, 2011). Among those are elements emerging from a recent meta-analysis of studies linking leadership to student outcomes (Robinson, Lloyd, & Rowe, 2008): the principal's efforts to establish goals and expectations; align resources to priority teaching goals; plan, coordinate, and evaluate teaching and the curriculum; promote and participate in teacher learning and development; and ensure an orderly and supportive environment. These practices align well with other research syntheses over the past two decades (Hallinger & Heck, 1996; Marzano, Waters, & McNulty, 2003).

From this scholarly work emerge broad categories of leadership activity that set the stage for instructional improvements, which ultimately translate into student learning. Pursuing more specifically who is leading, how they are leading, and what they are focusing on, recent research on distributed forms of leadership, teacher leadership, and instructional leadership have been especially helpful. In particular, these streams of research have helped to conceptualize and understand how leadership can be "distributed" or "collective"; clarify the nature and role ambiguity of teacher leadership; explore further what instructional leadership means and who does it; and develop more integrated understandings of leadership work.

Conceptualizing and understanding "distributed" and "collective" forms of leadership. First, fully acknowledging both the centrality and the limits of the school principal's leadership role, scholars have been working on clarifying the contributions that multiple educators in the school (and to less extent, beyond the school) make in efforts to improve teaching and learning, as well as other facets of the school's functioning. A spurt of theory-building and empirical work across the last decade has helped to identify dimensions of distributed leadership work, pinpoint what functions or responsibilities might be distributed (or not), and sketch the forces and conditions encouraging or discouraging the development of distributed leadership (see Leithwood, Mascall, & Strauss, 2009 for a good summary of this research). This scholarship has also clarified a fundamental divide between scholars who approach leadership distribution in descriptive and analytic ways (e.g., Spillane, 2006) versus others who view the matter in more normative terms and hence are more concerned with whether and how school system leaders are, or should be, intentionally distributing leadership responsibilities (e.g., Mayorowetz, Murphy, Louis, & Smylie, 2009). These lines of scholarship have helped to see the "leader" as more than one person and leadership as inherently and/or intentionally shared among many, in relation to situations that bear most closely on the improvement of teaching practice, though the kinds of distribution at work can clearly vary by situation or function.

Clarifying the nature and role ambiguity of teacher leadership and its role in school and learning improvement. Alongside attempts to theorize and document distributed leadership has come a line of thinking and some data-based investigations of "teacher leadership" and its place and practice in schools seeking to improve (e.g., Lieberman & Friedrich, 2010; Murphy, 2005; Stoelinga & Mangin, 2008; York-Barr & Duke, 2004). Some of this research explicitly considers how teacher leaders figure in intentionally "distributed" leadership arrangements (e.g., Firestone & Martinez, 2007). At the core of this work is the attempt to make sense of the ambiguous, and sometimes contested, role that teachers take on who are positioned "in between" the classroom and supervisory leaders at either the school or district level. While noting some clear advantages to having accomplished teachers who are either formerly or currently still practicing in classrooms (often part-time) exercise teacher leadership, the research is only beginning to detail how such individuals establish a secure footing for their work, actually engage problems of teaching practice and leadership practice, and stimulate changes in teaching practice that actually improve student learning.

Exploring further what "instructional leadership" means and who does it. The previous two lines of research have considered, respectively, where leadership responsibilities and practice sit among multiple educators, and how it is exercised by particular positions (teacher leaders). In contrast, continuing work on instructional leadership focuses on *what* leaders aim at (instructional practice and how to improve it). Research on instructional leadership across more than three decades has developed a robust set of insights into what individual leaders do, especially school principals, working closely with individual classroom teachers to bring about changes in teaching practice that, in turn, produce improvements in student learning (e.g., Hallinger, 2005). A body of research on teacher leadership and instructional coaching is beginning to offer us similar images, though the connections to student learning have not yet been systematically traced (e.g., Knight, 2009; Taylor, 2008; Mangin & Stoelinga, 2008).

These insights accompany a broader picture of instructional leadership that encompasses "setting the stage" for instructional improvement, often through the principal's efforts to establish a supportive climate, communicate high expectations, coordinate curriculum, and monitor performance (Hallinger, 2005). Recently, scholars have begun to visualize this "core work" of school-based instructional leaders as evolving to address several kinds of "new work" necessitated by the demanding environment for contemporary schooling (Halverson, Grigg, Prichett, & Thomas, 2007; Knapp, Mkhwanazi, & Portin, 2012). These new dimensions of instructional leadership include: guiding teachers' efforts to address growing diversity of learning needs, embedding teaching (and instructional support) practice in data and evidence, working within and through instructional leadership teams, and engaging the school's environment as a useful resource for instructional improvement.

Developing more integrated understandings of the leadership work. Building on these lines of research are several that productively merge them with each other or with adjacent scholarship. For example, a merger of instructional leadership with transformational leadership notions provides a picture of a more "integrated" approach to leadership, whereby school principals and teachers come to *share instructional leadership* and engage in interdependent ways on efforts to improve curriculum and classroom teaching (Printy, Marks, & Bowers, 2009). A recent look at efforts to help high school department heads assume an instructional leadership role has offered a springboard for conceptualizing *distributed instructional leadership* and within it "the situated tools, tasks, and routines required to change and maintain improved teaching" (Halverson & Clifford, 2013). Other scholars are trying to understand the merger of principal, teacher leader, and coach instructional leadership, viewed from a distributive lens (e.g., Neumerski, 2013). And by marrying instructional leadership with several strains of adult learning theory, a recent rendering of the territory identifies how school leaders facilitate, and design for, learning as a fundamental part of the work that adults, as well as young people, do in the school building (Breidenstein et al., 2012). These and other writers also continue to probe how leaders learn, and how their stance as learners might be part of the leadership equation (e.g., Donaldson, 2006).

Our Frame: Learning-Focused Leadership

Our own way of approaching learning-focused leadership offers another way of integrating what principals, teacher leaders, coaches, central office staff, and others do to collectively bring energy, effort, direction, and resources to bear on improving teaching and learning. Our participation in these streams of work has generated a multilevel model of leadership that maximizes learning in educational systems. As explicated first in an empirically grounded framework document (Knapp, Copland, & Talbert, 2003), later expanded to book form (Copland & Knapp, 2006), and subsequently elaborated in a series of literature reviews that were summarized in several venues (Knapp et al., 2006; Portin et al., 2008), this line of thinking has tried to explore the relationship between leadership and learning in both conceptual and practical ways, as a multilevel, distributed set of arrangements and practices that makes student and adult learning both an explicit goal of leadership work, and a means for achieving educational system goals.

Our frame assumes that, at its root, "learning" is both a *result*, demonstrable as knowledge gained or performance mastered, and a *process*, knowable in the ways people participate with others in learning situations. It is something that leaders aspire to support, and it is also something that leaders *do* on a regular basis, within themselves, out of sight; with others collectively; and explicitly and publicly in their leadership roles. Finally, we assume that learning is both individual and collective, attained and demonstrated in groups and even organizations. Hence, ideas about learning pervade our thinking about learning-focused leadership in multiple ways.

As we have explained in greater detail elsewhere (e.g., most comprehensively in Copland & Knapp, 2006), our take on learning-focused leadership asserts that its target is always and simultaneously the learning of students, of adult professionals at multiple levels of the educational system, and of the system itself, conceived of as a "learner" (as organizational learning theories do). We use a simple figure (see Figure 1.2 below) to represent this leadership target.

The figure also serves to highlight several essential ideas about leadership that aims at this set of targets. First, each learning target is surrounded be a set of learning opportunities—in effect these are created, or at least can be created, by leadership actions of various kinds. In this respect, leaders, wherever they sit in the organization, are potentially the orchestrators of occasions for others' learning, and even facilitators of it. An essential leadership question then becomes: what constitutes the ripest opportunities for student, professional, and system learning, and how can we set these up and motivate participation in them? What arrangements and practices are most likely to facilitate learning within them? Second, the

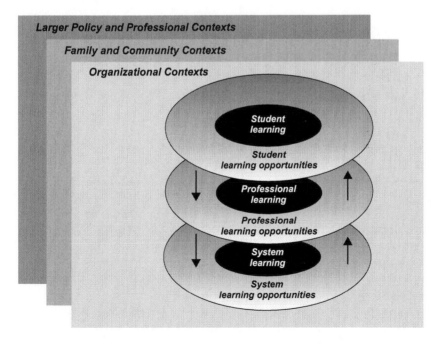

FIGURE 1.2 The Targets of Learning-Focused Leadership in Context

vertical arrows suggest that the learning within each domain potentially informs and can influence the others. The leadership questions become: in what ways does and can the learning in one arena shape or guide the learning in another, and how can we enhance the prospects for that to happen? Third, the learning occurs within multiple contexts that define the particular situations in which people and systems learn, offering resources and posing constraints on that learning, and giving everything particular local meaning. A different set of leadership questions arise: How can we attend to the events and conditions in the larger contexts that most permeate the work in the school or district? How can we constructively engage and respond to the aspects of these contexts that can enhance or impede learning?

Given a clear sense of the targets of leadership and how they are positioned in relevant contexts, our lens also draws attention to particular kinds of leadership actions that are most pertinent to fulfillment of the leadership promise to produce powerful equitable learning, especially five:

(1) Establishing a persistent public focus on learning (including the leader's own learning);
(2) Building professional communities that concentrate on issues of teaching and learning (including the professional communities to which leaders most naturally belong);
(3) Engaging external environments that matter the most for the learning of students, professional educators, and the system as a whole;
(4) Identifying strategic and mutually reinforcing "pathways" for exerting influence on learning targets, and collaboratively mobilizing effort along them to achieve learning goals; and
(5) Helping participants and constituents see how these efforts are coherently linked to each other and ultimate ends.

When leaders across an educational system act in concert in all these ways, substantial learning improvements are the likely result.

This basic formulation of premises and assertions left unexplored a number of more specific details about what learning-focused leadership might mean in practice. And in subsequent writing (e.g., Honig, 2008; Honig & Copland, 2008; Knapp et al., 2006), we tried to identify what these "loose ends" might be, and where the further work would lie. Six aspects of the leadership equation emerged and became a focus of one or more strands of the *Study of Leadership for Learning Improvement*. The first two concern the way learning-focused leadership work is arranged and what practices that work entails.

Leadership roles, structures, and arrangements in schools, district central offices, and how the two are connected. To realize learning-focused leadership as an attribute of the school system, not just an individual school, means paying close attention to existing leadership roles and arrangements (at the school and district levels); considering new roles and arrangements, where necessary; and redefining or repurposing others, so that throughout the system, there is a "persistent, public focus on learning" and learning improvement. Though structural changes, by themselves, are never sufficient to change behaviors, beliefs, capabilities, and ultimately outcomes, they are often a necessary step. The following are among the matters that shifting to a more learning-focused mode implies:

- *Examining the roles and positioning of teacher leaders inside of schools*, and sometimes across schools, to maximize their legitimacy in colleagues' eyes, access to teachers who need help, and ability to "lead from the middle."
- *Reconfiguring central office roles that sit at the interface between central office and the schools*, to provide a more consistent and useful connection to the school, while considering how other central office roles and arrangements serve the goals of learning improvement in schools.
- *Considering how to develop and sustain instructional leadership team arrangements within schools*, enabling them to operate as a team.
- *Growing the instructionally focused aspects of the principal's role* appropriately and feasibly to maximize this person's time and attention to instructionally related matters, while ensuring that the management of the school building gets taken care of.

Leadership practices. Structures, roles, and arrangements are empty shells, absent the attention to the actual work done within them. In this respect, leading in a learning-focused way means attending to the kinds of practices leaders in all of these roles engage in. In particular, within leaders' daily work are questions about how precisely one addresses both student and professional learning (as a target or reference point), how to do this work in ways that support others' learning, and how leaders use an explicit learning stance as a tool of leadership. Realizing these purposes is likely to involve a certain amount of reinvention, in areas such as these:

- In the ways members of school-based instructional leadership teams engage teachers, individually and collectively, in "instructional conversations" concerning current practice, student learning, and how either could be improved.
- In the interaction of school-based leaders and their counterparts in the central office, especially those who take responsibility for directly supporting school staff.
- In the ways school principals transcend the evaluative nature of supervisory practice, both in their direct work with teachers and through instructional leadership teams.
- At the interface of central office staff with each other, across traditionally established functional boundaries and divisions, and around issues that implicate their joint contributions to supporting learning improvement in schools.

Two more areas of activity implied by an attempt to realize learning-focused leadership concern leaders' orientation to information and resources and their capacity to bring these into line with priorities for learning improvement. Here, too, new practices likely need to be developed.

Data, evidence, and feedback on professional work, as part of leadership practice. Given that new practices are involved and new information are inherently part of learning, learning-focused leadership necessarily focuses on the information that actually flows among people and different units, how it flows, and what people do with it. The policy context for learning-focused leadership also demands increased and more formalized ways of working with data and evidence, and this adds to the imperative to build an appropriate data-related toolkit and make good use of data tools. Motivating and guiding any and all efforts with data is a climate supporting inquiry—the asking of questions that data can help answer. Leaders are in a particularly good position to foster this kind of climate and set inquiry related to learning improvement in motion. At least these issues deserve further understanding:

- How leaders on the "front line" of instructional improvement work use data, evidence, and related questions as part of their ways of engaging teachers, including those who are reluctant to consider data; simultaneously, how instructional leadership teams use data and evidence to understand their own work as productively as possible.
- How schools assemble various kinds and sources of data—what comes to them through official accountability routines as well as other sources—to address whatever questions they may have about teaching and learning.
- How school districts create an "infrastructure" supporting the use of data and evidence in instructional improvement—including timely and easily accessible data sources, and help with data interpretation.
- How data, evidence, and inquiry connect parts of the school system, and enable its "learning."

The equitable allocation and use of resources for learning improvement. Coherent leadership action along pathways leading to learning targets—not to mention the (re)deployment of leaders (some in new positions), support for their learning, and use of data and evidence in leadership work—all take time, money, expertise, and other resources, especially those bound up with staff, the basic human resource of school or district. Learning-focused leadership offers an important set of reference points for decisions about resources—student learning, adult learning, and the system's "learning"—which differ from those more conventionally referenced in resource decisions (e.g., last year's budget, the loudest voices in the staff meeting, the superintendent's pet projects). In an era of scarcity, with declining or stagnant sources of funding, these matters take on additional meaning if the school system is committed to maintaining or enhancing equity of opportunity and result. With this purpose in mind, learning-focused leaders need more detailed pictures of:

- How leaders can view resources as something that can be "invested" to yield a "return."
- What processes can be created for deliberating about the allocation of resources in relationship to learning improvement priorities.
- How resource allocations can enable the kinds of new practices learning-focused leadership entails, as well as the capacity to learn new practices.
- Whether and in what ways leaders can anticipate the inevitable pressures to direct resources disproportionately towards those who may need them the least (typically, the advantaged people in a school district community, who have the greatest visibility and voice).

Finally, two additional areas of leadership activity need attention if the principles of learning-focused leadership are to be realized: the first concerns the leaders' own learning and development, and the second, a system of supports for leadership work.

Leaders' own learning and development. To the extent that learning-focused leadership practice implies departures from prior ways of doing things, new professional learning is inevitable, as people in different leadership positions discover how to lead in a learning-focused way. If so, leaders' learning implies a supportive "learning environment," intentional efforts to facilitate their learning, resources and tools, and regular occasions for engaging in it. These learning needs are easily forgotten as school systems devote their time and attention to the primary categories of learners—students and teachers. But the system leaders will still need to figure out how leaders will get feedback on their own work that is meaningful and useful, not to mention how they will be introduced to new ideas about their work, no less be helped to try out and practice these ideas. Alongside these issues are others concerning how individuals are drawn into leadership roles (formal or informal) to begin with, so that they are positioned to "learn their way in" to leadership. In particular, the following need illuminating:

- Creating structures and regular occasions for the professional learning of teacher leaders or others in "mid-level" instructional leadership or coaching positions, especially those who are new to this role. Being an accomplished teacher is not, by itself, adequate preparation for being an accomplished guide for other teachers' learning.
- Engaging school principals in new learning about the practice of instructional leadership through individual and collegial avenues. This includes helping leaders learn what it means to do this work in the context of an instructional leadership team.

- Providing professional development support to central office staff, both those who interact with the schools directly and others who are reorienting their work practices to more explicitly support learning improvement in schools, albeit more indirectly.
- Creating more effective environments for ongoing learning about—and through—data related to student learning, teaching practice, leadership practice, and system functioning. Here, staff at all levels of the system are the learners.

A support system for learning-focused leadership work. The means for facilitating and supporting leaders' own learning, just discussed, comprise one crucial support for learning-focused leadership work, but there are others. To enact learning-focused leadership, especially for those who are new to it, means that leaders themselves need guidance, assistance, resources, and other forms of support. At both the school and district levels, then, systems are needed that anticipate the different kinds of support that can help leaders do their work, while identifying the means for providing the support. Here, too, new arrangements, routines, and practices are likely to come into play, and we need to understand better how leaders can:

- Intentionally develop lateral networks among educators at different levels of the system who can provide a range of peer supports (e.g., informal advice, encouragement, ideas and resources, and even "a shoulder to lean on").
- Formally legitimize and otherwise offer "political" support for learning-focused leaders' work, especially where these efforts are unlikely to be well understood or appreciated (e.g., for some "mid-level" teacher leader roles) or even resisted (e.g., where advantaged interests push back against efforts to allocate resources more equitably).
- Allocate resources to leadership work itself, alongside the allocations that go to the targets of that work.
- Discover the most effective means for providing regular, formative feedback to leaders on and about their work, preferably linked to the professional learning systems noted above.
- Develop teams and other arrangements that create collaborative work environments for individuals, in different positions and at different levels of the system, who share learning-focused leadership goals.

Learning-Focused Leadership in Action: Plan for the Book

The aspects of learning-focused leadership detailed above are as yet poorly understood. The field lacks images of what these can look like in practice, and what it takes to enable the exercise of this kind of leadership, especially in settings that face the most substantial challenges in educating young people. This book is our response to this need for more detailed and compelling images of learning-focused leadership in action.

In the ensuing chapters, we draw on the three strands of the *Study of Leadership for Learning Improvement*, supplemented by our subsequent writings that have extended the originally reported findings and our own work with school and district leaders, noted earlier in this chapter. We present what we have learned in three parts, each offering two chapters devoted to one of the three strands of the original investigation. Following that, we offer a concluding chapter that draws together threads from all the preceding ones. In specific terms, the chapters try to accomplish the following:

- *Part One*, addressing findings from the school-level strand, offers insights in to learning-focused leadership at the school level. The chapters deal with:
  1. The exercise of team-based instructional leadership in schools and the ways these teams pay collective attention to the improvement of teaching and learning in demanding contexts.
  2. How schools energize and sustain instructional leadership by creating a within-school system of supports for learning-focused leadership work.
- *Part Two* presents what we learned from the second strand of investigation, focused on efforts to fundamentally improve the ways district central offices relate to schools and attempt to enhance the quality of learning-focused leadership in the school. These chapters address:
  3. The way the district central office engages teaching and learning improvement system-wide, and what it means to fundamentally transform the central office to serve this purpose.
  4. Conditions that support central office transformation and its leadership of learning improvement, both within the central office and at its interface with schools.
- *Part Three* considers findings from the third strand of our investigation, concerning the allocation of resources at both the district and school levels, in the service of learning improvement. Specifically, the chapters address:
  5. What it means to invest in learning-focused leadership and to create a framework that supports this way of approaching leaders' work.
  6. Investing for equity in learning improvement at the school and district levels, in the face of predictable resistances and longstanding inequities in school systems.

A *Conclusions* chapter pulls together the joint story that these three strands of investigation surface. It reviews findings, first, concerning learning-focused leadership practices, arrangements, and investments, and second, those related to the system of supports for learning-focused leadership work. We then consider whether this way of approaching leadership across a school system really matters for the ultimate learning outcomes that everyone most wants from school systems, and what continuing challenges educators face who wish to create this kind of leadership system. We also step back from what the study revealed, to put these findings into context of ongoing efforts and debate about the improvement of teaching and learning in settings serving historically underserved students.

Notes

1 See Portin, Knapp, Dareff, Feldman, Russell, Samuelson, and Yeh (2009). Details of this case on this page and the next come from a school case portrait developed for this research.

2 These ideas build on others' work using similar terms, as noted in text. Others also use similar terms, though not necessarily in all the ways that we do—for example, Glickman (2002), who focuses primarily on the direct guidance that school principals (or others) offer their teaching staff; Schlechty (2009), who concentrates instead on how schools can be transformed into learning organizations; and Danzig, Borman, Jones, and Wright (2009), who emphasize leadership training approaches that foster learning communities. While these latter works do share some resemblances with our own, they were not central to the development of our thinking. More recent work, reviewed in this chapter, has continued to develop the idea in productive ways.

3 In addition to the original report of this investigation (Portin et al., 2009), subsequent publications that offer a more detailed look at specific aspects of the study findings include the following: Knapp and Feldman (2012); Knapp, Feldman, and Yeh (2013); Knapp, Mkhwanazi, and Portin (2012); Portin and Knapp (2011); and Portin, Russell, Samuelson, and Knapp (2013).

4 In addition to the original report of this investigation (Honig et al., 2010), more recent publications amplify what was found and offer further insights into central office transformation processes: Honig (2012, 2013); Honig, Lorton, and Copland (2009); and Honig and Rainey (in press).

5 A follow-up analysis has expanded on some of the report's work (Plecki et al., 2009): see Lochmiller (2012).

6 At the time of our study, all schools within the New York City Department of Education chose to be part of one of 14 "School Support Organizations" (SSOs), the segment of the District Central Office that offered the most direct support to the school. Our research concentrated on the largest of these SSOs, then called the "Empowerment Schools Organization" (ESO), which subsumed approximately 500 of the city's 1,500 schools. Our data came primarily from ESO schools and central office units, although some data from sources outside this SSO provided background to our analyses. Thus, we were not studying the whole of the Department of Education reform; NYC/ESO comprised the relevant "district" for most of our analyses.

PART I

Learning-Focused Leadership in Schools

This first part concentrates on the school, the unit most directly responsible for the education of young people. There, learning-focused leadership takes direct aim at the quality of teaching and learning in classrooms, and seeks to guide and support instructional improvement in a variety of ways. The resulting "instructional leadership" efforts, exercised by principals, assistant principals, instructional coaches, teacher mentors, data specialists, and others, engage teachers, both directly and indirectly, in reconsidering and renewing their practice in the classroom. Two facets of this school-level leadership are especially noticeable in schools that are improving how they work with students, and we devote one chapter to each. First, much, if not most, of the instructional leadership work in the school is *team-based* (Chapter 2), and second, this leadership work *itself* is well supported, at the same time that it provides significant support for instructional improvements (Chapter 3).

The chapters in this part explore these matters by assembling what we learned from school-level research in a set of 15 elementary, middle, and high schools across four districts about the way learning-focused leadership is exercised inside the school. This investigation, the first strand in the *Study of Leadership for Learning Improvement,* examined what it means for school principals, teacher leaders, coaches, and others to jointly take on and share instructional leadership in schools that are "making progress" (on locally determined measures) in their quest to educate a diverse, high-poverty student population more effectively. The schools were located in four districts—two of which were also included in the other two study strands (the Atlanta Public Schools and the NewYork City/Empowerment Schools Organization),[1] while two others (Norwalk-La Mirada, CA, Unified Schools, and the Springfield, MA, Public Schools) offered a comparable look at school-level learning-focused leadership in smaller or less urban settings.

The study design and methods, detailed in the Methodological Appendix and in the original study report (Portin et al., 2009), featured repeated visits to the sampled schools across a year and a half (the 2007–08 school year, and first part of the next) within a multiple-case design, relying largely on qualitative data sources. We repeatedly interviewed key participants in school-level leadership, observed them in various leadership events, and coupled that with a deep dig into archival sources for each case study school. In addition, we interviewed selected teaching staff, observed classroom instruction and classroom-based coaching, and solicited views of the schools from staff in the central office and reform support organizations that worked with the school. In sites that were shared with other study strands, we rounded out our understanding of what was happening in the targeted schools by drawing selectively on data collected for other study purposes.

We supplement what we reported in our original analysis of the study data with subsequent elaborations and further analysis that have appeared in print. Two book chapters clarify what we discovered about the learning of school-level supervisory leaders and nonsupervisory teacher leaders (Knapp, Mkhwanazi, & Portin, 2012; Portin & Knapp, 2011), and three articles appearing in journals focused on leadership and school improvement examine more extensively the teacher leadership dynamics in urban high schools, the response of learning-focused leaders in urban high schools to the demands of their environments, and the ways that leaders across all levels of schooling managed the intersection of external and internal accountability (respectively, Portin, Russell, Samuelson, & Knapp, 2013; Knapp, Feldman, & Yeh, 2013; and Knapp & Feldman, 2012).

This part focuses squarely on the school, with less attention to its numerous connections to a larger system of schools and the environment for public education. At the same time, we regularly acknowledge how learning-focused leadership in the school was intimately shaped by the district central office, external accountability expectations, and the other forms of interdependence with the larger environment. Because the ensuing two parts of this volume concentrate on the larger system, we leave a fuller discussion of the central office and its relationship with schools and the flow of resources through the system to later chapters.

Note

1 As explained in Chapters 1 and 2, we concentrated our research on a portion of this mega-city system, which had a distinctive organization for supporting the nearly 500 schools that were affiliated with it (see Methodological Appendix for a more complete explanation of the study samples).

2

TEAM-BASED LEADERSHIP OF INSTRUCTIONAL IMPROVEMENT IN DEMANDING SCHOOL CONTEXTS

Bradley S. Portin and Michael S. Knapp
With the assistance of Susan B. Feldman, Felice
A. Russell, and Catherine Samuelson

If nothing else, learning-focused leadership in schools concentrates on the act and quality of teaching—that is, on everything going on in and around classrooms that creates opportunities for learning and helps the full range of students take advantage of them. Some of the leaders' focus concerns the day-to-day interactions among teachers, learners, and content immersed in the "instructional triangle" within classrooms (City, Elmore, Fiarman, & Teitel, 2009). School leaders also concern themselves with what surrounds this interaction—such as an ethos across the school emphasizing learning improvement, the planning processes in which teachers engage both individually and in groups, and the forms and kinds of professional learning that all adults in the building do to make the instructional enterprise vibrant and productive. And all of this activity takes place in a demanding context, which leaders carefully watch knowing that they work in an environment of expectations, resources, and constraints that interact and cannot be ignored.

One thing is increasingly clear about learning-focused leadership in today's schools within the United States: it is not solo work. Various school-based staff within the school come together by design or more accidentally—sometimes in concert with each other, and sometimes not—and through joint effort set the tone and direction for learning improvement efforts in the school. These efforts among and with their colleagues constitute the primary *instructional leadership* of the school, whereby they foster instructional conversations, scaffold and motivate teachers' learning about their own practice, and introduce new forms of teaching practice. The school principal is—in principle—a central player in this work, as a robust line of research over the years focused on principals as instructional leaders has explored (see Hallinger, 2011 for a recent review). But as a growing body of work on distributed or collective leadership has begun to point out, the principal is not the only main player, nor necessarily the most central one (e.g., Bredeson & Kelley, 2013; Hallinger & Heck, 2010; Leithwood et al., 2009; Spillane, 2006). Any attempt to understand what high-quality instructional leadership entails means getting clear about how all participants in this function within schools organize themselves and do their work. That leadership activity, spread or "stretched" among multiple educators, can take many forms, some more intentional, coordinated, and coherent than others.

On the more coordinated end of the spectrum of collective instructional leadership activity lie *instructional leadership teams* of varying descriptions. Typically combining the efforts of school administrators with those of school-based instructional coaches, staff developers, and a growing cadre of teacher leaders, these teams bring together a potentially powerful combination of expertise and perspectives to bear on instructional and learning improvement in the school. But there is no guarantee that more cooks will make a better broth, and it is distinctly possible that the proliferation of these leadership resources in schools will yield much *less* than the sum of the parts, and be declared a waste of time.

Scholars have paid sporadic attention to instructional leadership teams over the years, but often as an attempt to coordinate decision making about instructional matters (e.g., Archibald & Odden, 2000), or to promote team-based school organization (Supovitz, 2002). In addition, advice and counsel to school principals often features discussions of team-building, support for professional learning communities, and the cultivation of an instructional leadership team as part of developing a strong school culture (e.g., DuFour & Marzano, 2011; Thacker, Bell, & Schargel, 2009). But rarely have researchers looked closely at how such a team—or multiple teams within a school—actually *lead* instructional improvement. We need to know much more about how instructional leadership teams form in schools, what they do, and how they become an effective force in moving a school towards achieving whatever learning improvement agenda it sets for itself. What conditions in the school support team formation and sustain its work over time? How do different kinds of participants, especially principals, assistant principals, designated coaches, and teacher leaders, work within and through the team to reach teachers? How do they influence instruction itself, and do so in a coherent way across the school? What challenges do they face in doing so, especially in schools located within demanding environments?

This chapter probes these questions, based largely on our work in the first strand of the *Study of Leadership for Learning Improvement* (Portin et al., 2009). In that investigation, we carried out intensive study of learning-focused leadership work in 15 elementary, middle, and high schools, located in four urban and exurban districts, chosen as schools that were making progress (by local measures) in educating diverse, high-poverty populations and that had configured their leadership resources to maximize attention to teaching and learning. In other words, we explicitly set out to get inside the exercise of collective instructional leadership in settings that would be likely to display it. Our investigation relied heavily on qualitative data sources gathered through repeated site visits to the schools across the 2007–08 school year and first half of the next (see Methodological Appendix for more detail on the study design).

Our argument unfolds in several stages. To begin with, we lay out the terms of our analysis and the background for doing so, based in several converging lines of scholarship. Following that, we review what we learned in three "layers" of activity, which we have identified in recent writings about instructional leadership (Knapp, Mkhwanazi, & Portin, 2012). The first we call the "groundwork" that provides a foundation for team-based leadership aimed at learning improvement in the school; the second is the "core work" of instructional leadership teams that engages teachers and others in rich conversation about their teaching practices and attempts to change it. Third, the "new work" of instructional leadership team activity reveals emerging dimensions of this facet of school leadership that the current circumstances of schooling demand. Finally, we conclude by reflecting on the challenges and prospects for effective instructional leadership teams as vehicles of learning improvement.

Because our focus here is on what happens inside of schools, the analysis and argument we present highlights the activities of school-based staff, as well as those shapers of activity that are most apparent at the school level. That said, we recognize and take note of the power and relevance of external forces for the instructional leadership work in schools. Chief among these "outside" influences are the efforts of the district central office staff, some of whom may provide a direct and continuous form of instructional leadership support for the principal and other school staff (see Chapters 4 and 5 in this volume; also Honig, 2012; Honig, Copland, Rainey, Lorton, & Newton, 2010; Honig & Rainey, in press). In this chapter, however, we concentrate on what school-based staff are doing inside of schools.

Thinking About Leadership in Schools That Prioritizes Learning Improvement

Making sense of instructional leadership teams in schools and what they can offer to improve teaching and learning has been greatly facilitated by a long line of research and working experience related to the way individuals—especially the school principal, but also others who take on "supervisory" functions—approach teachers in support of efforts to improve their craft. But more recent work, especially in the past decade, views school-based leadership in more collective or "distributed" terms, and paints a broader picture of instructional leadership that sheds new light on the players and the possibilities. Add to that a long established body of literature on team dynamics in organizations outside of education. All these sources help to illuminate team-based instructional leadership at the school level, and its simultaneous concern with student, professional, and system learning, as our overarching model of "learning-focused leadership" assumes (see the discussion in the introductory chapter of this volume; also Copland & Knapp, 2006; Portin, Knapp, Plecki, & Copland, 2008). A brief excursion through these views on the way school leaders focus on improving teaching and learning can help to characterize the groundwork, core work, and new work of school-based instructional leadership, especially as it is exercised by teams.

Instructional Leadership Exercised by Individuals: Principal, Coach, Teacher Leader

A stream of writing across the years aimed at defining and characterizing "instructional leadership" at the school level has concentrated on the school principal. This emphasis is natural enough, given that this individual has overall leadership responsibility for the school, and arguably can set the tone, direct resources, and engage this aspect of school leadership in many ways. The overall preoccupation of this stream of research and related practitioner advice is to sharpen the skills, knowledge, and mental frameworks of individuals occupying this central role in the school. The stream has deep roots in "effective schools" research (e.g., Hallinger & Murphy, 1985; Levine & Lezotte, 1990; Purkey & Smith, 1985) and represents an enduring idea, a "passing fancy that refuses to fade away" (Hallinger, 2005).

Over time, this line of work has helped to pinpoint key dimensions of the principal's instructional leadership and how it is practiced in schools (for a recent summary of these, see Hallinger, 2005). On the one hand, the principal's leadership can create a larger environment for instructional improvement activity by creating a shared sense of purpose emphasizing student learning, fostering continuous improvement cycles, coordinating curriculum or curriculum decision making, and developing a climate of high expectations, among other schoolwide activities (Hallinger, 2005). In addition, the principal's watchful eye (e.g., through monitoring of student learning and professional development cycles), visible presence, modeling the school's values, and shaping of a reward structure all can contribute, albeit indirectly, to instructional improvement. Taken together, these activities help to build the "groundwork" that supports efforts to guide, direct, and support instructional improvements.

On the other hand, the principal's instructional leadership implies some direct work with teachers, convening or engaging instructional conversations, as well as helping to scaffold and motivate teachers' professional learning about pedagogy, the content they teach, and how they assess learning. These forms of more direct engagement with teachers are all parts of the "core" work of instructional leadership. Principals have a natural opening for doing so in their capacity as staff supervisors, but a broadly construed instructional leadership role goes well beyond what might happen in the annual teacher evaluation cycle, a mainstay of supervision.

More recent lines of investigation have concentrated on other individuals, and their exercise of instructionally related leadership in schools—chiefly, as teacher leaders (Lieberman & Friedrich, 2010; Lieberman & Miller, 2004; York-Barr & Duke, 2004) and instructional coaches (Gallucci, Van Lare, Yoon, & Boatright, 2010; Knight, 2007; Taylor, 2008). From these lines of inquiry come descriptions of leadership practice as teachers and coaches engage in it, how teachers develop a "leadership identity," learn to do this work, and come to survive in their often fragile or ambiguous position within the school. Yet the focus typically remains on the practice and positioning of individuals occupying these relative new niches in the ecology of the school.

Emerging Collective Views of Instructional Leadership

By stages and in different ways, the field has begun to understand the exercise of instructional leadership in schools as a *collective* endeavor, distributed among multiple people by design or default (Nordengren, 2012). Accumulating ideas about distributed leadership (as assembled in Leithwood, Mascall, & Strauss, 2009) offer one vantage point on collective leadership, as do related ideas about "shared leadership" (e.g., Lambert, 2006), "collaborative leadership" (Hallinger & Heck, 2010), and several versions of "transformational leadership" which emphasize collaboration and the building of staff capacity and commitment (e.g., Bass & Avolio, 1990; Marks & Printy, 2003). Other research attempts to capture how various individuals, in aggregate, exert collective influence on student learning (Leithwood, Patten, & Jantzi, 2010). These and other converging lines of inquiry acknowledge that principals can't do it all, and they are—or need to be—intricately linked to others in efforts to focus leadership energy on both learning improvement and the school's *capacity for improvement* (Hallinger, 2011).

Visualizing instructional leadership as joint activity. At the heart of the emerging set of distributed leadership theories is a tension between treating "distributed leadership" or "collective leadership" as a conscious, intentional strategy (typically orchestrated by the school principal) or a fact of school life, a way of describing how multiple individuals, interacting with each other and with their immediate context, jointly "construct" guidance for instructional improvement, whether or not they intend to (Mayrowetz, Murphy, Louis, & Smylie, 2007; Spillane, 2006). These images of distributed effort also differ in how they visualize the participants project an instructional vision, mobilize instructional expertise, and engage directly with teaching and learning in classrooms.

Drawing on these roots in various ways, the field has begun to articulate models of instructional leadership that presume joint effort, though not necessarily overt collaboration. In one view, traditional instructional leadership theories join with transformational leadership thinking to characterize a "shared instructional leadership" in which principal and teachers develop an interdependent relationship in addressing matters of curriculum, instruction, and assessment in the school (Bellamy, Fulmer, Murphy, & Muth, 2007; Printy, Marks, & Bowers, 2009). This "integrated" model of leadership highlights the mutual influence that all participants exercise over instructional improvement processes. In another instance, a more descriptive model of *distributed instructional leadership practice,* specifically focused on high schools, offers a more developed picture of the social and situational "distributions of practice" that comprise leadership tasks and tool use (Halverson & Clifford, 2013). Together, these models of instructional leadership work refocus attention, away from the principal, instructional coach, or department head, and towards an interactive engagement of actors (including these individuals) in the joint enterprise of reconstructing how students are taught and how professional educators learn to do their work more effectively.

One way or another, these distributed images of instructional leadership—at least, those that presume an intentional distribution of effort—often imply that it will be exercised within and through a team structure of some kind. This can mean existing organizational structures, such as a school Site Leadership Council or Leadership Team, grade-level teams (in elementary schools and some middle schools), and subject departments (in high schools). However, by tradition and also mandate, these existing structures typically address a full range of administrative matters, and may not be particularly tuned to or focused on instructional improvement per se. As suggested by recent examples of the development of high school departments as instructional leadership teams led by a chair who takes on an explicit role as instructional leader chairs, the transition to an instructional focus is not a simple one (Kelley & Salisbury, 2013; Klar, 2013).

Understanding the dynamics of teams in schools. In a generic sense, organizational teamwork and team leadership are well studied, and we know a great deal about how they operate effectively (Larson & LaFasto, 1989) and what it takes to lead them (Hill, 2006). Here, the research base helps to establish basic principles of team building, group dynamics, and the maintenance of effort; and the research moves understanding beyond team structures for administrative delegation purposes. Regardless of task or purpose, successful work teams, for example, are characterized by a results-driven structure, competent team members, unified commitment, collaborative climate, standards of excellence, and external support and recognition, among other attributes identified through exhaustive study of a wide range of organizational team arrangements across sectors, not mainly in educational contexts (Larson & LaFasto, 1989). This line of scholarship also zeroes in on key leadership actions associated with the team, such as those related to defining and addressing the team's task (goal focusing, structuring for results, and training team members), others aimed at improving team relationships (e.g., building commitment, managing conflict, satisfying individual members' needs), and still others that help that team manage its relations with its environment (e.g., advocating, networking, buffering) (Hill, 2006). Seen from this perspective, "team leadership" refers to the guidance exercised by individuals who act as the team convener(s), supervisor(s), or facilitator(s). But these generic understandings don't address what it means and takes for the team to act as a *collective leader* in an educational organization, and more specifically what this entails when the focus is instructional improvement. And these views tend to treat the team in isolation from its context, relegating to the team leader the job of managing the team's interface with the outside world.

A More Demanding Context for Instructional Leadership

The context for school-based instructional leadership is asserting itself in increasingly prominent ways that are intimately connected to what instructional leaders try to do and how they approach their work. Research on the contemporary context of reform, especially related to accountability policies and the education of historically underserved populations, helps to define what makes the school environment "demanding," and underlies the efforts by some observers to describe instructional leadership in settings that serve a racially and culturally diverse and generally low-income population (Knapp, Feldman, & Yeh, 2013). In urban classrooms, for example, where growing student diversity is keenly felt, instructional leaders find themselves helping teacher colleagues develop classroom practices that recognize diversity and help students succeed who bring different needs, prior learning, and backgrounds to school (Ylimaki, 2007). This presents a different and inadequately understood challenge to instructional leadership: helping teachers imagine and enact instructional strategies that address the acute learning needs they face each day.

The local and state policy environment surrounding the school also adds to the demanding context for instructional leadership. Specifically, this environment offers instructional guidance (sometimes mandating both the content of instruction and how it should be taught). In addition, it sets up accountability systems and consequences for failing to meet expectations, at the same time pressing educators to engage in data-based practice (Knapp, Feldman, & Yeh, 2013). The presence of people exercising instructional leadership in schools may also be part of the state or local theory of action guiding reform efforts. These matters have already begun to reshape the nature of instructional leadership practice, as seen in the way leaders build and use data-driven instructional systems to more systematically guide teachers' efforts to improve (Halverson, Grigg, Pritchett, & Thomas, 2007). Taken together, the community served by the school and the policy environment are major forces in creating the new work instructional leaders undertake.

A Working Definition of Instructional Leadership

Drawing from these lines of scholarship, we fashioned the following definition of instructional leadership to guide our research: *the shared work and commitments that provide direction for instructional improvement, and that engage the efforts and energy of teachers and others in pursuit of powerful, equitable interactions among teachers, learners, and content, in response to environmental demands.* This way of conceiving of instructional leadership work embraces a collective vision of the leadership work—in fact, locating the "leadership" in the interactions among key participants—and takes full account of the school's environment as intimately connected to this leadership work. This definition prepared us to identify the groundwork, core work, and new work of instructional leadership teams in the schools we studied.

Our year and a half tracking of leadership work in schools that are "making progress" helps to paint a picture of the team-based instructional leadership in action and to identify conditions supporting its growth, as well as issues confronting this form of leadership in schools that take learning improvement seriously. We review below what we learned about the presence and work of team-based instructional leadership within the three broad categories, each of which differently emphasizes certain players and highlights particular practices.

Laying the "Groundwork" for Team-Based Instructional Leadership in the School

The groundwork, or foundational steps, that leaders take to set team-based instructional leadership in motion are part and parcel of broader, school-wide leadership work that has long been associated with high-performing schools. As such, the school principal figures prominently in all of these steps, if not being the main player in making them happen. In these ways, much of this work has been well anticipated by cumulative images of the principal as instructional leader and generic literature on team dynamics discussed above. In particular, we encountered four kinds of "groundwork" steps taken by school staff, which established: (1) team focus on learning improvement, (2) team-oriented school culture, (3) team formation and membership, and (4) team "space," including the time and legitimacy the team would need to operate with each other and with their colleagues across the school. Not all schools reflected these in equal degree, but all had addressed them to some extent.

Focusing the Teams on Collaborative Learning Improvement

Building a school-wide learning improvement agenda and prioritizing collaboration were basic building blocks for all team-based instructional leadership, as perhaps for all school leadership, as various scholars have asserted (Hallinger, 2011;

Robinson et al., 2008). In response to district expectations and their own visions of what their schools needed, principals and other instructional leaders typically approached their work with a vision of themselves as leaders of a school-wide and school-specific learning improvement agenda. This agenda involved many people and a range of activities that activated the school's efforts in pursuit of learning improvement priorities.

The learning improvement agenda created a common reference point for everyone's work in the school, especially the instructional leadership team, as it foregrounded the particular aspects of the instructional program that everyone in the building needed to work on. When coupled with a priority placed on collaboration, the stage was set for team-based effort, if not a more general belief that "we are all in this together," and "working together we can do better." Understandably, these matters were generally catalyzed by the school principal, but rarely imposed (doing so would have negated the emphasis on collaboration). Rather, they emerged from group deliberations of various kinds.

While the school-wide learning improvement agenda in the buildings we studied often featured goals aimed at specific subject areas, levels, or aspects of pedagogy (e.g., focus on writing skills, go after the lowest performing students in math classes, integrate special education services more effectively into primary grade classrooms), it also presumed that staff shared some broader priorities. The principals we studied actively articulated such an agenda, which communicated three basic priorities underlying all instructional improvement work: a belief in student *and* staff capabilities as learners and teachers; the alignment of curriculum, instruction, and assessment; and an assumption that collaborative dialogue and problem solving was a key to improvement.

Prioritizing belief in student and staff capabilities. As one anchor for the school's improvement work, principals communicated their deeply held core beliefs about student capabilities and the school's capacity to improve these capabilities. Echoing the notion that vision and goals are a central part of leadership for learning (Hallinger, 2011), the principals' high expectations for students and staff were rooted, first of all, in a persistent and publicly declared belief that all students can succeed, and to do so meant improving both academic performance and behavior. A number of principals across our sites emphasized discipline and order at their schools in addition to prioritizing student support and academic rigor, in line with another well established dimension of school leadership that positively affects student outcomes (Robinson et al., 2008); others inserted "character education" or its equivalent into the curriculum as a means of teaching appropriate ways for students to manage their behavior. The combined message about students was powerful, and how it was heard by teachers echoes the conclusions of a long line of research on the role of beliefs in effective schools and schooling (e.g., Corbett, Wilson, & Williams, 2002; Levine & Lezotte, 1990;

Zohar, Degani, & Vaaknin, 2006). A middle school teacher described how the administrative team's high expectations had translated into what she expected of herself and her students:

> My expectations have increased every year. I've learned that as long as you support them, there is really nothing [the students] can't do, no matter what their language level is. I know the expectations in my class have changed. I think they've changed school-wide. The conversations I now have with my colleagues are no longer resignation with low scores—instead of "They are still just writing summaries," now it's "How do we get them to analyze?"

Prioritizing the alignment of curriculum, instruction, and assessment across grades and content areas. The alignment of curriculum, instruction, and assessments across grades and content areas held high priority as a means to improve instruction and test scores. Though teachers were playing the primary role in this work, at most schools, administrators or other instructional leaders were working alongside teachers to guide and support them in achieving this alignment. One middle school teacher acknowledged that during her first two years of teaching, staff meetings and team meetings sometimes felt like a waste of time because "everyone was doing something different." Once she and her colleagues developed grade-level "curriculum maps," their team meetings had greater focus and teachers began asking for more team time.

Prioritizing collaboration. The method for achieving alignment, let alone developing norms that emphasized high expectations as a school-wide value, often meant working together to figure out where and how to coordinate effort. Mirroring activities characteristic of a transformational approach to leadership (Printy, Marks, & Bowers, 2009), principals and other instructional leaders commonly expressed a desire or expectation for the school to work together as a team, a community, or as a family. A school administrator in Atlanta explained this emphasis on collaboration:

> From what I have seen with collaborations . . . those teams that come together and they collaborate and plan and make those decisions and bring their problems or ideas to the table, I'm saying that they work like a well-oiled machine, and the result of that you can see that in student behavior, student conduct, and student achievement.

Specifically, principals expected teachers to collaborate with one other and with administrative staff on various activities geared towards improving instruction and student performance, such as developing and aligning curriculum, instructional practices, and assessments; problem solving; and participating in peer observations.

Many schools also expected collaboration among administrators and across the school in general.

Fostering a Team-Oriented School Culture

Efforts by leaders to develop trust and community, and within that a team-oriented culture, extended the priority placed on collaboration to the point at which it became internalized and assumed by all or most of the school staff. Relational trust has been well established as an attribute of high-performing urban schools (e.g., Bryk & Schneider, 2002), and the dynamics of cultivating trust among staff, between staff and administrators, and between the school and community have been explored extensively (see Tschannen-Moran, 2004). By extension, this foundational element undergirds instructional leadership team effort, both as part of their internal work with each other, and in their efforts to engage colleagues across the school in instructional improvement efforts. School leaders, and especially the principal, were central to the process of building and affirming a culture that emphasized trust in each other.

Trust building. Taking specific steps to build trust was one key to achieving a sense of community in support of school-wide learning improvement work. The principal and other supervisory leaders worked at changing the supervisory relationship, for example, from one largely concerned with formal classroom visits for performance evaluation purposes, to a relationship emphasizing informal connections in the classroom (Orr, Byrne-Jimenez, McFarlane, & Brown, 2005). In many of the schools, leaders espoused the idea that "everyone is a teacher," and that understanding the work and experiences of teaching and bringing the teacher's perspective into instructional leadership work can be very powerful for the development of trust and credibility between instructional leaders and teachers.

Having or creating open-door policies across their schools also enhanced the leaders' prospects for engendering a sense of trust. Leaders in many instances were continually accessible to staff, students, and families, and teachers opened their doors to other teachers and instructional leaders. One middle school principal in New York City described his open-door approach to his own leadership and its connection to fostering leadership across the building:

> I try to model, and I really do use, feedback in all its forms to make my decisions as a school leader. So in that sense, the idea is that there's access, pretty much open access to me. And the fact that I listen to the staff and I take what they say pretty seriously means that anybody who is willing to open their mouth can be a faculty leader of the school and be in an influential position. You know if I don't hear you, it's hard for me to know that, but if I do, then your concerns are definitely going to be heard and probably acted upon, in the sense that it will affect school policy.

Other principals and supervisory leaders described communicating attention to teachers' needs and respect for their concerns through regular hallway conversations, casual interactions, invitations to accompany them to a meeting out of the building, and other means of maximizing the communication between supervisory leaders and staff. The net effect appeared to be more connected and trustful staff.

Building team-oriented cultures. Building trust among school staff depended on the school leaders' efforts to realize the school-wide priority placed on collaboration. The idea or value of working collaboratively—on teams, working groups, standing or ad hoc committees—had not always been well established in the schools we studied. The reasons for dysfunctional working cultures in urban schools are understandable and have been well documented (e.g., Payne, 2008). Alongside their efforts to prioritize collaboration and address trust in the building, the principals, aided by other administrative staff, made improvement of the work culture a central target of their efforts to lead a learning improvement agenda. Some had arrived at their job feeling that they needed to change a toxic culture at the school to do what they needed to do. Others spoke of "building a culture," "moving toward a culture," or "leading a culture change."

Some schools had already made significant cultural changes, while others continued to be a work in progress. Some of the cultural challenges, or what they identified as needing to change, included teacher isolation and closed doors, "negative teachers," "maverick teachers," uncommitted teachers, and teacher resistance. To counter the tendencies toward teacher isolation, negative energy, and fragmented effort in the school, school leaders worked to develop team-oriented cultures, where everyone was expected to do their part as members of one or more teams and work together toward the same goals.

To foster this kind of culture, leaders focused on both creating a positive school climate and building a sense of community in the school. At schools where teamwork across the school was evident, principals were deliberate about creating a positive environment and encouraging school staff to work together and help each other. One teacher noted that her principal "cares about the climate of the whole school," a comment that could have been made about most the principals we studied. Key aspects of positive school climates included a sense of student and staff safety; respect for all members of the school community, without regard to the professional status or position; an upbeat, welcoming, solution-oriented, no-blame, professional environment; an effort to invite and involve staff in various school-wide functions; and a parallel outreach to students that engaged and involved them in a variety of activities.

Team Formation and Membership

While in a few cases teams that exercise instructional leadership may form spontaneously and informally, the vast majority come about by conscious assignment or invitation. Following a decision that such a team needs to exist, the principal in most cases lines up participants by inviting, cajoling, pressuring, or simply telling them to join XYZ team. Team formation and the initial terms of the team's mandate may well reflect more than the principal's design and orchestration of staff; in more than half of our schools, the impetus for a specific kind of instructional leadership team came from decisions made outside of the school, whereby district leaders encouraged or compelled the school to create school-based teams with an explicit focus on instructional improvement, leaving it to the principal to make this happen. In a few instances, the districts even created and filled new instructional leadership positions and assigned them to schools, thereby forming the nucleus of an instructional leadership team (see Chapter 6 in this volume and Plecki et al., 2009 for more detail on this kind of district-level investment process).

Teams of various kinds were formed in the schools we visited. Consider the following range:

- *School-wide professional development team.* At one elementary school in New York City, the instructional coaches were major participants in the school's professional development team, along with the principal, assistant principals, assessment coordinators, and mentors. This team met weekly to discuss the professional learning needs and strategies for meeting them. Led by the principal, the team represented a reconfigured and expanded version of the former school leadership team, which had been devoted largely to administrative matters.
- *Principal's "extended cabinet."* In a different school serving grades 7–12 in the same district, teacher leaders joined what the principal called her "extended cabinet," comprising the principal, two assistant principals, the lead math teacher, the literacy coach, and the teacher leaders responsible for subject departments. The cabinet's task was to figure out how to guide and support teachers' classroom practice.
- *School literacy teams.* In Norwalk-La Mirada, an elementary principal planned building-level professional development activities in literacy with her administrative TOSA (teacher on special assignment) and the district literacy coach, but involved teacher leaders in three grade-defined "literacy teams" to develop particular professional development sessions that occurred several times across the school year.
- *Inquiry teams.* In all New York City Schools, a district-wide mandate (see Talbert, 2011, for a more detailed account of this city-wide initiative) required each school to constitute an "inquiry team" to "increase the sphere of success" of a group of struggling students they identified, and then to develop and assess a targeted intervention designed to improve these students' achievement. In all the New York schools we studied, inquiry teams formed and took on their task of inquiring into the learners' struggles, using a variety of inquiry tools— e.g., low-inference observations, teacher and student interviews, review of

student work—that heretofore they had not used extensively or at all in that setting.

- *Team Time.* In one Springfield, MA, elementary school, a team of three "instructional leadership specialists" (ILSs) worked in collaboration with the principal and assistant principal to lead weekly grade-level meetings called "Team Time." Leadership was shared among members of the team with the ILSs providing most of the organization and maintaining the focus solely on instructional improvement and student learning.

The membership of these teams thus varied considerably across schools and, often by design, brought together people with expertise in different subject areas, knowledge of data tools and how to work with data, and working experience in various leadership roles. Teacher leaders of several descriptions worked alongside principals as members of these instructionally focused leadership teams. In most cases, these teams met on a regular, often weekly, basis. As members of an instructional team, the participants took on the task of diagnosing and addressing instructional improvement issues on the school's learning improvement agenda, or even identifying these issues to begin with.

Especially in the larger schools in our sample, more than one instructional leadership team came into being with overlapping or otherwise linked mandates. For example, the schools with multiple "Lit Teams" (each with teacher leaders located at a different grade level, a literacy coach and regular participation of at least an assistant principal and sometimes the principal) tightly connected the work of each team to an overarching literacy improvement thrust anchored to notions of balanced literacy. Some other multiple team configurations implied a looser relation among them, as in the school that featured a professional development team and a school-wide inquiry team, alongside several curriculum redesign teams.

Creating "Space" for the Team to Work

Composing instructional leadership teams was only meaningful if steps were taken to dedicate time (and sometimes physical space) for team members to work with each other on a regular basis, and also for particular events (e.g., professional development sessions) they would want to undertake with teachers around the building, where these events were other than the normal routine of school life. Other resources such as money and materials were also implied, though the availability of the right kind of time threaded through the complex scheduling of everything else in the school was paramount. Schools were remarkably creative in creating the time and space for team activity—among them, adjusting the master schedule so team members had common prep periods, taking over other meeting slots, carving out early or late-in-the-day periods, taking advantage of early release days (where these existed), negotiating the use of "prep periods" for meetings, and using enrichment teachers, in effect, as "substitutes" to allow some core academic teachers to attend their team's meetings. Generally in the hands of one of the school administrators, whoever was adept at managing and adjusting the master schedule, the creation of space for teams to work together was a high priority matter in these schools.

But beyond having or making the time to work as a team, the team's existence and potential success as a collective instructional leader depended on them being legitimized, occupying an understood and accepted position in the building, and undertaking a kind of work that all saw as important to the school's success. Efforts to legitimize and normalize the work of the instructional leadership team thus became a central part of the "support system" school principals created to enable this kind of work to continue (we elaborate on this issue in Chapter 3 of this volume).

The "Core Work" of the Instructional Leadership Team

Though their team mandates differed somewhat, all of the teams tackled the core work of instructional leadership on two levels. First and throughout, team members *engaged each other*, as collaborators in the enterprise of leading others toward more powerful and equitable forms of instruction. As part of this, they had to figure out what each other thought and assumed about good instruction, what it meant to lead, how to confront the various problems of leadership practice they came up against, and finally how they could be a *team* as contrasted with a collection of individuals, a task that was relatively new to many participants. In addition, in some instances—especially true of the New York City inquiry teams—team members needed to figure out exactly what their joint task was, as it had no precedent in their working experience. Second, team members *engaged teachers directly* in a variety of ways, both individually and in groups. Through these encounters, they projected their collective capacity for supporting improvement work around the building in a variety of venues—often one-on-one in the classroom or prep room, sometimes in group professional development sessions or staff meetings, and sometimes in "professional learning community" (PLC) groupings, where these had been established. In these settings, team members tried to focus teachers on instructional improvement issues, motivate and scaffold professional learning, and otherwise engage in the instructional conversations that are so central to reconsidering and improving one's practice.

Engaging Each Other

To be a team rather than a gathering of individuals took effort, group awareness, and team leadership, often by the principal, but not always. Lead coaches took on this responsibility, as did assistant principals in some instances, and occasionally outsiders (consultants, district office staff). Leading a learning improvement agenda meant working with—and through—a group of individuals, all of whom brought different ideas, experiences, and expertise together in the service of instructional improvement work.

Melding these into a cohesive team effort was not a simple task. For all these things to happen productively and in a mutually reinforcing way, principals or their counterparts needed to act, and see themselves, as leaders of an instructional leadership team—a "leader of instructional leaders" (Glickman, 2002, p. 6)—as much as, or more than, the sole or chief instructional leader of the school. It is not a foregone conclusion that multiple people in the building exercising some form of instructional leadership will be a net benefit to the school, especially if not tied to a larger system plan to spread leadership for learning beyond the principal. In fact, given the ambiguities and tensions that frequently accompany emerging teacher leadership roles (Lieberman & Miller, 2004)—it would be easy for different individuals to work at cross-purposes, fail to take advantage of each others' expertise, or simply miss the opportunity to be a *team*—that is, more than the sum of the parts. This question confronted those who took on the leadership of instructional leadership teams, such as the principal of a large New York City elementary school, whose main instructional leadership team contained four different kinds of instructional leaders. His assistant principals had considerable supervisory experience working in conventional staff evaluation capacities; three content coaches brought instructional expertise related to math and literacy, three "assessment coordinators" were experienced teachers with particular training and expertise in reading and interpreting student data, and several Inquiry Team members (who also participated in the main team) were simply experienced teachers from different grade levels. How were they to understand the work that each other was doing, and meld their efforts so that teachers were receiving consistent and coherent guidance and support across the building?

Alluding to the groundwork described earlier, which set the stage for collaborative work, this principal and other instructional team leaders we studied took steps to create and sustain viable teams by:

- *Managing the distribution of expertise.* By recognizing and formalizing complementary strengths and expertise, members of the instructional leadership team could develop interdependence. In the case above, particular individuals had extensive experience working with data, while others did not; some were steeped in balanced literacy instruction, while others were not; and so on. The team structure created regular occasions for the members to tap each others' expertise and to bring their collective expertise to bear on central problems of instructional improvement practice.
- *Structuring and hosting regular team dialogue about teaching and learning.* While the members of the team participated on different team structures across the building, all were members of a cross-cutting Professional Development Team

that met weekly, convened by the principal. He saw this team as his primary vehicle for guiding the instructional improvement work of the school, and used it as a teaching opportunity on numerous occasions.

- *Adjusting team members' roles to accommodate their experience and learning.* In part as a way of managing the ambiguities in learning-focused teacher leadership roles and in part as a response to unanticipated developments in the school's improvement work, the principal was in a position to reconfigure the team members' roles as needed. Two such reconfigurations were necessary moving into the 2008–09 year: a redefinition of the Assessment Coordinator position so that it could assume a greater staff development function, and the creation of a Curriculum Coordinator position to help manage some of the cross-cutting improvement work that the content coaches were unable to handle.

In addressing these matters, the person assuming the leadership of the instructional leadership team often took on a *teaching* role, that of teaching others how to lead. One high school principal created a systematic way of teaching team members a certain approach to instructional leadership, in a situation in which he shared instructional leadership responsibilities (beyond formal supervision) with his assistant principals [APs]:

> Well, the first week I walked through [classrooms] with each one of my APs. I took one AP with me and we walked through and I asked them what they saw to see if they were looking at the same [thing as me]—plus we have a little guide that was kind of developed by a couple of administrators and throughout the district. It's just a check-off list, and these are the things that we're looking for, and then we make little comments down at the bottom—what we saw the teacher doing and what we observed the students doing, and we leave it in their box. And the reason we don't . . . photocopy it, is because we shared with them that we were not going use this as an evaluative tool.

In this instance, school administrators who had formal supervisory responsibility were using that position as a platform for a more informal, non-evaluative support to teachers. As such, this more descriptive exercise lent itself to the professional development of leadership team members. Here, and elsewhere, the principal was doing this work in the context of an instructional leadership team, and using the opportunity to meld the efforts of different instructional leaders into a more cohesive influence on instructional practice than they might otherwise be. Not all principals were as comfortable in such a direct teaching role, nor felt they had sufficient expertise to be the primary voice in the building on instructional improvement matters. Where this was the case, the principals delegated or otherwise ceded the team lead to others, while watching carefully to make sure that the team was doing its job.

Through these kinds of steps, principals or others could bring team colleagues with different talents and experience together into a functional working relationship with one another and with the overarching learning improvement agenda to which they were—or could become—committed.

Engaging Teachers Directly and Indirectly

As they worked on becoming a team, the members put the bulk of their effort into their main work itself: connecting with teachers around the school building, in a variety of modes, seeking to help the teachers recognize and confront problems of instructional practice and experiment with resolving these problems. This direct work with teachers took many forms. Supervisory and nonsupervisory team members tended to approach the work somewhat differently, bringing their differing strengths and positioning to bear on the task at hand, while facing different challenges.

How supervisory team members engaged teachers. Whatever their skills at and propensity for working directly with teachers, in and out of the classroom, the principals and other supervisory leaders understood the limits of their own capacity to serve the instructional improvement needs of the entire school, as established by research on the principalship (Portin, DeArmond, Gundlach, & Schneider, 2003). As one assistant principal in an elementary school put it:

> My intention for the day is always to be in classrooms. The reality of my day, most of the time, is dealing with discipline problems or going to meetings, or like today, I'm meeting with you and this afternoon I have the [arts organization meeting]. . . . As far as my informal [interaction] or the walk-throughs that I plan, a lot of times those are disrupted by discipline problems, a parent's here, or we have to do this meeting, or this has to go out today—those kinds of things.

The size and complexity of this school, not to mention limitations on the principal's base of instructional expertise, prohibited him from providing direct instructional support to all teachers who needed it. Furthermore, the sharing of a learning improvement agenda presumed and was nurtured by a team-oriented culture, which principals were fostering, as noted earlier.

But even with these limitations, the principals in the schools we studied and assistant principals (where their role was explicitly focused on instruction) tended to remain active in direct instructional leadership work with teachers, both as part of the formal teacher supervision process required of their jobs and in a variety of more informal ways. And they made a conscious effort to push this set of connections beyond the annual evaluation cycle, while using it as an entry point. Formal observation processes in the annual cycle can support capacity-building efforts in a number of ways. For example, having identified teacher or grade-level and content area team strengths and weaknesses, supervisory leaders were able to address areas of weakness in follow-up conversations and support activities as a means for improving teacher practice. They also could tap areas of strength to direct peer support to other teachers, grade levels, or content areas. Further, school leaders could identify staff members with particular leadership qualities to further develop instructional leadership capacity in the school.

Outside any formal evaluation process, principals and other supervisory leaders tried to be present in classrooms on a regular basis, often somewhat spontaneously and lasting only a few minutes, though sometimes these occasions were more structured. One assistant principal in Atlanta offers an example of the former:

> If I'm only in the classroom for 5 minutes—that's observation by walking around. It doesn't have to be 20 minutes or 30 minutes. You can go in and just scan the room and see what you need to see or what you're looking for. . . . I try to organize it such that I'm touching on a little bit of everything daily.

Informal observations were often treated as part of the leaders' daily or weekly routines, in response to identified needs or staff requests or as follow-up to professional development, as a New York elementary principal put it:

> Every day we're in classrooms, not teaching, but it's part of our culture that we just walk in all the time so they're used to us. . . . I will sit and I just take notes and the times—see, 3:02; 8:55—so I just walk in and I just sit and see, and then they don't get intimidated because they already know.

An elementary school principal in Norwalk-La Mirada reviewed the different reasons she might observe a classroom—just to stay in touch ("pop in to classrooms"), respond to requests (teacher says: "I'm doing this today . . . can you come in?"), or to check on a particular practice ("I haven't seen you do a shared reading for a while. Can I? When are you doing one?"). Regular "learning walks" following a preset observation-and-debriefing protocol were used in some instances to check more systematically across classrooms for a particular practice, such as objectives written on the board or particular instructional strategies leaders wanted teachers to be using. The point of both the formal and informal interactions between supervisory leaders and teachers was to generate instructionally specific conversations that gave teachers a clear sense of what to work on and how.

Supervisory leaders also connected with classroom teachers through professional development, both as leaders and participants. One principal explained how he works with new teachers through study groups in the fall and spring. During each series of sessions, he and the teachers read a book focused on a particular content area, such as writing in the fall and math in the spring, then met regularly and discussed the book together. A teacher from another school described monthly professional development led by an assistant principal intern:

> I think it's once a month we have a morning session—and they do it by subject area—so we have a group of all the math teachers, and it's led by [our intern assistant principal], so he leads our professional development and basically talks about different strategies of differentiation and then has us take our lesson plans and insert or alter them so that they include those strategies, and we kind of practice doing that. Then we bring them in and teach them in our own classes, and then, in the next session, we'll talk about how it went or how we've been able to work those strategies into our teaching on a more consistent basis.

The supervisory leaders' professional development work could happen in classrooms as well, though their time was typically limited to observing teachers. Some of these leaders modeled instruction or coached teachers, working with small groups of students or teaching lessons, as an assistant principal recounted:

> And so I provide teachers with support, and that support could be in the form of doing professional development or one-on-one. It could be in the form of having a workshop or an eighth-grade and Special Education team meeting. It could be in the form of modeling for a teacher, co-teaching with a teacher—really whatever the teacher's needs are in order for him or her to work with students. I'm here to make sure they get whatever they need.

While most supervisory leaders described these kinds of practices as professional development for teachers, one principal highlighted the kind of professional learning she experienced through her work with teachers and students in classrooms: "For example, when we had the reading and writing workshop, in order for me to supervise anybody, I had to understand what the teachers were going through. They were learning it, I was learning it." Echoing the established relation between positive student outcomes and the principal's promotion and participation in teacher learning and development (Robinson et al., 2008), she used her engagement as a participant in professional development as a way of modeling the learning she wanted them to do, while also establishing credibility in their eyes ("She knows what she is talking about!").

How nonsupervisory team members engaged teachers. The other members of the instructional leadership team (e.g., teacher leaders, data specialists, assessment coordinators, instructional coaches), who lacked a supervisory role and who were more numerous, did the heavy lifting on most of the direct coaching, professional development, and teacher support. They typically worked as individuals, often one-on-one with selected teachers, sometimes in small groups or larger groups. Here, their positioning—as teacher colleagues, not administrators—both created challenges for their work while allowing them to reach teachers more directly than their supervisory colleagues. At best, their efforts complemented that of their supervisory counterparts.

As nonsupervisory staff occupying positions that were often new or poorly understood, and not necessarily well accepted, nonsupervisory members of the instructional leadership team spent a great deal of energy forging relationships and gaining acceptance. When teachers take on leadership roles, they are positioned in complex ways between their own and others' frameworks, beliefs, and understandings about instructional work (Leander & Osborne, 2008). Assuming a teacher leadership role for the most part challenges traditional norms of school life, such as norms of privacy and noninterference that exist among many teachers (Lortie, 1975; Murphy, 2005), which can be a source of tension between teacher leaders and their classroom-based colleagues. What the teacher leaders we were studying encountered mirrors the findings of descriptive studies of instructional coaching: to be effective in their role, coaches need skills in communication and relationship building (Gibson, 2006; Knight, 2006), and their learning is mediated by the relationships that they are able to establish on the job (Lowenhaupt & McKinney, 2007).

Building such relationships hinged on establishing trust and providing supportive conditions for teachers' professional learning, and helped to mitigate the tension that arises in their work. A teacher leader in an Atlanta elementary school noted:

> The main thing is to give support and instruction so that we can have student achievement . . . whatever it takes. . . . If it's resources you say you need, we try to get that. If you want an idea or suggestion, [you can ask], "What do you want me to do with . . . this comment on my lesson plan? What do you mean by that and give me an example?" As I said, the thing that gives me the most joy is when I can get into that, because . . . [then we're] making a difference. I really think that's what the district wants us to do and I think that's where we're trying to go with all of our many, many other tasks. . . . That's what we're here for—to support the teachers.

Providing support for teachers—"whatever it takes, whatever you need"— facilitated the relationships and trust that the teacher leaders sought to foster with the teaching staff. Even so, by acting as a source of support, teacher leaders could be seen as more of a supervisory administrator; in such instances, helping teachers to understand that they played a supportive rather than supervisory role was a challenge, as a teacher leader in Springfield noted, "Some of [the teachers] think that I am [the principal], but I'm not; I am a teacher like them."

Understandably, the ability to connect with teachers on a teacher-to-teacher level and form comfortable relationships where evaluation was not a factor seemed to contribute to the ability of teacher leaders to have an impact on teaching and learning at the classroom level. In this respect, they had an advantage that principals and other supervisory staff did not possess.

Assuming they could strike the right relationships, nonsupervisory members of the instructional leadership team created a wide range of occasions for engaging teachers' thinking and learning about their teaching practice. These occasions included professional development activities that involved individual teachers, groups of teachers, or whole-school professional development. In all cases, these professional learning activities were centered on a set of goals related to the school's (or district's) learning improvement agenda. Although some teacher leaders engaged groups of teachers in more traditional organizational structures, such as content area, department, or grade-level teams, they also worked with groups of teachers in newly conceived structures focused on specific aspects of the school or district learning improvement agenda. Groupings of teachers such as these provided numerous opportunities for discussion and dialogue, thus encouraging professional learning; in these settings, teacher leaders were especially well situated to prompt and guide that discussion, as noted in recent research on instructional coaching (Gallucci et al., 2010).

A key to these forms of engagement with teachers in the building was the degree to which the efforts of different members were well articulated with each other, and thereby seen by staff as part of a larger course of action across the school with school-wide and district-wide backing. Given the large amount of time that they spent interacting with their other team members, more often than not, the different members of the team were, relatively speaking, "on the same page," articulating a common vision of improved instruction and in line with the overall learning improvement agenda. While there was no guarantee of this, the result in these schools was a high degree of coherence.

The "New Work" of the Instructional Leadership Team

Three other forms of engagement, intertwined with those just described, characterized the work of the instructional leadership teams in the schools we studied. Because these forms of engagement have been seldom recognized in writings about instructional leadership, and driven to some extent by relatively recent developments in the schooling enterprise, we refer to them as the "new work" of instructional leadership (Knapp et al., 2012). In a curious way, they may represent a response to forces and conditions that have pushed for a more expanded and coherent instructional leadership presence in the school. The three concern: (1) the growing intensity and diversity of learning needs in these schools, as in many schools across the country; (2) the growing availability of, and press for, the use of data and evidence in instruction itself, as well as in instructional leadership; and (3) the greater intrusion of external demands and constraints, as well as some opportunities, in the larger environment of the schools. Instructional leadership team members engaged each one in noticeable ways.

Engaging Diversity

The growing diversity of student populations, not only in urban settings like the ones we were studying but also in exurban, suburban, and rural settings, is widely recognized as a major set of challenges facing classroom teachers. The issues this fact raises are nowhere more clearly seen than in the rapid increase in English Language Learners (ELL) (National Clearinghouse for English Language Acquisition, 2011), all of whom speak another language at home, and many of whom struggle at various stages of English language proficiency in schools, compounded by race and poverty (Ladson-Billings, 1999). Though we did not sample for this, 12 of the 15 schools we studied served a substantial population of ELL students. Understandably, lacking specific training for this population, teachers in the schools we studied, as elsewhere (Lucas, 2011; Moll, Velez-Ibanez, & Greenberg, 1990), were often at sea, wondering how to reach and teach this specific group, as well as worrying about how to effectively engage the full range of students who had been historically underserved by their schooling. This concern was only one example of a broader pattern in which teachers were puzzled about how they could meet the variety of learning needs they confronted each day.

The instructional leadership teams took this challenge on by focusing teachers' attention on individual student needs and differences, and the ways that a teacher could address those differences within the same classroom. In simplest form, the differentiation of instruction that school leaders sought to inculcate addressed low test scores by targeting instruction to measured gaps in particular students' knowledge, identified by test score item analysis or some in-class assessment. The approach was straightforward, as a teacher leader in one of the Atlanta schools explained:

> Let's say we did a skill last week and some students didn't do well on the quiz—that would be their focus in their center activities. And then I kind of monitor and see … some teams are … reassessed the very next week, and some students I wait maybe two weeks to reassess them. So they're working on the skills—that's what their homework is about, because every student doesn't have the same homework. So they may have that homework as practice and they get reassessed either the following week or the week after that. So it just depends on how they're grasping it.

Instructional leaders pushed teachers to seek out a strategy the student might respond best to, then use it to re-teach the material, and following that, determine the results by retesting the students. In some schools, students were regrouped for interventions or given additional help (e.g., through after-school tutorial, extended-day enrichment classes), while in other schools differentiation was individualized within the classroom.

Instructional leaders' effort to promote differentiated instruction often embodied a broader logic than helping each child reach proficiency on particular gaps identified through testing. In one school in New York City, school leaders and staff spent a year in multiple professional development sessions exploring the meaning of differentiated instruction, stimulated first by reading a book on this topic, and then by making the differentiation of classroom lesson plans and instructional activities a focus of supervisory visits to classrooms by assistant principals, all of whom looked for this facet of instructional practice in a series of informal observations. One assistant principal gave this example of her feedback to a teacher in an informal classroom visit late in the school year:

> There was a fourth-grade teacher who gave a lesson and I didn't see much differentiation in instruction and that's what we had focused on this year. So I said, well let's sit down and talk about how could you have made this lesson a little different for the high group or the low group? Could you have incorporated maybe some more hands-on activities? How could you have changed it for the kids who finish early? What could you have done for the lower-point group who couldn't quite get it?

All of this took place in the context of a larger set of conversations across the school about students' multiple intelligences and a move to restructure the school into separate academies defined by different configurations of these intelligences—thereby allowing instructors to adapt their teaching to these systematic differences in the way their students approached learning. This kind of structural response to enabling the differentiation of instruction, mirrored in the efforts of elementary, middle, and high schools in three of our four districts, set the stage for the instructional leadership team's work in this regard.

Instructional leadership teams engaged diversity differently across schools. Some schools targeted particular kinds of differences, such as those reflected in second language learners' needs, specially, while others did not. In schools within the same district, leaders chose different approaches to addressing gaps in students' knowledge in a differentiated way. For example, one school leader explained his choice to end homogeneous classroom grouping in his school, while another school in the same district determined that ability grouping (through homogeneous within-classroom groups) was exactly the tool they needed to meet external expectations. We found contrasting choices in many areas: scripted curriculum versus teacher-made units of study, co-teaching arrangements versus serial teacher arrangements, extended-day instruction versus interventions inside the school day, pullout interventions versus push-in interventions. The contrasts among these efforts to differentiate student learning experiences may reflect different theories of how to help a diverse student population learn, a casting about for alternatives that might work, or a lack of clarity about what differentiation might mean. But the common denominator was a clear focus on what it means to ensure that *all* children would learn in a setting in which students arrive at the schoolhouse with varying degrees of preparation, home support, and cumulative experiences in schooling. As other case study research in urban high-poverty settings has begun to identify, intelligent approaches to differentiation of instruction is an important focus for instructional leadership work (Ylimaki, 2007).

Anchoring Instructional Improvement to Evidence

Related in part to the growing diversity of students and enabled—even pushed—by district, state, and federal pressure to anchor teaching and learning improvements to actual evidence of learning needs and progress towards meeting them, instructional leadership teams in the schools we studied had many data resources to work with, and a clear mandate to do so. Not only did the policy environment push for this, the rapid sophistication of data tools (software and hardware) and infrastructure made data-based forms of practice much more realizable. In natural ways, noted by other recent research (see Halverson et al., 2007), data and evidence became a central medium for the instructional leadership work of the teams we studied.

As literature on school-level data use has demonstrated elsewhere (e.g., Supovitz & Klein, 2003; Wayman, Midgley, & Stringfield, 2007), administrators and teachers consistently alluded to this focus on data, often the testing data on which accountability rested, but also other forms of data that the school staff found meaningful. In leading learning improvement, instructional leaders used data extensively to focus and anchor their improvement work. Specifically, they used data as a means of understanding what was happening in classrooms, both school-wide and in particular rooms; as a basis for decisions about instructional improvement activities; and as a tool to assist teachers (and each other) in their own teaching or leadership practice.

Of particular use to instructional leaders was the way data helped them connect to and understand what was happening in classrooms. In the kind of accountability environment these leaders are working in, student progress is measured primarily through tests—state tests, local or periodic assessments, and chapter or other in-house tests—and principals, administrative staff, and teachers spoke consistently about their use of test scores to guide their own teaching or instructional support work. In addition to using data to inform their decisions, supervisory leaders found various ways of encouraging or expecting teachers to use data as a means for informing their practice. One principal in Norwalk-La Mirada explained how she and teachers are using certain types of data at their school:

> I have modeled the value of having test data, and also in demonstrating for the teachers and modeling how we're keeping track of our attendance, our suspension, even if it is not achievement data, having that. I have been very pleased with it. . . . I believe that there are teachers in grade levels that are using and talking about pre and post [assessment] more on their own initiative than I thought they would. When I spoke to them in December about their benchmark assessments and I met with each of them for about 45 minutes, I was surprised to see what assessments they were using. They will not call it pre and post, but they're calling it assessment. I can tell you that out of 36 teachers, 30 are doing pre and post assessment using the benchmarks.

In various ways, the instructional leaders we were studying meant for data to become a medium of instructional practice, and they took steps to encourage its use through specific requirements and tools. As such, it also became a medium for their leadership work. As a result, active engagement with data of various kinds, often in a collaborative team context (e.g., Wayman, Midgley, & Stringfield, 2007), seemed to prompt a more focused, improvement-oriented conversation. Our fieldnotes from a grade-level teacher meeting in New York City illustrate something that was common in the schools we studied:

> *We are observing a grade-level teacher meeting in which the teachers each have spreadsheets in front of them to track the progress they and their students are making on a unit of study they had planned together. Conversation quickly moves to what they are going to do next to bring struggling students up to the proficiency level of the rest of the class. Being all on the same page with common measures, this team of teachers decides to assemble a small group of struggling students into an intensified weekly "learning hour" with one of the teachers before the gap in understanding continues to grow.*
>
> *It isn't clear whether or not the data they are considering accurately represent the students' learning issues, but the presence of the data is clearly structuring a different kind of conversation among these teachers than would have been likely or even possible without it. When a teacher strays into the territory of blaming a student for their lack of learning, the group leader redirects the teacher back to the data, asking the teacher what the data tell them their next instructional move should be to support that student.*

While their uses of data varied, as did their sophistication with data use, instructional leadership teams in all the districts had learned to ask useful questions of the data, display data in ways that told compelling stories, and use the data to both structure collaborative inquiry among teachers and provide feedback to students about their progress toward graduation goals.

Engaging Environmental Demands and Resources

Intertwined with their focus on serving a diverse student population more effectively, and using data to further this end, is the recognition by instructional leadership teams that the outside world is demanding that they do so. The expectation that the school help all students succeed was clearly embedded in the federal, state, and local accountability systems, if not local community expectations, to which they responded. The various data tools and infrastructure, accompanied by varying degrees of training and support, clearly pressed school staff to engage in a more fully data-based practice. In this respect, instructional leadership teams were making a virtue out of a necessity.

In some instances, the instructional leaders' work can be seen as way of bridging the daily practice of classroom teachers and the larger set of reform expectations and resources originating outside the school (see Portin et al., 2009; Portin, Russell, Samuelson, & Knapp, 2013 for a more complete discussion of this phenomenon). Teachers who were members of the instructional leadership team often carried out this bridging function by *personalizing* the system's policy demands for teachers, as has been noted elsewhere (e.g., Firestone & Martinez, 2007). Administrative members of the team also translated external expectations into terms that engaged school staff in attempts to realize more accountable practice (see Knapp & Feldman, 2012).

The key to the instructional leadership teams' response to external demands was to go beyond merely communicating them to school staff and insisting on compliance. Rather, they used the external expectations as *occasions* for engaging in learning improvement work that aligned with the school's own priorities and improvement agenda. This process took several forms:

- *Anchoring the improvement work to evidence* (e.g., by using district-provided data and press for data-based practice as a reference point).
- *Engaging in inquiry related to the performance issues that arose in relation to external demands* (e.g., by converting district, community, or state expectations into questions for the team to pursue).
- *Helping school staff internalize high expectations* that mirrored what external systems were calling for (e.g., modeling commitment to the principles of social justice underlying district policies).
- *Building professional development work and coaching around the issues that district-wide reforms were highlighting* (e.g., various supports for professional learning about differentiated practices).

- *Seeking out external helpers* (e.g., searching out expertise in the district central office or support organizations concerning the ways to understand and use data in improvement work).

In short, when they were taking full advantage of the context of demand in which they worked, instructional leadership teams were able to use this environment as a resource for their leadership work.

Challenges and Prospects for Team-Based Instructional Leadership

As the preceding discussion makes clear, the instructional leadership teams in the schools we were studying were busy engaging each other in efforts to become a more coherent, instructionally focused team, while engaging teaching staff across the school in the direct work of reconsidering classroom practice and trying to make it better. As they did so, their efforts took direct aim at the diverse and often specialized learning needs in the student population they served, and made extensive use of data in their efforts to target their leadership work appropriately and as an addition to teachers' repertoires. Finally, their efforts were linked to the environment of demands in which their schools were positioned, while using these demands as a resource for learning improvement more than as a set of constraints or directives to comply with.

But their efforts raised several questions about instructional leadership teams' ability to persevere and ultimately succeed in this enterprise. First are questions of team support. Who or what would support *their* work, at the same time that they were offering their respective schools a support system for improvement efforts? Exactly what would such supports entail? Some answers to the question have been hinted at in the analysis and examples above, as it was clear that certain individuals and activities within the school (e.g., the principal, other individuals with particular expertise, peer support through other team members) could be instrumental in supporting the professional learning of the instructional leadership team or offering it guidance of several kinds (see Chapter 3 for a further discussion of the within-school "support system"). But others home-based outside the school could be equally helpful—in particular, central office staff (as we explore in Chapters 4 and 5 in this volume, as well as Honig, 2012), but also staff of partner organizations with which some schools were affiliated. In this project, we quickly discovered that team approaches to instructional leadership were neither spontaneous nor rooted in "super principals." Instead, the schools' choices were guided and supported by a contextual theory of action that supported differentiated roles and emerging capacities for teacher leaders.

A second question concerns the resources the instructional leadership team depended on to come into being in the first place and carry on over time. Once again, some of the answers lie inside the school, and we have already touched on this matter in our discussion of groundwork, by highlighting the way principals or others created "space" (in time, facilities, and legitimacy) for the instructional leadership team activities. But here the roots of the school-based instructional leadership work go deeper, including in many instances the initial creation of, or call for, the positions of key team members, and the wherewithal to fund these positions. As we explore in Chapter 6 of this volume, the instructional leadership team was often an expression of a district-wide investment in instructional leadership. And over time, by providing tools, expertise, data, and discretion to fashion school-specific solutions to the instructional improvement challenge, district leaders and staff were central players in the school-level instructional leadership work. Not insignificant, in three of our four districts, district leaders were a continuing voice for the legitimacy of team-based instructional leadership activities—no small matter for teacher leaders, in particular, who faced continuing questions about their "rightful place" in the school.

Finally, there was an ongoing question of best practice: how were team members to learn how to do work that was new to many of them, and to do it collaboratively, taking full advantage of the collective resources of the team? How were they to know what was working? In this regard, our data revealed an ongoing process of experimentation and learning, often by trial and error, and with plenty of room for improvement. While they often displayed many of the attributes of effective teamwork, generically construed (e.g., Larson & LaFasto, 1989), they were not always clear about what instructional vision(s) their efforts reflected, and there were many unaddressed questions about whether good instructional leadership might mean different things in particular subject areas.

These questions underscore that there is still much to learn about effective deployment and practice of instructional leadership teams in the overall equation of learning improvement in schools. But in schools such as those we studied—all of which were making noticeable headway in improving student learning under circumstances that educators would widely consider adverse—one or more instructional leadership teams were an undeniable centerpiece in the schools' efforts to make good on a learning improvement agenda. Taken together, their efforts begin to help us characterize the kind of groundwork laid to enable the teams' existence and practice, the nature of the core work they did with teachers directly, and the ways these efforts reflect new dimensions of the instructional leaders' practice.

3

LEARNING-FOCUSED LEADERSHIP SUPPORT WITHIN THE SCHOOL

Michael S. Knapp and Bradley S. Portin
With the assistance of Susan B. Feldman, Felice
A. Russell, and Catherine Samuelson

A new teacher mentor in a large urban elementary school—herself an accomplished twenty-five-year veteran in the same school—described the central office staff person who regularly visited her to help her settle into her new role: that of guiding new members of the school's teaching staff through their first and second years in the classroom:

> Okay, he shares the assessment tools and how to use them in the classroom with the new teachers, collaboratively or in the log. The selective scripting I've never seen. I'm sure I saw people writing things down, but I never knew what it was actually for. He explains all of these tools. . . . He'll let me know about workshops for new teachers. [He'll] support me if I don't understand something, if there's a situation that comes up, like if I see something happening, do I go to the principal about it? Do I just talk to my mentee about it? Do I go to a coach to ask them? Who do I go to for support? He's there in case I have a problem. He's always available. I can e-mail him whenever I want or call him whenever I want. He's going to come in later this month to walk with us through some of the new teacher's classrooms, talk to us afterwards. Is this classroom up to what it should be at this point? As a new mentor, I need instruction—where should I be now, what should I be doing with my mentees? Am I supporting them enough? He's my go-to person if I have problems. . . .

Not only in this new mentor's descriptions of her work, the language of "support" is everywhere in daily discourse within schools, in school district central offices, and in the writings of those who study leadership and school improvement. Teachers complain of little "administrative support," value the "support" they get from colleagues and some parents, and wish for more "support" from the central office as the School Improvement Plan is being developed. Administrators talk about "supporting" teachers who are struggling with professional growth plans, as well as accomplished teachers who are developing interesting innovations. Scholars and others who give advice and counsel to administrators frequently refer to support dynamics in the school as they examine supposedly "supportive" structures (e.g., Critical Friends Groups or Professional Learning Communities), approaches to handling "nonsupportive" parents, or styles of leadership that do or don't "support" a district-wide reform thrust. The word and its synonyms are everywhere, yet they often elude clear and helpful meaning, even though audiences generally assume they know what is being talked about.

The term is especially noticeable in discussions of school leadership, which is widely assumed to be about "supporting" effective education for students. But one application of the term is generally missing, and in reference to learning-focused leadership, its meaning is crucial. To grasp how learning-focused leadership can flourish in a school, especially one facing significant challenges, it is one thing to identify key leadership practices and how various members of a school community take them up in the service of a learning improvement agenda, as we have done elsewhere (Knapp & Feldman, 2012; Portin et al., 2009; Portin & Knapp, 2011; see also Chapter 2 in this volume) and as other scholars have done over the years (Hallinger, 2011; Leithwood et al., 2004, 2010; Murphy, Elliott, Goldring, & Porter, 2006). It is quite another—and easy to miss—to show how the leadership work is *itself* supported, guided, and led. This chapter takes on that task, by tracing the ways that those who exercised learning-focused leadership in a set of urban schools we studied intensively were themselves given technical, intellectual, emotional, political, moral, and material help and direction, by key players inside the school (and to an extent by outsiders, who we will briefly acknowledge here, but treat more fully in other chapters).

The question of leadership support becomes all the more critical as districts and even states direct resources to various forms of instructional leadership in schools, often through the development of a cadre of individuals who exercise this leadership in the name of an overarching system-wide instructional improvement agenda (e.g., Firestone & Martinez, 2007; Michelson, 2013). Such individuals include an array of full- and part-time teacher leaders, instructional coaches, teacher mentors, data specialists, and others who have strong backgrounds in teaching, often in particular subject areas. The cadre often includes school principals, who are widely being urged to concentrate more on instructional leadership, and also assistant principals, where these individuals have been assuming an instructionally focused role.

While it is easy to assume that all of these individuals are "leaders" and therefore should know what to do and not need any particular support, the assumption misses several essential dynamics. Many of these individuals, even established administrators, are relatively new to the role of "instructional leader," a role for which they have little or no specific training—the teacher mentor quoted above is a clear case of this. The roles themselves are often organizationally ambiguous, not well understood or accepted in the traditional ecology of the school workplace, and hence raise a number of complex issues about how to gain and sustain the legitimacy and goodwill that are necessary for effective leadership work. Finally, with or without experience in the role, instructional leadership is difficult work, raising a host of issues that basic instructional expertise and administrative know-how are insufficient to resolve. For all of these reasons, there is no guarantee that the people who provide school-based instructional leadership will be particularly helpful to the teachers they work with.

To get inside the idea of "instructional leadership support" in schools—that is, the ways that schools try to shape and assist leaders' own work as guides for instructional improvement—we ask: what does "support" for learning-focused leadership in the school mean? What kinds of support do the different players in the (generally) team-based instructional leadership arrangements inside of schools need? And who or what does (or can) provide this support? In what ways, if at all, does this support enable instructional leadership in the school to thrive?

We answer these questions by drawing on what we learned from the first study strand of the *Study of Leadership for Learning Improvement* (Knapp et al., 2010; Portin et al., 2009). The 15 schools on which our investigation concentrated were making progress (as locally defined) on their respective learning improvement agendas and were experimenting with leadership arrangements that might further this work. As such, they offered a particularly good opportunity to explore these questions. Because these school staff were self-consciously considering what it took for learning-focused leadership to bring constructive and continuing attention to the instructional improvement issues their schools faced, they were both willing to experiment and reflective about the results. Our intensive qualitative design took advantage of this fact: by repeatedly visiting the schools across the 2007–08 school year and the first half of the next, we were able to observe a number of different kinds of leadership events and potentially supportive activities (e.g., professional development), as well as interview the participants multiple times, and thereby were able to develop a good sense of support needs and how they were or might be met (see the Methodological Appendix for more detail on the study design and methods).

This chapter explores these matters by, first, providing background on issues of "support" in leadership work within schools, derived from leadership research and related literatures, and then examining five themes that emerged from our data concerning leadership support. These themes concerned the creation of a legitimate "space" for instructional leadership work to take place in the school; attending regularly to the leaders' own professional learning; guiding and aligning the instructional leadership work, rather than assuming it would direct itself;

ensuring the right kinds of resources were available to enable leadership work; and developing routines for mentoring, debriefing, and troubleshooting leadership work as it unfolded. In examining these matters, our focus remains on the schools; however, we note periodically various ways in which support for school-level leadership work, in the fullest sense, entails actions and conditions at other levels in the system and also in the surrounding professional and organizational environment—especially in the school district central office, but also in networks of nonprofit or professional support-providing organizations and other community-based resources. We close the chapter with some further discussion about what this larger environment of support might entail, referring the reader to other aspects of the *Study of Leadership for Learning Improvement* (Knapp et al., 2010) that bear on this issue (for example, later chapters in this volume).

Framing Ideas

Several sets of ideas converge to give a useful way of framing the slippery and vague notion of "support," especially as it applies to instructional leadership work. Once again, we set our frame assuming a "learning-focused" leadership stance (Knapp & Copland, 2006; Portin et al., 2008; and the Introductory Chapter to this volume). In a nutshell, this line of argument about leadership asserts that, to improve learning outcomes for students, leaders need to address the learning of professional adults and even the "learning" of the system itself. And they do so by persistently and publicly focusing on learning as central to everyone's work, building strong professional communities among all adults working within the school, engaging relevant groups and individuals in the school's environment, and mobilizing coherently linked streams of activity down "pathways" that reach learning targets most effectively for the given context.

Roots of the Idea of "Leadership Support"

But if we are to think usefully about the kinds of support that leaders engaging in this work would find helpful, we need to be much clearer about what we are talking about. Classical leadership theories are one place to start, though they quickly lead one to a limited and limiting conception of support. Especially, in situational theories of leadership (e.g., Blanchard, Zigarmi, & Zigarmi, 1985), the idea of support and supportiveness get regular play, though primarily as a way of describing how leaders' behaviors do or do not concentrate on the quality of relationships between leader and followers. In this view, "*supportive* behaviors help group members feel comfortable about themselves, their coworkers, and the situation. Supportive behaviors involve two-way communication and responses that show social and emotional support to others" (Northouse, 2006, p. 93). This theory contrasts "supportive" with *directive* behavior, which focuses on goals, tasks, role definitions, concrete strategies, and evaluation methods. Related theories (contingency theory, path-goal theory), which assert that leadership is most effective when it acknowledges the characteristics of the subordinates, the task to be done, and the situation in which it is done, rely on similar characterizations of "supportive leadership"—for example, "being friendly and approachable as a leader and attending to the well-being and human needs of subordinates" (Northouse, 2006, p.130). While these perspectives show that different combinations of "support" and "direction"—participative involvement, on the one hand, and push for results, on the other—may be more or less appropriate in certain situations, it needlessly separates the two, thereby disallowing the possibility that clear "direction" might be the most helpful "support" that anyone, leaders included, might want.

By shifting focus to the processes and conditions enabling leaders' own learning, as in research on leaders' learning (e.g., Donaldson, 2008; Lieberman & Friedrich, 2010; Michelson, 2013) and mentoring (e. g., Southern Regional Education Board, 2006; The Wallace Foundation, 2007) or coaching (e. g., Gallucci et al., 2010; Taylor, 2008), a more useful merger of the principles of direction and support appear. These lines of investigation into leaders' learning help to surface important dimensions of the learning problem faced by newly emerging leaders, especially principals and principal interns. In particular, the research distinguishes *cognitive* leadership challenges (What do I or we know about the problem we are trying to solve? What do the data or literature say? What strategies are likeliest to pay off?), *interpersonal* challenges (Are our working relationships strong enough to let us take this issue on? How to approach staff so they develop ownership of this problem?), and *intrapersonal* challenges (How does this course of action square with my beliefs? Am I up to it? Where do I need to adjust behavior or attitudes to prevail?) (Donaldson, 2008). The research base also underscores the importance of an ongoing relationship between emerging leaders as learners and others who can teach, guide, and assist their efforts, often through ongoing mentoring or coaching relationships closely connected to the new leaders' daily practice (Swinnerton, 2007), while noting that this kind of relationship is more often absent than not. To be sure, the focus of this scholarship to date has been on individual leaders' learning, mostly in the context of preservice preparation for administrative roles, but the principles and insights emerging from it suggest different meanings and forms of support for leaders' professional learning that are applicable as well to team-based or collective learning.

Other scholarship, variously focused on school improvement dynamics, change processes, or particular issues facing school leaders, alludes to kinds of support these leaders may need in addressing the instructional challenges in their school contexts. For example, classical work on the "human side" of school change underscores the kinds of emotional work that any staff, leaders included, may need to do, as they "grieve" the loss of a long established, familiar way of doing business and attempt to develop new practices (Evans, 1996). A more pointed form of emotional work has been documented for white school leaders encountering and trying to manage interracial conflict in their schools (Ford, 2011). These instance of internal work that leaders must do—and often need help to do—echo and extend the "intrapersonal" learning that new leaders undertake as they try to settle their sense of themselves as leaders and own what leadership means to them (Donaldson, 2008). Paralleling these lines of work are others that underscore the kinds of leadership learning that most pertain to instructional leadership. Of particular note, immersion in the content areas of instruction helps school leaders get better grounded in the subject-specific nature of instructional change (Stein & Nelson, 2003).

Meeting and managing conflict and resistance involves more than internal work on the leaders' part, and as such brings into view another kind of support, more political in nature. Within the "micropolitics" of the school is a constant tugging and hauling among competing interests, which can never be permanently and harmoniously aligned (Blase & Blase, 1997; Flessa, 2009; Malen & Cochran, 2008). School leadership, then, inescapably entails the search for *political* support—for example, provided by allies, alliances, or coalitions that can help keep a fluid course of action on track, especially when it raises unpopular prospects or shifts the within-school balance of power appreciably.

These different lines of scholarly work help to identify various actions and conditions that are likely to figure into the equation of instructional leadership support—among them, help with the hard intellectual work that leadership inevitably entails, the nurturing of interpersonal relationships, the development of alliances and other forms of political backing, and assistance with the more internal and emotional dimensions of leadership work. Taken together, it is clear that the old distinction of "support" and "direction" holds little water, as the two are intertwined throughout these forms of support. Few scholars to date have tried to either describe or assess attempts to put in place a "system of supports" for leadership work that combines most or all of these. Some notable exceptions occur in studies of comprehensive or whole school reform models (Murphy & Datnow, 2003), such as a recent account of the Modern Red Schoolhouse's (MRSH) strategy for developing and sustaining reform-focused leadership in this comprehensive school reform initiative (Kilgore & Jones, 2003). There, the interaction of school staff with the MRSH organization combined leadership diagnostics, principal mentoring, customized leadership team training, and technical assistance, offered over a period of years, as the schools became more comfortable with the MRSH reform. Recent research on the learning of instructional coaches has also begun to visualize what a system of support might entail (Michelson, 2013).

Across all these lines of investigation, leaders and leadership are most often construed as *providers or sources* of support for others, rarely as *objects* or *recipients* of support (the leadership mentoring and coaching literatures are an exception, as are accounts of comprehensive school reform processes such as the one noted above).

And these more generic literatures do not yet help to pinpoint the different kinds of support that instructional leaders and leadership might require. In addition, the work of instructional support has traditionally encountered a firewall between learning and evaluative activities. As such, direction and support have been dichotomous—administrators direct and peers support. What we suggest in this chapter is that the firewall is becoming more permeable, albeit at a cautious pace.

A Typology of Supports for Instructional Leaders and Leadership

With the ideas noted above as building blocks and with the specific case of instructional leadership in view, we can suggest a set of supports for leadership work that are especially likely to matter to individuals and teams of school-based staff who are engaged in instructional leadership work. As a starting point, we treat "instructional leadership" as collective work undertaken by various school staff, often through a formalized team structure, that seeks to motivate and engage teachers to reconsider and renew their instructional practice, in line with school and district's learning improvement agenda (a more extended discussion of the literature base for this view of instructional leadership appears in the Introductory Chapter of this volume; see also Hallinger, 2005; Printy, Marks, & Bowers, 2009; Robinson, 2010). The consequence of this view for questions of leadership support is that more than one kind of staff is involved, with different roles and support needs; what is more, their work as members of an instructional leadership team raises a further dimension to the question of support. With this as the reference point for support needs, at least the following five are inevitably present, as any instructional leadership activity unfolds.

1. *Legitimizing and normalizing the work*, as a normal part of daily practice in the school building that potentially touches all members of the school community.
2. *Enabling and motivating leaders' professional learning,* about learning (of both adults and children), leadership, and instructional improvement.
3. *Guiding and aligning the work,* so that the leadership activities of multiple players relate in coherent ways to a school-wide learning improvement agenda and vision of instructional improvement, if not to a larger district or state improvement agenda as well.
4. *Allocating resources* necessary for instructional leadership work to proceed, so that individuals and teams have the time, funds (if necessary), materials, space, data, and outside expertise (if necessary) that their leadership work entails.
5. *Trouble-shooting and crisis management,* to help instructional leaders and leadership teams process and respond to the unanticipated logistical and operational matters that get in the way of instructional leadership, as well as the overt resistances that leaders encounter among those they work with.

All five of these represent "essential supports" for instructional leadership to continue. A few comments about each of these dimensions of the instructional leadership support problem in a school will set the stage for what we learned about them in our study sites.

Legitimizing and normalizing instructionally related leadership work is a pressing issue for schools that wish to engage in instructional leadership. To be sure, principals and other supervisory leaders have long had an understood role in "instructional leadership" of a limited sort—defined and constrained by the annual staff evaluation cycle in most instances—and otherwise expressed through school-wide goal setting or the orchestration of professional development for teaching staff (Glickman, 2002; Hallinger & Heck, 1996; Smith & Andrews, 1989). But an expanded vision of instructional leadership work, featuring various staff, is not well established, understood, or accepted in many schools, and has only begun to be explored in the last decade of scholarship, through examinations of distributed or collective leadership (Hallinger & Heck, 2010; Printy, Marks, & Bowers, 2009; Spillane, 2006; see also Chapter 2 in this volume). The lack of acceptance is especially true of teacher leaders who seek to guide their colleagues, thereby bringing on their "quest for legitimacy" in the school workplace (Lieberman & Miller, 2004). Given the organizational fragility of many instructional leadership positions, but also the lack of precedent for ongoing and focused instructional leadership work beyond what has been assumed by conventional cycles of instructional supervision, school leaders need support from others who can help them establish an accepted basis for their work. In part, their legitimacy ultimately derives from their own ability to establish their "warrant for leadership" through their expertise and vision (Lieberman & Miller, 2004), and in part through the actions of overall school leaders and outside groups who publicly endorse and underwrite their work, as well as structure, guide, or fund it.

Enabling and motivating leaders' professional learning about leadership and instructional improvement. It is abundantly clear that individuals and teams engaged in instructional leadership have much to learn about learning (both adults and children), leadership, teamwork, and instructional improvement. What is more, their learning needs may differ depending on the positions they occupy in the building and how they have come to that role (Donaldson, 2006). Principals, on the one hand, are often not as expert in classroom teaching, direct work with teachers, or other dimensions of the instructional leadership as they may need to be, one reason frequently cited for their lack of presence in instructional leadership work (e.g., Cuban, 1984; Portin et al., 2003). Instructional coaches, teacher leaders, and data experts, on the other hand, are unlikely to be well versed in what it means to lead, no less to handle the "intensification" of teachers' work that is accompanying many contemporary reforms (Valli & Buese, 2007). And as educational systems embrace ambitious learning standards for all (e.g., the Common Core Standards), people working as instructional leaders are themselves learning what instructional practice can and should look like. As learners, leadership staff need occasions and experts that will support their own learning.

Guiding and aligning instructional visions and practices. Instructional leadership inherently involves one or more visions of excellent instructional practice (Hallinger, 2005, 2011). When multiple individuals are part of a more distributed instructional leadership effort, where does that vision come from? The school principal is often a source (in many cases guided by an explicit district vision), but others with particular expertise or positional authority may fulfill this responsibility, and in many cases better than the principal. But seen from the vantage point of collective leadership effort, the various players need a common reference point for their work—and leaders are particularly well positioned to provide this learning focus (Hallinger, 2011). While the body of evidence to date has most fully substantiated the import and impact of the principal's vision and goal setting (e.g., Hallinger, 2005; Robinson et al., 2008), the same process is likely to apply at all levels of a multi-layered leadership system that provides a different kind of support: one that *directs* school leadership activity, both that of the principal and others in the school, when needed. This kind of guidance could come from "above" (e.g., from the central office) or from elsewhere outside the school (e.g., from a reform support organization with which the school is affiliated), or it can come from the continuing interaction among leaders within the school, who mutually construct a guiding vision for their efforts. Either way, multiple players have people to turn to—themselves or others—as well as occasions, tools, and other elements of a "leadership infrastructure" that help them relate their efforts to each other in coherent ways, and to a school-wide learning improvement agenda and vision of instructional improvement.

Allocating resources necessary for instructional leadership work to proceed. Several kinds of resources are central to school-based instructional leadership work, and evidence has accumulated that "strategic resourcing," which aligns the allocations of resources with learning improvement priorities, positively affects student learning (Robinson et al., 2008). Especially important for the practice of instructional leadership are: *time* for instructional leaders and teachers to work together beyond what may take place in classrooms during actual teaching time; additional *time* for instructional leadership teams to put heads together for planning, coordinating, or professional learning; *materials and other conceptual tools*, if any, that go beyond what teachers are already using in their instruction; *data and other informational resources*, including tools that help people gather or process data; and *outside expertise* (if necessary) that may be needed to enhance or bolster their own expertise (e.g., related to subject matter, new standards, or even leadership strategies). Outside expertise (or key internal figures such as the school principal) may offer more than the people, time, and money that are normally considered in questions of resource allocation; these more intangible resources may include a source of vision, energy, hope, trust, and ideas—an essential "glue" for school improvement work (City, 2010). Several other resources, such as appropriate space and occasional funds beyond what are implied by salaries and material costs, may also be necessary. Thus, instructional leadership work in schools demands particular kinds of people, time, money, and other resources (see Chapters 6 and 7 of this volume for a more extended discussion of resources in learning-focused leadership).

Trouble-shooting and crisis management in instructionally related issues. To help instructional leaders and leadership teams process and respond to the unanticipated logistical and administrative matters that get in the way of instructional leadership, as well as handle the overt resistances that leaders encounter among those they work with, school leaders can benefit from a source of troubleshooting help. Part of this may entail technical assistance or interventions that deal with what are essentially operational problems (e.g., by providing suitable materials to address second language issues facing the third grade teachers). Another part responds more to the emotional dimensions of leadership work (e.g., helping an instructional coach work through the appropriate response to overt refusal or passive aggressive behavior by teachers she is working with), a matter that leadership scholars have paid relatively little attention to until recently, inside or outside education (e.g., Goleman, Boyzatis, & McKee, 2002).

Taken together, these elements of the typology can be summarized in terms of several essential questions that can be asked of any school's instructional leadership efforts. Who or what makes the exercise of instructional leadership legitimate and accepted, in this school context? Who or what, beyond trial and error, helps the leaders learn to be effective leaders, both individually and as a team? What vision(s) of good instructional and leadership practice guide their work and keep it aligned with the school's (and even district's) learning improvement agenda? Where and how do instructional leaders get the resources they need to do improvement work? Who or what protects their time and enables them to pursue their work in a focused way, and helps them cope with the unexpected challenges and frustrations they will inevitably encounter?

What We Learned

The 15 schools we studied offer some beginning answers to the questions just posed. Specifically, the five types of leadership support reviewed above appeared in varying degrees, both as needs expressed by participants and in the arrangements and dynamics whereby leaders did (or sometimes didn't) receive such support. Using various illustrations from our data, we consider below how this supportive activity was set in motion and manifested itself (or was wished for and never found) in different school contexts.

Clarifying, Normalizing, and Legitimizing the Work

Supporting the presence of school-based instructional leadership by making it a legitimate and expected part of the worklife was especially problematic in the case of teacher leaders. The work of teacher leaders was in the process of unfolding in the schools we studied. Previous research suggests that such teacher leader roles are likely to be emergent, multifaceted, and often ambiguous (Blachowicz, Obrochta, & Fogelberg, 2005; Coggins, Stoddard, & Cutler, 2003). Accordingly, what these teacher leaders were actually doing, what they thought they should be doing, and what they would like to be doing varied both across the schools and across time. Subtle dynamics were at work in positioning their work within the school, as schools leaders sought to *clarify* what that work could and should be; "*normalize*" it—developing among school staff a widespread understanding of the work and expectation that it belonged there; and *support* it, helping the teacher leaders establish themselves and refine their own practice. Several conditions affected the ability of the teacher leaders to find a secure footing in the school—among them, role clarity, cultural norms, and the support of the principal as well as peers engaged in teacher leadership work.

Positioning teacher leaders' work within the school and clarifying their role was heavily influenced by the principal. In some of the schools, the principals had a clear vision for these roles, whereas in other cases the principals seemed unsure how they might take advantage of the roles and the individuals in them to ensure their efforts were part of a coherent reform plan. We know from previous research that successful school leaders articulate a vision for shared organizational purpose and shared authority and that the ability of principals to envision new ways to do this is critical to the work of teacher leaders (Donaldson, 2006; Leithwood, Louis, Anderson, & Wahlstrom, 2004). The work of learning-focused teacher leaders was clearest in instances where the school principal held such a vision and, based on it, took steps to grow staff into these roles.

Principals with such a vision noticed teaching staff members who had potential and took steps to invite them into leadership roles, while legitimizing them in the eyes of their colleagues. One principal in New York City had a habit of taking promising classroom teachers with him whenever he left the building to visit other buildings, resource organizations, or the district central office, and then had the teachers report back to their colleagues. Over time, these informal experiences were sometimes parlayed into more formalized roles (e.g., an assessment coordinator position, an advocate for a new student support system). Sometimes the process worked in reverse, with individuals who were already in a formalized leadership role, as in a middle school in which the principal and the math coach decided that it would be best for the coach to take on some teaching responsibilities to better legitimize her work in the face of some teacher resistance. The principal noted:

> She's even talked to me about . . . teachers who really wouldn't really take advice or talk to her beforehand, because they see the coaches more as part of administration rather than purely supportive. [They would think] someone's coming in my classroom to check on me, as opposed to help with my stuff. And so that's something we're trying to [change]. Once she became a teacher again in people's eyes [it helped]—and also she even says to me that it helps because she knows what works and what doesn't in the curriculum. So she could give advice better if she was actually doing it.

Rather than, or in addition to, growing one leader at a time, principals could create a school-wide expectation and norm that supported the exercise of leadership in many forms and by many individuals. For example, in a very large elementary school in New York City, the principal communicated the idea that a large number of teachers could and should become involved in the leadership of the school. The whole staff of teachers were invited to a leadership meeting in the spring of his first year as principal to discuss an ambitious new academy plan for the school; half showed up, and many took on roles in the ensuing academy development effort. The math coach summed up a widespread feeling among staff at this school: "He's big on leadership. They want us to have as many leaders as possible in every role that's possible, which is a great thing, I think."

Here the support providers (both school leaders and district-level policymakers, in some cases) sent messages concerning the desirability of designated people inside the school engaging in regular instructional leadership work. Continual messaging and action by the principal were obviously key here.

Supporting Instructional Leaders' Professional Learning

The steep learning curve many, if not most, instructional leadership team members encounter, both in settling into their mostly new roles, as well as figuring out how to become a team and how to do new forms of leadership work, prompt a continuing professional learning challenge. This meant attending to the structures and occasions for ensuring the leaders' own learning, as well as the quality of "teaching" they encountered. The team meeting structure was often one vehicle for this kind of learning, as well as other kinds of coaching or outreach, including work with fellow instructional leaders.

What instructional leaders were learning that they didn't already know how to do. In this regard, leaders in supervisory roles were learning somewhat different things from their nonsupervisory counterparts (principally teacher leaders). Specifically, principals and assistant principals found themselves:

- *Expanding their knowledge of instruction in particular subject areas,* often by participating alongside teachers and teacher leaders as learners in whatever professional development sequences were created. As has often been noted in research on the principalship, individuals in these roles often lack the rich understanding of high-quality teaching practice that would support their work as instructional leaders (e.g., Fink & Markholt, 2011; Stein & Nelson, 2003).
- *Developing greater fluency in the use of data as a leadership tool.* Though most of the principals we studied had some idea how to use data in their instructional leadership work, most had much more to learn—about the new data systems their districts had created, for example, or about effective ways of translating and presenting data to teaching staff, not to mention learning from regular consultation with data about what was needed by whom in the school building.
- *Building a different image of formal supervision of staff performance.* They were reinterpreting their supervisory work as one component of a larger vision of instructional leadership and support, and often as an entry point for engaging teachers in improvement work.
- *Learning how to operate in partnership with nonsupervisory staff,* to pursue a collective learning improvement agenda through the work of one or more instructional leadership teams. Building, guiding, and working through these teams was new work for many supervisory leaders, which entailed helping emerging instructional leaders assume and own a new framework for approaching their work with a new set of skills, while developing an unfamiliar and sometimes problematic set of relationships with their teaching colleagues.
- *Finding ways to create the "space"—that is, conditions of trust, openness to critique, and focus on instruction—for learning-focused teacher leaders to do their work.* Given the lack of understanding of, and predictable resistance to, their work in the school, teacher leaders could find themselves sitting at the margins of classroom practice, rather than closely connected to the challenges teachers face. Putting those cultural conditions in place was a major responsibility of supervisory leaders, thereby implying that cultural leadership was as important as what they did to manage their schools.

The professional learning diet of nonsupervisory staff differed in noticeable ways, though in certain respects their learning overlapped with that of their supervisory colleagues. For one thing, all members of the instructional leadership teams were developing comfort and expertise in team-based leadership. For another, both supervisory and nonsupervisory staff faced similar challenges in becoming more expert with data and in using it to prompt instructional conversations with teaching staff. Beyond that, teacher leaders, instructional coaches, and other individuals in nonsupervisory roles found other learning challenges that were more particular to their expertise and positioning within the building, among them,

- *Learning to "generalize" their already well developed knowledge of a particular content area and the pedagogy related to it.* Unlike supervisory leaders, who were more typically generalists without a deep grasp of teaching in particular content areas, teacher leaders and others like them had an opposite need, in those instances where their work was meant to extend to teachers beyond their own subject area (a frequent occurrence in these schools). As such, they needed to learn how to be useful to teachers across a spectrum of subject areas—not a small task.

- *Developing an instructional leadership repertoire that would respond to a range of expertise and experience in the teachers they worked with,* from novices new to the classroom to veteran teachers with many years of experience. For understandable reasons, their veteran colleagues were often least amenable to the help that teacher leaders could provide.

- *Learning to build instructionally focused leadership relationships and navigate the "middle ground" they occupied in the school workplace.* Even in schools they had been working in for years, newly anointed teacher leaders or others in nonsupervisory roles had to find productive ways to work with teachers, when their entry was by invitation or gentle persuasion, not because teachers were "required" to work with them.

- *Communicating, as well as translating, school and district learning improvement agendas.* Their "middle ground" position, among other things, meant that nonsupervisory staff were often the means by which teaching staff came to understand what district or overall school leaders hoped they would learn, and in return a route by which their issues could be expressed to other leadership levels. This fact put a premium on their capacity for "simultaneous translation" of reform intentions into actual daily classroom practices, and vice versa. This work could sometimes complicate the relationship-building task that teacher leaders faced, and required new learning that they were unlikely to have experienced in their prior work.

Arrangements for supporting the professional learning of school-based instructional leaders. To support all this professional learning, schools (and also district central offices, to an extent) created different arrangements for supporting the professional learning of instructional leaders. First, participants took advantage of the leadership team structures that most schools had created as a venue for informal as well as formal learning by team members, often entailing ongoing peer-to-peer support, although also arranging more formal "teaching" situations when the team convened. The principal or assistant principal was often the chief orchestrator and "teacher" in this setting, but other team members sometimes filled this role. Teacher leaders who were part of peer-alike teams were a particularly useful resource for each others' learning, as well as helping each other navigate the emergent and ambiguous nature of their work. When they were able to connect regularly with peer-alike colleagues, they became more confident in their work and less isolated in their role. In a Springfield, MA, elementary school, the Instructional Leadership Specialists (ILSs) shared a large workspace that con-tributed to their sense of camaraderie, as one of them noted:

> Well, as you see, we have a "dorm room" here—it's all four of us stick-ing together, and actually when [one ILS] was across the hallway at the beginning of the year, that made no sense . . . because we spent our time in the hallway trying to find each other . . . but I can just [call my colleague's name] across the room versus being lazy and have to get up and walk across the hall. . . . We all meet once a week for Leadership Team, which is tomor-row. It's definitely a working team, and the whole cliché of there's no "I"—there really is no "I" in team. [The principal] has a clear vision, but it's a vision that we all share, so it's okay. It's easy for us because, there are bumps, but we talk through the bumps, if it doesn't work.

Proximity seemed to enable this group of teacher leaders to share the ongoing work and to bounce off one another ideas and issues that come up. Another one of this group described what enables her professional learning:

> I think the collaboration of the team, for one. Sharing with Megan, Carter, and Jeannie [*pseudonyms*] as well. Although Megan is math, there is a lot of collaboration in this room, a lot of expertise in this room. People I so value working with. We read, we talk about what we read, we share ideas, we sup-port one another. We certainly don't leave anyone out.

The presence of peer-alike colleagues in teacher leadership roles in this school seemed to impact positively the professional learning and development of the individuals in these emerging roles. By working in a common space, in which they continually interacted informally as well as by design, these learning-focused teacher leaders were able to understand their own work through the lens of their peers' experiences, in ways that helped buffer the inherent tensions in their roles.

Peer-alike colleagues need not be working in the same building to provide some ongoing support for each others' professional learning. A number of the learning-focused leaders in New York City schools participated actively in pro-fessional peer networks that spanned a number of schools (for example, in the 25-school "Networks" that were the basic organizing unit of the Empowerment Schools system in the city). Here, greater autonomy granted to schools, along with facilitation by Network leaders, enabled this kind of cross-school connection, though there was no guarantee that such relationships would form or be produc-tive. One math coach, who lamented the lack of a mandated professional devel-opment structure in the Empowerment Schools system, said he had not found as many occasions to meet with other math coaches to learn what they were doing as he had in the past (when required to go to regional coach meetings).

The team structures also provide many occasions for more formal teaching by the principal, another team member, or an outsider, typically through professional development that supervisory leaders facilitated, or took part in as participants. One principal explained how he works with new teachers through study groups in the fall and spring. During each series of sessions, he and the teachers read a book focused on a particular content area, e.g., writing in the fall and math in the spring, then met regularly and discussed the book together. A teacher from another school described monthly professional development led by an assistant principal intern:

> I think it's once a month we have a morning session—and they do it by subject area—so we have a group of all the math teachers, and it's led by [our intern assistant principal], so he leads our professional development and basically talks about different strategies of differentiation and then has us take our lesson plans and insert or alter them so that they include those strategies, and we kind of practice doing that. Then we bring them in and teach them in our own classes, and then, in the next session, we'll talk about how it went or how we've been able to work those strategies into our teaching on a more consistent basis.

The supervisory leaders' professional development work could happen in classrooms as well, though their time was typically limited to observing teachers. Some of these leaders modeled instruction or coached teachers, working with small groups of students or teaching lessons, as an assistant principal recounted:

> And so I provide teachers with support, and that support could be in the form of doing professional development or one-on-one. It could be in the form of having a workshop or an eighth-grade and Special Education team meeting. It could be in the form of modeling for a teacher, co-teaching with a teacher—really whatever the teacher's needs are in order for him or her to work with students. I'm here to make sure they get whatever they need.

This important form of professional learning support was embedded in the leadership practice itself, as when a coach or other knowledgeable person accompanied another coach in classroom work. Informal mentoring arrangements appeared in several of the schools, in which a first-year coach "apprenticed" with a more established coach, sometimes working jointly, sometimes engaged in debriefing conversations on a periodic basis to "process" the experiences of the more junior member.

While most instructional leaders described these kinds of practices as professional development for teachers, one principal highlighted the kind of professional learning she experienced through her work with teachers and students in classrooms:

> For example, when we had the reading and writing workshop, in order for me to supervise anybody, I had to understand what the teachers were going through. They were learning it, I was learning it. So, I taught because I wanted them also to see, because I knew [they would be thinking], "You don't know how to teach it; you don't know what we're going through." So the assistant principal and I both taught lessons. And also when I've seen in the past teachers struggling maybe in testing grades, and I'll go there . . . and I start teaching the class.

This principal also attended professional development sessions with teachers to ensure they were up to speed instructionally and could provide effective modeling and coaching in classrooms. Not all the principals were equally adept at guiding professional development or modeling effective instruction. In such instances, they tended to delegate this work to others in the school who had these skills, while still exercising a measure of instructional leadership.

In addition to the range of professional learning opportunities that occurred within school walls, the school districts we studied frequently created occasions for leaders' professional learning in cross-school groupings and venues. In Norwalk-La Mirada, leaders from all the district's schools met monthly in "principal cadre" meetings to gain a deep immersion in balanced literacy teaching, combined with instructional leadership strategies related to this major curricula initiative. The professional peer networks noted above for the New York City system were only one of a variety of mechanisms this district employed for enhancing school-based leaders' skills. While staff of reform support organizations were sometimes the primary "teachers" in such events, the central office staff were often central players, too, especially in districts that were intentionally seeking to transform their relationship with schools, but by establishing "learning partnerships" between school principals and dedicated central office staff who we have referred to elsewhere as "Instructional Leadership Directors" (see Chapter 4 in this volume; also Honig, 2012 and Honig & Rainey, in press).

What support for leaders' professional learning entailed. Across these various instances, "support" for leaders' professional learning entailed a series of things. By participating in these various occasions for professional learning, instructional leaders got access to new ideas, about content, learners, pedagogy, and leadership practice. They were able to replay and seek to understand their own attempts at instructional leadership in the presence of a supportive audience, who could help them understand what had and had not worked, and could offer new ideas. Feedback on practice could be even more immediate in the job-embedded work, where an instructional leader was accompanied by another, more experienced colleague, who could offer comments and suggestions in "real time." In some instances, others were able to demonstrate better forms of practice, helping the instructional leaders as learners to visualize what they might do in the future. Their counterparts in these exchanges, whether a mentor, more experienced coach facilitator, principal, or peers, were also able to offer emotional support when things went badly (as we discuss at more length below). And in these interactions, the direction of leadership work in which all would engage was confirmed, or in many cases debated and clarified to begin with.

Guiding and Aligning the Work

While professional learning experiences were one vehicle for guiding the learning of instructional leaders in the school, there were others, and all traced back to one or more sources of a guiding instructional improvement vision. The keepers and promoters of the vision might reside within the school (typically the principal or another well established school leader would play this role) or come from outside (e.g., from the central office or a reform support organization). Whatever the source, the instructional improvement vision offered a common reference point for everyone's efforts to lead the school toward more effective teaching practices and improved student learning. In this respect, guidance for leadership, even overt direction for this work, provided an essential kind of support.

The guiding vision for instructional leadership work in the school sometimes took the form of a district-wide initiative to improve some aspects of instructional practice, as in Norwalk-La Mirada's multiple-year investment in improving balanced literacy teaching in grades K–12. In such instances, numerous communications from the district central office, coupled with periodic meetings of school principals and tools that they were expected to use, offered a directive form of support for school-based leadership work.

Still originating in the central office, the vision for instructional leadership could be more tailored to a specific school's improvement needs, as determined from data about school performance that suggested how effective teaching and leadership in the school had been to date. Principals in the Atlanta schools noted that their own leadership for instructional improvement very much reflected the direction that their central office leaders were promoting, as the principal of an elementary school explained:

> We have our math initiative. You might say that is a district learning goal or a School Reform Team goal, and not only for our school, but you know we could look at our data and see "Oh on this grade level, we need to improve here." We can look at our data and see that measurement in geometry is a problem. Problem-solving—well that's a problem for everybody—but we could look at that and see that. . . . So the math and science—especially the

math, that is a district-wide learning goal this year, but even if it were not, you would still be looking at your data to see what you need to do in your school.

In this instance, the district leadership was a source not only of an emphasis on mathematics, but also a thoroughly data-based way of focusing the school's improvement efforts and monitoring progress.

But the school itself could be the primary source of direction for instructional leadership work, as school leaders generated a school-specific learning improvement agenda. This was especially noticeable in situations where the district's improvement policies emphasized school-level discretion and flexibility, albeit within an overarching accountability structure, as in New York City/Empowerment Schools. In some instances, this took the form of an ambitious school-wide vision, derived from the nature of the student population and embracing all aspects of the academic program, as in a middle-high school serving a heavily Latino immigrant population in New York City. There, prompted by the school principal, the school had evolved a focus on creating a fully bilingual program emphasizing English and Spanish biliteracy in all aspects of the school's program: "Two languages, one vision, many successes." But a more modest and specific improvement vision, providing clear direction of instructional leadership work, could be developed by school leaders in relation to a particular weak link in the school's program, as an Instructional Leadership Specialist at a Springfield high school noted:

> . . . And as a school we have a focus. The focus for our team from [the principal] is to focus on open-response—writing, crafting, implementing, assessing—all that kind of stuff, because that is the area we perform the weakest on [the state assessment] tests. So we definitely have that as a mandate of something we need to work on within our departments and with teachers, and we're working with them. . . .

The school might even entertain multiple visions, all within an overarching improvement agenda, as in the large elementary school in New York City that decided to organize itself into four thematically defined "academies," each pursuing a different theme within a structure based on a "multiple intelligences" vision.

Whatever their sources, these visions of good instructional practice and good leadership practice simultaneously focused the school leaders' efforts and *aligned* them with each other, and with other relevant aspects of the school's academic program (e.g., assessment, curriculum, student support services). The ultimate reference point for alignment was often state expectations, expressed in learning standards and assessments, and districts were careful to align their learning improvement agendas with these expectations. Doing so sent clear signals to school leaders, as a district leader in Norwalk-La Mirada noted while describing his district's intentional effort to align curriculum, pedagogy, and assessment:

> There's more deliberateness about what we do. And it was [deliberate] before, but now there's a . . . deeper deliberateness. The principal's accountability is deeper. My work with the principals is deeper. We are also looking at the match with our assessment pieces to make sure that our [state] benchmark assessments are the benchmarks that had the highest payoff, and the questions in those benchmarks are going to give us the real information we need to make certain that [the students] can be successful on their state testing.

The pattern in this district and state resembled that in the others we studied. In the Atlanta schools we visited, for example, teacher leaders spent much of their time aligning school curriculum plans and resources with district goals and the Georgia Performance Standards. Similarly, in the Springfield Public Schools, school-based teacher leaders occupying the Instructional Leadership Specialist role were central figures in the district-led efforts to align curriculum through pacing guides and model lesson materials. In both districts, school reviews and improvement planning prominently featured state standards and district curricular priorities.

As the examples imply, instructional leaders in the schools often took their cue from the guidance or requirements of others, inside or outside the school, whose efforts to promote a particular image of good teaching practice and desirable learning became the guiding light for instructional leadership. That said, the dynamic of directional support for leadership work did not generally imply blind adherence to the mandates of an organizational superior. Especially noticeable at the school level, learning-focused leadership sought to encourage ownership and active response to the guidance, as one principal who sought to build leadership capacity around her, explained:

> I want to kind of let [the leadership team] run the show. . . . Because . . . when that happens, they hold each other accountable. And you know, it's one thing, disappointing or not, coming through for your principal, but I feel like they feel more responsible when they all come through for each other.

Allocating Instructional Leadership Resources

Resources of various kinds enabled the school's instructional leadership work. Here, the support providers (often the principal or others who had their fingers on money, time, materials, information, content expertise, etc.) made various things possible for the ongoing work of the instructional leadership team. The success of the team's efforts often depended on the presence of these resources.

Instructional leadership team members accessed and used a wide variety of resources. Most obviously, time and space to do their work as a team was especially appreciated, not to mention other slots in the school schedule to meet with groups of teachers or individuals outside of class time, to carry out instructional improvement activities of one kind or other. But other resources were equally valuable in one situation or other, among them: money (e.g., to purchase substitute time that freed up certain teachers for extended professional development activities), equipment (e.g., computers and software that helped track special education students' progress towards IEP goals), data and data translations (e.g., timely access to district data systems that had been converted into formats that were easier to work with), and specific expertise (e.g., in particular content areas or on working within "inquiry cycles" to identify and diagnose instructional problems and track progress in addressing them). Instructional leadership expertise (e.g., in the details of instructional coaching) was also in demand by leadership teams and much appreciated when it was available. In ways that were both obvious and subtle, these allocations of resources operated as essential supports, especially when they became available at times of felt need.

Trouble-Shooting and Crisis Management

The development of routines for monitoring leadership work itself, and for debriefing and "trouble-shooting" problematic situations that arose, constituted a different kind of support. Here, the unpredictable nature of instructional leadership work raised questions about how anyone knows if the work is being done well, and what anyone does when things aren't going well. The principal, and sometimes others with particular expertise and "supervisory" purview, were in position to monitor and guide instructional leadership team activity; all team members were also contributors to a team culture that could offer help and mutual accountability for the work being done.

The districts that we were studying set the tone for this kind of support by establishing close, ongoing relationships between central office staff and the school principals. In the two districts that were purposely setting out to transform their central office and its relationship with the schools, these "learning partnerships" had multiple functions, chief among them to help the principals improve their instructional leadership skills (see Chapter 4 in this volume; also Honig, 2012 and Honig & Rainey, in press) for a much more detailed discussion of these partnerships). But alongside that goal, and in some respects prerequisite to it, the partner relationship provided much needed emotional support when things were going wrong. An Atlanta principal commented:

> The partnership piece was a very important piece because it meant we built a relationship where [the School Reform Team leader] even knew my expressions. She'd come into the school and say, "How ya doin'?" I'll

say, "Oh I'm great. Fine." And she'll say, "No, you're not—come on in here and tell me what's going on . . ." And she was truly there to support us—not to tell us what we were doing wrong or this is how I think you should do it.

Central office staff were not always the one a principal could turn to in such instances, as the same principal noted about her early years in the principalship, when she had a partner principal who came in once a week: ". . . And her shoulders were shoulders that I cried on, because that was a moment when I just wanted to scream, cry, shout, pull, kick. But you know I had her to talk to."

While principals naturally turned to outsiders, whether from the central office, peers, or staff from reform support organizations, other instructional leaders (and even the principal, sometimes) within the school often experienced a support system created inside school walls. School administrators were often central figures in this kind of support, as were experienced and well-established instructional coaches, or sometimes veteran teacher leaders who had gained the respect of their peers. The support could evolve organically out of relationships with trusted colleagues who were sharing the leadership work, as one principal in Springfield noted:

I am incredibly fortunate to have a terrific assistant principal. So she and I do an awful lot of——I mean I can say to her—have I lost my mind? Does this sound like something that's going to make sense? And she is able to say yes or no and give me some feedback. So that's—she is very, very savvy that way. She and I are very different . . .

Because instructional leadership—indeed, all school leadership—so often involves the unexpected and necessitates complicated adjustments on the spot in the face of significant uncertainty, having this kind of relationship is a great resource.

Schools were often more purposeful in building support systems for their instructional leadership teams. Regular team meetings, professional development activities designed for them alone, and coaching for coaches were among the devices created to offer regular touchbase points at which troublesome issues could be aired. The configuration of leaders also lent itself to natural pairings (e.g., two half-time math coaches in one middle school, the upper primary and lower primary literacy specialists in an elementary school), and these arrangements fostered these interactions, within which leaders got help coping with the unexpected. An experienced Instructional Leadership Specialist (ILS) in Springfield commented about how she was helping several newer colleagues manage their new ILS roles:

. . . Larry's [*pseudonym*] very new to leadership this year, Michele's very new to leadership this year—I said to them as a joke at the beginning of the year, something didn't happen the way they expected it to and you had to do something else. I said welcome to leadership—that's what leadership is: being able to swerve and dodge and weave and be able to stand through it all. I still have that face on, like no big deal, I can do this, no big deal. It's exhausting some days. . . .

With a system in place within the school that encouraged these kinds of mentoring relationships, members of the instructional leadership team were better able to handle the unexpected, at the same time that they were developing the more predictable skills and dispositions for their work.

The Contours of Learning-Focused Leadership Support in the School

Putting these lines of evidence together, an integrated picture of support for instructional leadership in the school emerges. First of all, the architects of these schools' instructional leadership arrangements clearly understood that leadership was always a work in progress, a continual process of developing and adapting strategies for helping a school realize its learning improvement agenda, no less have such an agenda in the first place. And especially because many of the instructional leaders were relatively new to their roles, they would need considerable help becoming effective in these roles. Accordingly, each school created some kind of "support system" whereby all participants in the instructional leadership team received guidance, help, and—at a minimum—someone else to talk to about their work. The system also communicated expectations for their work and established an internal basis for accountability.

The Nature of Within-School Support Systems for Instructional Leadership Work

In essence, the support system for instructional leadership in the school did three things: it provided direction and legitimacy, it created ongoing leader–leader relationships that could help leaders manage both the interpersonal and intrapersonal dimensions of their craft, and it taught people how to be better leaders. Though it could take many forms and was not always as fully realized as it might be, the support system addressed these three things as part of routine daily work within the school. While leadership provided essential support for instructional improvement, it was itself supported.

The *directional* dimension of leadership support is perhaps the easiest to miss, as it is so widely assumed that leaders are the ones who provide direction for others. In the schools we studied, no one assumed that the members of an instructional leadership team automatically knew where they were all headed or what to prioritize in their efforts with others. Rather than "turn them loose" in their various interactions with teaching staff, these schools took pains to guide the work of their instructional leaders in common directions, through regular interactions, jointly developed mission statements, and repeatedly examining data, among other common devices. And as the system communicated direction for their work, it also established a more legitimate basis for their presence in the school's staffing configuration. Generally, the principal's persistent emphasis on the importance of instructional leadership as part of the school's overall improvement efforts, along with messages from elsewhere (e.g., the district central office) that instructional leadership and accountability went hand in hand, laid the groundwork for all members of the instructional leadership team to be accepted, or at least expected, as part of the school's learning improvement efforts.

The *relational* dimension of leadership support embodies for leaders the same kinds of relationships leaders establish with followers, and underscores the notion that leadership—and leadership support, which is itself another level of leadership—happens inside relationships. In this regard, the schools we studied set the stage for leader–leader relationships by forming teams of individuals who would take on instructional leadership, rather than relying on a single individual to be The Instructional Leader. But having multiple individuals engaged in this work within a school building is no guarantee that supportive leader–leader relationships would form, as years of isolated teaching practice in school would attest. In these schools, however, principals and sometimes others took steps to nurture the relationships between them and other individuals engaged in leadership work, and among the members of the instructional leadership team. Where these relationships developed, in most of the schools, many benefits ensued, ranging from enhancing capacity to plan collaboratively, enabling mutual accountability for practice, guiding further learning, and offering emotional support when things don't work out.

The *teaching* dimension of leadership support acknowledges what any honest leader knows, which was so clearly announced by the teacher mentor quoted early in this chapter: instructional leaders have a lot to learn about what to do and how to do it well and the need for professional learning continues over time. In this image of learning-focused leadership, leaders are learners, not only in the beginning (as novices), but forever (as inquiring leaders who are always querying their work, as they are trying to figure out what will work best in each new situation they face). The "teaching" could be direct and even didactic, as more experienced leaders taught instructional team members particular techniques and shared insights into new content, but more often the teaching was more indirect, conveyed through modeling, sharing of experiences, and analyzing problems (the mentor teacher quoted early in the chapter alluded to both kinds of teaching at the hands of her central office Lead Mentor). But however it was done, the teaching that instructional team members experienced reflected attributes of high-quality professional learning: among them, active engagement with the material to be learned, embedded in actual leadership practice, and connected to overall reform goals (Donaldson, 2008; MacBeath & Dempster, 2009; Reeves, 2006).

The Larger Environment of Support for School-Based Instructional Leadership Practice

Though it may appear largely self-contained, the school's support system for instructional leadership work reflects, and can benefit from, a larger environment of leadership support. As this chapter has periodically noted, others positioned outside the school but with a regular presence in it were sometimes part of the school-based support system for instructional leadership work, especially for the school principal (here we anticipate a topic that is explored extensively in Chapter 4, with data sources from the second strand of the *Study of Leadership for Learning Improvement*). Conversely, we have also noted how leaders within the school recognized and participated in a larger improvement agenda developed by educators and others at the district level and beyond, and often reflected in a district-wide theory of action that features instructional leadership teams in schools. In short, the schools' instructional leadership work did not and could not take place in a vacuum.

Though this chapter's purpose is not to explore the contours of the larger instructional leadership support system in detail, we will comment briefly on school-based instructional leaders' response to this aspect of their environment, with particular attention to how it shaped their efforts to lead others in instructional improvement activity. As we have shown in other writings derived from this study (e.g., Knapp, Feldman, & Yeh, 2013), school leaders worked at the intersection of four external systems that intimately affected what teachers taught and how, and by extension what instructional leaders in the school would and could do to support the teachers. These systems, lodged in the district central office but reflecting state and federal requirements, (1) offered instructional guidance and support, especially through curriculum and learning standards, but also emphasizing certain aspects of preferred pedagogy (e.g., differentiation); (2) anchored teaching and leadership across the district to a particular set of assessments and accountability expectations; and (3) pressed for and sought to facilitate data-based practice at all levels, from the classroom to the principal's office. In addition, indirectly related to classroom teaching and learning, district central offices offered operational support to school leaders, on issues large and small, many of which had important implications for classroom work (e.g., the timely presence of materials, the ordering of equipment, the quality of the physical facilities), and all of which taken together could pose a major distraction from instructional leadership work. These features of the larger environment were a constant presence at the school level which could not be ignored.

Although their responses differed in some respects, leaders in the schools we studied responded to these environmental influences in remarkably common ways. Specifically, they engaged the environment of instructional guidance and support by searching for coherent images of instructional practice and instructional leadership. They responded to the external assessment and accountability system by developing the school's *internal* accountability system and culture (see Knapp & Feldman, 2012). They engaged the district's press for data-based practice by modeling and promoting engagement with data in their everyday work. And they interacted with external operational demands and support systems by trying to keep their operational and instructional responsibilities in balance and constructively related to one another.

Cumulatively, the larger instructional leadership support system had a focusing effect on leaders' efforts and, through their work, on the instructional practice of the schools. In the ways these leaders interpreted what the outside world expected and offered them, and how they professed it through their own value commitments, the performance of particular children mattered. How certain segments of the school population fared on a particular assessment instrument mattered. Mastery of particular demonstrable skills mattered. And tools (often rooted in data) were available for generating specific insights into these issues, at least for identifying where work needed to be done. By treating these matters as central and related aspects of the school's work, the leaders' response to these environmental forces, and conditions appeared to have identifiable implications for instructional practice.

As they worked within the demands of a larger environment, astute school-based leaders made good use of the resources, requirements, and expectations that surrounded the school. Rather than reacting to outside pressures and simply complying with them, they proactively used these demands as opportunities to further the work of the school, and in so doing judiciously adjusted external expectations as needed. The response of a school-based Instructional Leadership Specialist in Springfield voiced a widespread sentiment among the leaders we studied:

> We have scripted lesson plans from the district. I don't agree with them. I think that there's a place for them, I don't agree that every person needs to have a scripted lesson plan. I think that struggling teachers need it and I think that if someone's skilled, and this is their profession, I don't think they need it. I think it's a great resource, but we've been mandated to use them, and quite frankly we don't. I have used them with teachers when they've really needed to see the lesson plans and the block of time, but then we've moved away from them again. I think they have their place, but I don't think that—to me that's cookie-cutting and I hate cookie-cutting teaching . . . for example, 3rd grade, I know they're all working on the same thing when I

walk through their classrooms, but they're not all teaching it the same way, and to me that's much more powerful. . . . I just think that you got to take pieces of it that work and make it work for your school and work for your teachers because you don't want a revolt. I don't.

This leader put learning first—the learning of both students and teachers. And he made good use of what the system provided him, but was not a prisoner of it. The school-level system of leadership support enabled him to take this stance, and kept his practice learning-focused.

PART II

The Central Office as Learning-Focused Support System for Instructional Improvement

In the following two chapters, we shift focus from the school to the school district central office, with special attention to the way the central office and the schools relate to one another and to fundamental changes in central office leadership and work practices that turn it into a more effective support system for instructional improvement in schools. To that end, central office staff become more continuously connected to schools, through "learning-focused partnerships" with school principals and various other ways of responding to school needs. Such a shift represents a big departure from traditions of central office structure and work practice, which have a long history and a less than stellar track record in enabling schools across a district to improve in measurable ways.

The two chapters draw primarily on the second strand of the *Study of Leadership for Learning Improvement*. This strand concentrated its data collection and analysis on three large urban districts, each of which was well along in a process of what we are calling "central office transformation." Though their stories and circumstances differ in many ways, their approaches and discoveries about what transformation means and how to make it work are strikingly similar. Two of them, the Atlanta Public Schools and the New York City/Empowerment Schools Organization, were shared with the other two study strands. The third, Oakland (CA) Unified School District, provided an additional vantage point on the transformation process that complemented the other two, given Oakland's years of experience with a major renewal process undertaken under adverse circumstances (including a state take-over of the district's superintendency). All three demonstrated a pattern of gradually improving student achievement leading up to and during the time we studied them; although our analysis made no formal link between the practices we identified and these outcomes, there is good reason to believe the two are related.

The design of this study strand, described more fully in the Methodological Appendix, resembled that of the other two in many respects, but with differences that enhanced its ability to get inside the practice of the central office staff who were main players in the transformation process. To better understand what such reform strategies involve, we asked: Who participates in central office transformation? What are they doing to increase central office support for teaching and learning improvement? What conditions help or hinder them in the process? We explored these questions with an in-depth comparative case study. We grounded our study in two strands of learning theory, and focused the largely qualitative data collection and analysis on particular dimensions of central office work that seemed promising for supporting school-level teaching and learning improvements. We collected the data through repeated visits across the 2007–08 school year, and the first half of the following year, allowing iterative cycles of data collection and analysis. Our resulting data set includes over 220 interviews, 252 documents, and verbatim notes from over 300 hours of observations, including meetings and shadowing central office administrators as they went about their daily work.

We supplement what we have learned from this investigation with the experiences from partnership work we have undertaken over the last three years with other districts across the country that are embarking on attempts to transform their central offices, albeit at an earlier stage in the process than the three districts we studied. Those more recent experiences, in rural, suburban, and urban settings, have afforded a way to informally "test" and in some ways refine the findings of the main study, while enabling us to illustrate the findings in a wider range of cases.

The two chapters offer different perspectives on what we learned about central office transformation. The first (Chapter 4) provides an overview of central office transformation, defining its distinguishing features and locating them in the context of research and historical trends concerning the school district central office in relation to reform efforts. The second (Chapter 5) steps back from the learning-focused partnership work in schools and associated practices in the central office itself, to describe the ways that transforming districts build and maintain a "support system" for this work. It highlights five conditions that transforming districts create and try to maintain as they undertake the hard and long-term work of making fundamental changes in practice.

4

TRANSFORMING CENTRAL OFFICE LEADERSHIP FOR INSTRUCTIONAL IMPROVEMENT[1]

Meredith I. Honig
With the assistance of Michael A. Copland, Lydia Rainey, Juli Anna Lorton, and Morena Newton

Federal and state policies place challenging demands on school district central offices—the local governmental bureaucracy that sits hierarchically above schools—to realize ambitious achievement goals, but these policies seem designed for failure. For example, No Child Left Behind largely mandated that districts help schools dramatically improve their performance, including significantly shrinking decades-old achievement gaps. This emphasis on central offices reflects reams of research and experience that show, absent central office leadership, school reforms lumbering or failing at single schools and at scale across districts. But such policies hardly attend to the mismatch between the new performance demands and traditional central office work and capacity that generally have focused on business and compliance functions along with limited activities related to curriculum adoption and development, while not helping schools realize improved results. Not surprisingly, in part given this mismatch, the percentage of schools failing to realize adequate yearly results has been on the rise. Efforts to turn such results around are right to invest in central offices but generally tinker with surface changes, and they fail to attend to how the work practices and capacity of central office staff matter to such results yet are ill-suited for achieving them. Unless educational leaders tackle this mismatch head on, they will continue to expect the near-impossible from school district central offices and realize disappointing results.

As this chapter will demonstrate, promising experiments are underway in school districts across the land that offer hope for a better match between central office capacity and school improvement needs. Drawing extensively from our recent research from the second strand of the *Study of Leadership for Learning Improvement* (Honig et al., 2010) in three such districts—Oakland, CA; Atlanta

Public Schools; and the New York City/Empowerment Schools Organization[2]—
and supplemented by partnership work we have done with half a dozen more, we
show that district central offices *can* lead for better school performance, and also
how. To that end, such leadership requires that districts shed old ways of working
and fundamentally transform their core work and their capacity to help all their
schools improve teaching and learning. The experience of these pioneering districts suggests this transformation should proceed along three main fronts:

- Creating learning-focused partnership relationships between principals and
  central office staff, aimed at helping principals build their capacity to lead for
  improved instruction in every classroom.
- Developing and aligning central office services to support improved teaching
  and learning in all schools.
- Engaging in new forms of central office leadership that help all staff perform
  continuously better.

We develop these ideas below by first reviewing the historical circumstances
and policy developments that have brought about the mismatch in the first place.
Then, we delve into each of the three dimensions of transformation, explaining
what changes in the central office's core work, how it changes and why, along
with glimpses of the evidence that supports our thinking. Finally, we reflect on
what it may take to realize these changes in the contemporary educational reform
environment.

Current State of Affairs

Since around the mid 1990s, school district central offices have faced increasingly challenging and high-stakes demands to help all their schools and students
realize ambitious improvement goals—that is, to exercise significant leadership
for district-wide teaching and learning improvement. Calls for reform from the
federal level offer a clear signal of this trend. For example, the Goals 2000 Educate
America Act of 1994 extended an effort by state governors in the 1980s in calling
for bold improvements in school performance by the year 2000. As part of this
initiative, school district central offices became responsible for the development
and implementation of a district-wide plan for helping all schools meet or exceed
the standards. The Improving America's Schools Act of 1994 (the 1994 reauthori-
zation of the Elementary and Secondary Education Act of 1965, ESEA) provided
funding for schools to help them realize such goals. Whereas past federal and state
policies called on schools to help students reach basic minimum standards, the
new initiatives required schools to help all students to reach high learning standards. And while for decades, prior federal and state governments skipped over
district central offices and channeled resources and attention to schools, with these

new initiatives, federal and state leaders ushered in a new era of requiring that central offices play more central roles in helping schools achieve the ambitious results. No Child Left Behind only amplified these demands by imposing progressively higher consequences for schools' failure to improve. Many of these consequences fell directly on schools but some significantly affected districts, including the possibility of funding cuts and other sanctions such as district takeover by state agencies.

The Central Office Role to Date: Impediments and Possibilities

In addition to what is currently required by state or federal government, there is ample reason for seeing the central office as having an important, but as yet unrealized role to play in improving the performance of schools. The reasons reflect the negative evidence of central offices that clearly impeded reform, historical origins of the central office that precluded any role in instructional matters, and emerging evidence from unusual counter cases that show how the central office can make a positive difference in instructional improvement.

Clearly, the central office can be an obstacle to reform. Though there are various root causes of the generally limited yield of school improvement initiatives, many agree that the absence of a positive role by the central office is a contributor. Evidence shows that school reforms of various stripes tend not to take root at single schools or get to scale district-wide when district central offices do not participate productively in implementation (Bryk, Sebring, Kerbow, Rollow, & Easton, 1998; Chubb & Moe, 1990; Malen, Ogawa, & Kranz, 1990; Ravitch & Viteritti, 1997). For example, the effective schools movement of the 1980s revealed how features of effective schools were difficult to realize within single schools, let alone across multiple schools, when school district central offices did not participate productively in their implementation (e.g., Purkey & Smith, 1985). In the 1990s, reforms to scale-up promising comprehensive or whole-school reform models likewise ran into central office roadblocks that curbed implementation (e.g., Berends, Bodilly, & Kirby, 2002). More recently, the implementation of standards-based curricular reform initiatives have been impeded in part by central office administrators' limited understanding of and support for new teaching demands (Spillane, 1998, 2000; Spillane & Thompson, 1997; Stein & Nelson, 2003).

Even though central offices have the potential to provide the support necessary for schools to realize the new performance results, given their proximity to schools, such results are not materializing. By the year 2000, the Goals 2000 Panel that monitored progress on the goals concluded that, while school readiness and achievement in mathematics and middle school reading were showing some modest gains, none of the eight educational goals had been realized. In the case of two goals, teacher quality and school safety, results worsened (Honig, 2013). The number of schools not making adequate yearly progress under the No Child Left

Behind law increased between 2001 and 2010. By 2011 almost half (48%) of all U.S. schools fell into that category. The Center on Education Policy reported the 2011 percentage as an "all-time high and an increase from 39% in 2010" (Usher, 2011). While many factors no doubt contribute to such outcomes, they suggest that district central offices have not been able to help schools turn such results around.

The limited performance by central offices is hardly surprising, given the job this organizational entity was given to do. Central offices were set up at the turn of the last century not to address teaching and learning but mainly to bring control and order to schooling, and especially to help manage burgeoning public school enrollments in growing metropolitan areas (Cremin, 1982). From their inception, rural district central offices had similar regulatory functions plus the added challenge of raising tax revenue often required as a condition for receiving state funding on which they were significantly dependent (Mirel, 1990; Steffes, 2008). And for much of the 20th century, both urban and rural school district central offices continued to focus on a relatively limited set of business, regulatory, and fiscal functions with little attention to teaching and learning. As federal and state governments increased their involvement in schools, they positioned district central offices as fiscal pass-throughs for that funding and otherwise amplified the central offices' noninstructional role. Accordingly, central offices generally did not develop work practices or capacity consistent with supporting schools in improving the quality of teaching and learning for all students.

Yet there are counter-examples indicating the central office can transcend its history and take on a different kind of role, more squarely focused on instructional improvement. The experience of some urban school systems is beginning to demonstrate in broad terms what central office leadership for district-wide teaching and learning improvement may require. For one thing, their experience shows that *what central office administrators know and do* is consequential for the implementation and success of teaching and learning improvement efforts. For example, research on the implementation of various school improvement efforts including new small autonomous schools initiatives, shows that their success hinged substantially on how central office administrators thought about and engaged in their work (Honig, 2003, 2004b, 2009). Many of the most promising central office work practices were nontraditional and outright counter-cultural for some school district central office administrators, and required new forms of capacity throughout the central office for taking on and occasionally inventing new work practices (e.g., Honig, 2009). District-wide teaching and learning improvement efforts in New York City Community School District #2 and in the San Diego Schools likewise depended heavily on the ready capacity of central office administrators to engage in new work practices supportive of district-wide teaching and learning improvements (Elmore & Burney, 1999; Hightower, Knapp, Marsh, & McLaughlin, 2002; Hubbard, Mehan, & Stein, 2006). There and elsewhere, central office administrators' knowledge of high-quality instruction has been emerging as fundamental to implementing ambitious standards-based curricular reforms (Spillane, 1998, 2000; Spillane & Thompson, 1997; Stein & Nelson, 2003).

Research also supports the importance of central office administrators' work by negative example. For example, efforts to achieve district-wide "alignment" of formal goals and strategies fall short in many districts without substantial, increased capacity of central office administrators to change how they work with schools within those formal structures to support school improvement (Corcoran, Fuhrman, & Belcher, 2001).

These efforts have begun to underscore some of the essential features of productive central office work. For one thing, the success of these reform efforts often depends substantially on central office administrators engaging in new *partnership relationships* with schools and community agencies, to build the central offices' and schools' collective capacity for implementation (Honig, 2004a; Honig, 2009). The emphasis on partnership relationships moves beyond long-standing debates about whether schools or the central office should direct educational improvement efforts. Rather, both parties—the central office *and* the schools—possess knowledge and skills essential to expanding students' opportunities to learn. These relationships are fundamentally dynamic (Murphy & Hallinger, 1988) and rooted in notions of reciprocal accountability (Fink & Resnick, 2001) where central office administrators do not abdicate their traditional regulatory functions, but rather redefine them so that they operate in service of partnership relationships that help build both school and district capacity for learning improvement.

Researchers have variably called such changes in central office practice "central office administration as learning" (Honig, 2008); a "learning stance" (Gallucci, 2008; Swinnerton, 2006), "inquiry" (Copland, 2003), and "reform as learning" (Hubbard et al., 2006). In so doing, researchers have underscored that central office leadership for teaching and learning demands ongoing learning on the part of central office administrators as well—ongoing learning about the kinds of capacity, work practices, and relationships that might enable demonstrable improvements in teaching and learning.

In sum, central offices and the people who work in them are not simply part of the background noise in school improvement. Rather, school district central office administrators can exercise essential leadership, in partnership with school leaders, to build capacity throughout public educational systems for teaching and learning improvements. Such leadership requires new capacity, work practices, and relationships throughout central offices. However, a host of forces work against such central office leadership. As noted above, school district central offices have operated for most of their history in ways distinctly different from what efforts to improve teaching and learning across an entire district demand. Accordingly, efforts to engage urban district central office administrators in the kinds of leadership that district-wide teaching and learning improvement demands are akin to trying to reverse the direction of a large ocean liner cruising full-speed ahead. Inertia from long-standing institutional forces coupled with demanding job conditions and limited research-based and empirical guides work against the kinds of fundamental changes that such leadership seems to demand. Adding to the challenge, just as some urban systems have begun to take up the mantle of leadership for district-wide teaching and learning improvement, they are facing severe budget shortfalls (Bach, 2005; Davis, 2008; Garber, 2008; Song, 2009), the threat or reality of state takeover (Goertz & Duffy, 2003; Katz, 2003), and desegregation and special education decrees that focus more on compliance with external mandates than on learning support (Boghossian, 2005; Chute, 2007; Haynes, 2007). These conditions obscure, but don't refute, the fact that central office participation in ambitious education reform strategies may be more consequential to successful implementation than formal policies (Honig, 2004a, 2009). The question remains: how to enable this kind of participation?

Limited Prospects for Current Strategies Aimed at Improving the Central Office Role

To an extent, educational reformers have recognized both the impediments and the potential, and have devised various strategies for realizing improvement goals through augmented, restructured, or otherwise reimagined central office roles. These strategies include a spectrum of attempts: from those that streamline the central office (e.g., by bolstering its responsiveness to schools) or expand its capacity (e.g., by increasing central office professional development staff and resources), to those that downgrade, recast, or even eliminate central offices (as in some chartering schemes, and a recent spate of "portfolio management" arrangements). Yet, when examined closely, these strategies only tinker with central office activities and staffing and do not engage central offices in the deeper changes in their work practices and capacity that are necessary for improved teaching and learning at scale. In this respect, these strategies are too limited and incomplete to realize instructional improvement goals across the district.

Improving central office responsiveness. Take, for example, the emphasis placed by many superintendents on improved responsiveness to schools, by having central office staff return calls and otherwise address schools' requests promptly. Such efforts deal with a major complaint from school people over the years: the central office bureaucracy is hard to deal with, slow, inattentive, inefficient, or downright incompetent. But such strategies fail to meaningfully confront the mismatch between what staff do day-to-day and contemporary performance demands. For example, in one district, the director of Human Resources (HR) reported that principal satisfaction with HR had skyrocketed in recent years thanks to her efforts to respond quickly to principals' request. We asked: "But are principals asking you to do the right work?" Her replies suggested that principals were simply asking HR to perform routine functions, such as processing their paperwork for teacher hiring and leaves. While HR staff in this district were engaging in such functions with better customer service than ever before, they were not necessarily providing principals with better services—those actually likely to help them improve the quality of instruction.

Bolstering the central offices' professional development role. In recent years some districts have pursued instructional improvement by increasing the number of central office staff providing professional development to schools and substantially ramping up the district-wide professional development function. These attempts may be part of a larger initiative to increase mathematics scores, literacy, or science, and as such may include curriculum upgrades and technology assistance, along with more intensive training for teachers and sometimes administrators across the district. While the emphasis of these efforts on district-wide teaching and learning improvement is on the right track, they generally do not yet engage *most* central office staff in new ways of working with schools likely to realize teaching and learning improvement at scale. For one thing, those responsible for training teachers often operate out of a different unit from those who provide the line-supervision of school administrators, who in turn are responsible for teachers' supervision and annual performance review. Without ensuring these administrators are sufficiently knowledgeable about and supportive of the new instructional reforms, the potential is high for mixed messages to teachers—or simply lack of support when needed.

Alternatively, as part of the reform effort, the central office may bolster its professional development support for school principals, but not necessarily in ways that complement the instructional improvement thrust, as in one typical district with which we have worked, where the district supports retired principals to coach sitting principals in strengthening their leadership. As the director of this unit admitted, the retired principals weren't necessarily instructional leaders themselves and had received little coaching on how to work effectively with principals. Analysis of their actual work suggests the coaches tended to help principals with operational rather than instructional matters and had little interaction with others in the central office. One principal commented that in an effort to emphasize instruction, the central office kept putting more coaches and others in schools and that keeping track of all the coaches, ironically, took her time away from supporting instructional improvement.

Maximizing school autonomy while minimizing the central office presence. On the other end of the spectrum, some reform strategies aim to improve central offices by significantly lessening or even eliminating them, allowing schools to operate autonomously. Such initiatives seem to assume that a central office is more likely to be a hindrance than a help, and so better to dispense with it. Yet doing so seems to ignore how successful schools rarely go it alone but instead rely on their central offices and other outside organizations for essential supports. In a comprehensive review of research on school autonomy initiatives, we found that, paradoxically for some, an *enhanced* role for the central office may be essential to helping schools make good use of their autonomy (Honig & Rainey, 2011). Perhaps not surprisingly, charter school leaders who aim to create more than one such school outside central bureaucracies have invariably formed their own "central offices," sometimes called Charter Management Organizations (CMOs), to serve a network of charter schools and realize economies of scale with some operational and instructional supports (Woodworth et al., 2008). But as alternatives to traditional central offices, the CMOs do not necessarily offer better support for instructional improvement in the schools they serve. Some charter school leaders express the same dissatisfaction with their management organizations as public school principals do with their central offices, or even worse; they may even experience *less autonomy* from their CMOs than their regular public school counterparts (Finnigan, 2007). Such realities suggest that the question reformers and policymakers should be asking isn't whether or not to have central offices but what do high-performing central offices look like?

Recasting the central office as "portfolio manager." One relatively recent set of answers to the question resides in "portfolio management" arrangements (e.g., Hill, Campbell, & Gross, 2013). Such strategies vary but typically involve amplifying the central office's role as identifying and contracting out with external organizations to support schools in a differentiated fashion, while enhancing choice, autonomy, and performance-based accountability within the system. As part of this process, the portfolio strategy seeks to develop strong roots in a wider set of constituencies than other forms of district-focused reforms, especially among a range of community-based actors and "diverse independent providers," which schools are encouraged to access (Hill et al., 2013). While such cultivation of external supports and constituencies could be part of the core work of a high-performing central office, the experience of districts pioneering this reform strategy suggests that it does not provide a full enough picture of high-performing central offices to guide improvement (Honig & DeArmond, 2010). For instance, New York City's ambitious portfolio management effort suggests that even in contexts relatively rich in external support providers, external organizations have the capacity to serve only a small fraction of city schools and have hardly supplanted traditional central office operations. To launch such initiatives, central offices typically designate offices with such titles as "portfolio management" to leverage necessary changes throughout the central office. However, research on similar central office change approaches underscores that such single offices are hardly up to the task (Honig, 2003, 2009).

All of these strategies recognize that the school district central office is potentially a key, though they take radically different approaches to reconceiving of its role and operations. But while there is promise in some of what these reforms have advocated, all of them miss the point to some degree.

A More Promising Alternative: Central Office Transformation

To move beyond debating whether or not to keep the central office or mounting strategies that amount to tinkering with its structure, presence, or portfolio of functions, district leaders and reformers are more likely to achieve success when they fundamentally rethink the core work of their central offices and essentially transform it to align all that staff do with what matters most—helping schools build their capacity to help all students learn at high levels.

The three school systems we studied closely, and others we have been working with since then, got the central office problem right: leaders of these systems understood that they faced a fundamental mismatch between what it would take to realize improved teaching and learning at scale for all students and how their central office worked. We call their efforts "central office transformation" in part because they involved leaders initiating a process of completely disbanding their long-standing central offices and erecting new performance-focused organizations providing high-quality services to support school results.

Three core elements characterize central offices that are on track to perform in ways that help schools build their capacity for improved teaching and learning in every classroom: (1) learning-focused partnerships between executive-level central office staff and school principals, aimed at helping principals grow as instructional leaders; (2) central office services aligned to support the work of the partnerships and teaching and learning more broadly; and (3) central office leadership for continuous improvement.

Core Element 1: Establishing Learning-Focused Partnerships Between the Central Office and Schools

The staff of successfully transforming districts understand that they exist to help schools build their capacity for high-quality instruction in all classrooms and that their support of school principals' development as instructional leaders is essential to realizing those results. While definitions vary, "instructional leadership" here refers to principals' work with teachers inside and outside classrooms to help them continuously improve the quality of their teaching. Although others participate in instructional leadership (see, for example, discussion of school-based instructional leadership teams in Portin et al., 2009 and Chapter 2 of this volume) and exercise it from different levels of the system, what principals do is indisputably central to school-level instructional leadership work.

Central office participants: the "Instructional Leadership Director." Learning-focused partnerships develop between school principals and executive-level central office staff whose work is dedicated to enhancing principals' growth as instructional leaders. In all three systems we studied, and others we are working with, the heart of the transformation effort involved creating these ongoing, personal relationships specifically focused on helping every school principal become a stronger instructional leader. To be sure, central office administrators interacted with schools in various other ways, including direct work with teachers. But a striking feature of central office transformation efforts is the focus on building the capacity of school principals to lead for instructional improvement within their schools. To carry out this capacity-building, some districts for years have routinely contracted out to external groups who provide supports for school principals in building their instructional leadership practice. In transforming districts, however, responsibility for ongoing support for principals' instructional leadership became the main, if not the sole, work of specific central office leaders, whom we call, collectively, "Instructional Leadership Directors" (ILDs).

Several things about the positioning and deployment of such staff are essential to understanding their role. First of all, their existence elevates the importance of principal instructional leadership by making its support the responsibility not of occasional coaches located within a professional development unit but of staff who report directly to the superintendent or his or her cabinet. Beyond the symbolic effects of such a move, the creation of those dedicated positions at the executive level effectively shrinks the distance between the principal and the superintendent, increasing communication between the two and the focus of executive-level decisions on principal support. Second, the staff participating in the partnerships are given ample, dedicated time for intensive work with principals. In mid-sized to large urban districts (those with at least 20 schools) that take transformation seriously, supporting principals' instructional leadership is the sole responsibility of the executive-level staff in ILD roles. In smaller systems, superintendents and chief academic officers can function effectively as ILDs themselves, provided that they reshuffle or eliminate enough of their other responsibilities to help them focus on direct work with principals. Third, the executive-level of the position helps ILDs engage in the work—enabling them to protect their time and marshal necessary resources—in ways not typical of part-time principal coaches located elsewhere in the organization.

In the districts we have studied or worked with, ILDs are typically assigned to a manageable number of principals, often 15–25 individuals, who may be located in a geographically defined network or in other arrangements that cluster the principals in logical ways. The central office staff engage these principals individually on the school site in job-embedded interactions focused on various instructional leadership tasks or problems. Some of the time, ILDs engage the principals to whom they are assigned in groups, as in the "principal professional learning communities" that can form among members of an assigned network. In both one-on-one contacts and in group settings, ILDs can thus return repeatedly to the same individuals, and thereby, are able to fashion and enact a cumulative "curriculum" of learning experiences that help their school principals, individually and collectively, engage in progressively more challenging instructional leadership practices.

High- and low-quality learning-focused partnerships. Not all partnerships help principals become better instructional leaders, and simply creating ILD positions is not sufficient to ensure principals' growth. Our research and ongoing work on central office transformation—based in observations of actual leadership work, probing interviews of both the central office staff and the principals they work with, and analysis of how ILD practices converge with research-based principles of support for professional learning—enables us to pinpoint what makes the difference between partnerships that do and do not help principals develop as instructional leaders.

As we have described much more extensively elsewhere (see Honig, 2012; Honig & Rainey, in press), high-quality ILDs understand their work as *teaching* and they engage in specific practices typical of high-quality teachers in other settings, in particular, the following:

- *Differentiating supports for principals' instructional leadership* consistently over the entire academic year. ILDs' individual attention to principals' learning needs went beyond the obvious fact that inexperienced principals might need more help with many aspects of their work. Rather, as good teachers, the ILDs figured out, with each principal, what specific issues and aspects of instructional leadership should become the focus of further learning.
- *Modeling ways of thinking and acting* that exhibit the exercise of effective instructional leadership practice. Here, the ILDs were ready to walk their principals through the thought processes of an experienced instructional leader as he or she diagnosed the instructional improvement needs of the building, planned how to address them, and engaged teachers in bettering their craft. In addition, ILDs would demonstrate, as appropriate, what a difficult conversation with a teacher or parent might entail, how one might set up a productive professional learning community dialogue, or use data to focus on particular issues in the school's instructional program.
- *Developing and using tools* that helped principals engage in instructional leadership practices. High-quality ILD practice created and made frequent use of various learning "tools"—that is, materials representing ideas that the principals were seeking to incorporate into their practice and helping them engage with these ideas in practical ways. Classroom observation tools, data use protocols, and inquiry tools were common examples of these tools; when used in conjunction with a principal, such a device could prompt conversations about

good teaching practice, connect principals to heretofore invisible aspects of instruction, and structure their attempts to guide teachers' improvement efforts.

- *Serving as a broker between principals and external resources,* by connecting principals to sources of assistance, while at the same time buffering them from negative external influences—both in service of supporting principals' instructional leadership. For example, ILDs might link the principal with other staff in the central office who could help solve a particular problem—some with particular curricular or instructional expertise, and others who could help with an operational matter, thereby enabling the principal to stay focused on instruction. Just as important in some instances, ILDs were able to deflect an external demand (usually emanating from the central office), or else to "translate" it into terms that were more streamlined, understandable, and compatible with the principals' ongoing instructional leadership work.

Each of these practices is well established in scholarship on learning among adult professionals and others (see Honig, 2012 for a detailed discussion of the relevant scholarship).

These practices were evident both in ILDs' one-on-one work with principals at their school sites and in interactions with groups of principals. Additionally, in the principal networks, one other high-quality practice was common: ILDs engaged *all* principals in the professional community or network as resources to their peers in support of each others' instructional leadership. In this way, the ILDs took advantage of the "distributed expertise" apparent in the groupings of school principals to maximize the possible sources of their principals' learning.

By contrast, in low-quality learning partnership work, ILDs tended to view and approach their work as a traditional form of principal "supervision" or "evaluation." For example, one such ILD occasionally visited his assigned schools, checked on the quality of classroom teaching, and sent principals written summaries of what he saw and what the principal should do. ILDs such as this one did not model ways of thinking and acting but rather stepped in and essentially did the principals' work for them or told them what to do without creating intentional opportunities for their principals to observe or practice the work. While such activities resulted in some principals' work getting done, they did not seem in any way tied to building principals' capacity for instructional leadership (or other activities, for that matter). When asked how she helped a school principal fund a particular instructional program, one such ILD described opening up a school budget and making adjustments herself. When asked directly to what extent she also demonstrated these budgeting strategies to her principals or thought such demonstrations might be important for the principals' development, this ILD responded that it was easier for her to just go in and make the change. Similar missed opportunities for actually teaching principals occurred with respect to tool use, as where ILDs engaged their principals with data but not as part of a protocol for helping principals meaningfully grapple with implications of the data for their own instructional leadership practice. In such instances, the ILDs were presenting principals with data, in effect, to help justify why principals should follow the ILD's directives when making particular decisions, rather than helping the principals fashion data-based strategies of their own.

None of the districts we studied or have worked with since have yet succeeded in getting all the individuals occupying ILD roles to embody high-quality practices equally well. Needless to say, however, where ILDs understood what high-quality practices entailed, their efforts were more likely to be rewarded, in both the changes in principals' practice and their satisfaction with the partnership.

Core Element 2: Differentiating Central Office Services and Aligning Them to Partnership Work and Instructional Improvement

As noted above regarding the history of the school district central office, many of its functions and practices bear no clear relationship to teaching and learning— the core work of schools—at least as far as current staff understand it, even some staff located within curriculum and instruction units. This is especially true in larger districts, in which multiple functions easily become "silo'd," and the left hand almost literally doesn't know what the right hand is up to. Furthermore, districts typically lack an evidence base that might connect their work to learning improvement in schools, no less to each other. For instance, in some districts that we have worked with, staff tell us that they open every school year with an intensive workshop for all district teachers in a subject area such as math or reading. We then ask, "To what extent does offering that workshop actually help teachers teach better?" More often than not, staff lack evidence to investigate the effectiveness of such professional development and sometimes admit that they host such workshops because that's what the district has always done, rather than because doing so might actually improve results. Our analysis of staff assignments in most central offices shows that staff tend to be assigned to manage particular funding streams or programs—with federal, state, and private foundation funding sources driving staffing rather than an analysis of what staffing and work patterns might actually improve school performance.

Organizing for performance. An alternative, more apparent in the three districts we studied closely and in some others we have been helping with transformation, is to organize deliberately for performance, and to develop a set of practices and culture that make teaching and learning performance everyone's core concern. Doing so implies system-wide reconsideration of all district functions, to determine what is essential and how each relates to the improvement of instruction.

Based on such an analysis, leaders of transforming districts strategize how the central office can deliver those services, with a corresponding (re)allocation of resources and even elimination of some services that have been around a long time. In the course of doing so, leaders build out the work of their staff to support the delivery of such services. Such efforts, like many portfolio management reforms, aim to provide schools with a differentiated set of high-quality, relevant services to help them build their capacity. However, unlike most portfolio management reforms, which depend on the availability of such services outside the district, central office transformation strategies engage all central office staff in the creation and ongoing quality-monitoring of such services for all schools.

For example, in one district, the head of the curriculum and instructional services unit engaged her staff in a comprehensive planning process to scour research, district performance data, and their own experience to identify services they could provide that were likely to improve teaching quality. They used that information to develop "service packages" that school principals, with support from the ILDs, could draw on to support the implementation of their school improvement plans. Like performance-oriented service menus in other sectors, the instructional services menu differentiated services for different users. For example, a "low-end" service package in elementary mathematics involved occasional coaching for experienced teacher leaders in leading the improvement of mathematics instruction. A more intensive service package in the same area involved more coaching days to build a team of teacher leaders who could work for those results. Schools had some choice (in consultation with ILDs) about the service package they saw as most suited to their needs.

Similarly, leaders in transforming districts are likely to engage in a major overhaul of the human resources function, again, by starting with a blank page and asking themselves: What supports can our central office provide to schools so that, as a system, we are recruiting, selecting, developing, and retaining top talent in all positions? How can we work from data to fit teachers and principals to the right schools at the right time in ways that are likely to accelerate the improvement of teaching quality and student learning? In the process, many leaders find that, to realize such results, HR staff must let go of some old work and engage in fundamentally new work, such as building pipeline relationships with colleges and universities so that both parties are working together strategically to grow and place highly-qualified staff.

Leaders of transforming systems scrutinize all central office functions in these ways and remain open to eliminating those that are not contributing to improved school performance. And they engage all staff in challenging and meaningful processes of aligning their work to such results. For instance, in one system, staff in the facilities department were able to quantify that by providing certain services to schools, they were able to shrink the amount of time school principals spent on facilities issues. They translated that time savings into a dollar value, which they argued school principals could reinvest in time with teachers on instructional matters.

Aligning work and reconsidering practices *across* the central office. Identifying essential work and its "through-line" to instructional improvement in the school represents a first step towards a central office that actually serves the most important needs of school staff and their students. But another step, clearly at work in the districts we studied closely, were arrangements and practices that aligned the work of different central office units with each other, as well as with the schools, thereby counteracting the natural tendency to remain in uncoordinated, often unresponsive "silos." Case and project management arrangements and associated practices were a prominent example.

On the surface, the case management approaches we observed looked like the simple reassignment of individual staff members in human resources, budget, facilities, and other units to work with small groups of individual schools rather than serving all schools with a specific kind of need, such as processing paperwork for all new teachers. However, such structural changes do not automatically mean that the reassigned staff will actually work with schools in smarter and better ways specifically connected to teaching and learning improvement. By contrast, when staff in our three districts worked in a case management fashion, they became experts in the specific needs, strengths, goals, and character of each individual school in their "case load" and worked to provide high-quality, responsive services appropriate to their individual schools. Central office administrators who took a case management approach focused their work on such questions as: Who are the individual principals in the schools I am—in fact, *we* are—responsible for? What are these school principals and their staff trying to do to improve teaching and learning? What kinds of resources do they need and how can we help them secure them?

When central office administrators took a project-management approach to their work, they shifted their focus from primarily delivering the services that they controlled to taking responsibility for solving problems that promised to help schools improve teaching and learning, even if those problems cut across multiple central office units. Through this approach, central office staff did not simply take on discrete tasks but rather engaged with their colleagues to solve specific problems around supporting schools' focus on teaching and learning improvement. This shift to project management reflected a recognition, expressed by one central office administrator in Atlanta, that when a central office changes focus from delivering services to solving problems, staff begin to see that they have to work with their colleagues in more integrated and collaborative ways than they had in the past:

> No one department can accomplish anything by themselves. Even HR— they need technology, they need finance. You all need us to get it to the board. So we all kind of need each other and so why don't we get together on a project team and figure out how to do it together. . . . We're in the

beginning stages of really solidifying that as a way of work. And it has been, I must say, the most effective way in which we are beginning to get buy-in from people at the central office. What we found is that people really like to collaborate with other people. And it has been amazing the problems that we have been able to at least identify.

The creation of the operations support unit in Oakland provides one example of how project management called on central office staff to solve problems, even if responsibility for those problems and promising solutions did not fall neatly within any one central office unit. Central office leaders launched this unit in 2005 in direct response to a problem with how the central office worked with schools: demands to manage operational issues were keeping many principals from focusing on teaching and learning improvement, not only because of the sheer number of demands, but also because schools did not have efficient systems or staff in place to manage those demands. As the central office began its transformation effort and its emphasis on principals focusing on instructional improvement, central office leaders realized that the approach, as one said, "places a lot of emphasis on [other school staff] as . . . the operational manager [of the school]. The reality is most of our schools do not have support staff that can function at that level." Building the capacity of school-based administrators other than the principal to manage various noninstructional school operations did not fall neatly into any one long-standing central office unit. Nor did staff in those units typically have current capacity to help schools with their myriad noninstructional demands.

To address this problem, central office leaders convened a project management team consisting of some new and veteran central office employees around the problem of how to provide operations support to schools. Rather than tinkering within the central office's traditional departments, team members asked more fundamentally what kinds of support they could provide to schools to address that challenge. The result, Operations Support, brought together 12 staff people from within and outside the central office to help build more effective systems for handling various operational functions. The Oakland principals we interviewed were unanimous in naming Operations Support as the part of the central office that provided them with vital supports for addressing their challenges and freeing up their time for focusing on teaching and learning improvement. Operations Support also received consistently high marks on district-administered surveys of principals' satisfaction with central office services.

Developing performance management systems. To support the development of central offices into true performance-oriented service organizations, central office leaders develop performance management systems. Such systems help staff develop meaningful metrics of their own performance and, importantly, also use performance data to improve the relevance and quality of what they do. Specifically, in the districts we studied closely, central office administrators developed and used new mechanisms that held them accountable for improving the quality of support provided to school principals either directly or through their ILDs. As the high-level administrator in Atlanta reflected,

> . . . [W]e came up with a school reform team model, which was to decentralize the central office, place them in schools within their clusters, give them a lot of instructional support and whatever other support they need for central office. So the services would be closer. And there would be more accountability. [The Superintendent] would know who was responsible for those schools. For everything from facilities to improving instruction, there was a person, an entity that was accountable. And that, perhaps has been, again, one of the most strategic things we could have done.

Each district had always had some mechanisms for holding central office staff accountable for their work. But under central office transformation, the new accountability tools called for holding central office staff *accountable for providing high-quality and relevant services to school principals.* Some central office leaders also reinforced accountability measures with sanctions and rewards for employees.

As part of these new accountability tools, central office administrators in all three districts created or were in the process of developing specific metrics for central office performance. In Atlanta, for example, staff responsible for facilities decided that a meaningful metric of their performance vis-à-vis support for teaching and learning would be whether or not work projects came in at or under budget and on time, thereby freeing up central office staff and central office funds for other projects. Similarly, leaders in New York City described developing a clear set of measures for gauging individual central office administrators' performance. In the words of one, "We went into great detail about what exactly it is that we wanted them to do and how we define low performance, high performance, mediocre performance, and those in between." Likewise, in Oakland, central office leaders launched a major effort to develop score cards for staff throughout the central office that defined high-quality work performance with specific measures and made those measures public throughout the system. These metrics were an essential part of organizing for performance: they oriented central office work to specific results, and more to the point, to results that mattered to schools.

Core Element 3: District Leadership Supporting Continuous Improvement

Leaders in transforming systems engage in forms of leadership characteristic of those in high-performing private firms. They lead by continuously *learning and teaching*—learning what is and is not working in the organization to realize results, and teaching staff how to build their capacity for the right work. In the process, they are hands-on with staff, actively and directly cultivating the leadership of others by encouraging all staff to take risks and innovate in service of better performance (Tichy, 2002). Such leadership is counter-cultural for some leaders, who view their roles mainly as delivering and enforcing directives and largely hands off—a form of leadership we call leadership as *telling*.

As an example of leadership as teaching and learning, one superintendent realized that his cabinet meetings involved announcement after announcement about policies and procedures and did not help his cabinet members lead for results. He threw out the old way of working and began to organize those meetings more like learning seminars. He began his planning with learning goals for individual members and the group as a whole. He then constructed a series of meetings to help staff reimagine their own responsibilities as leaders of service teams responsible for contributing to the improvement of instruction. Now, all staff in the district, from teachers to the central office, engage in evidence-based improvement processes, called cycles of inquiry, that challenge them to work from performance data to interrogate and continuously improve their work.

In another district, a chief operations officer convened all staff, from clerical to professional, in a series of intensive development sessions to help them understand what it means to work as part of a service culture and that truly serving schools involves not just "service with a smile" but actually providing a higher quality service. She then worked alongside staff at all levels to deepen their understanding of how their current ways of working compared with the system's new performance expectations and to help them better align their work with what performance demands.

These district administrators were engaged in leadership that assumed continuous improvement was their goal, and that the organizations or organizational units they lead could always do a better job. In this respect, they were attempting to realize, at the central office level, principles that have been well established in organizations outside the education sector, and more recently at the school level within education (Smylie, 2010). Such organizations pay close attention to investments in human capital, the organization of people and work, accountability and reward systems, capacity for data analysis, and internal management systems, to mention several prominent features of organizational designs that emphasize continuous improvement goals. The districts we studied were attending to these matters, and as such their prospects for realizing improvements, both short-term and over time, were bright.

Conclusion

Taken together, the three core elements just described form an integrated strategy that promises to radically improve the role that central offices can play in supporting instructional improvement. First, the strategy anchors everything to the improvement of teaching and learning in schools, and to support this, builds a direct and strong bridge between the central office and the school principal as instructional leaders. Relying on executive-level central office staff with dedicated time and the appropriate expertise, the central office works continuously to build the principals' instructional leadership capacity through learning-focused partnerships that support principals both individually and as collectives (whose members become peer support systems as well). These arrangements work optimally when the central office staff engage in practices that reflect what is known from research about powerful professional learning.

Second, the learning-focused partnership work is paralleled and supported by a substantial shift in the way the entire central office works. Here, district leaders (re)organize the central office for performance, by reconsidering all district-level functions, pinpointing those that are the most essential while also identifying how all do—or can—serve schools' instructional improvement needs. Then, central office work is aligned across separate units, to further the purpose of supporting schools, and appropriate metrics are developed and used that can demonstrate how well everyone is doing in this regard. As part of this effort, central office staff in all units work to develop new practices that encourage joint responsibility and problem solving on behalf of schools.

Finally, leadership at all levels proceeds from a different set of premises than is typical at the district level, premises that the Instructional Leadership Directors enact on a daily basis. From the superintendent down to central office unit heads and to the school level, those assuming leadership roles become *learners* (figuring out how things are working or not to serve improvement purposes) and *teachers* (helping others learning how to work for performance). Doing so departs in many ways from a more usual leadership stance adopted by many central office leaders and staff, which emphasizes "telling" more than teaching, compliance over adaptive problem solving, and adherence to routine over mission-guided efforts.

This strategy makes good sense in many ways. It honors what we know from research about school district roles in reform, on the one hand, and what we know about creating organizations that maximize performance, on the other. Furthermore, it is anchored to a robust research base on the nature of professional learning and the kinds of practices that foster it. The strategy is also beginning to stand the test of practical feasibility: it can be done in large complex school districts (and smaller ones, for that matter), which are beginning to offer working examples from which others can learn.

As our evidence and experience also suggest, there is no denying the difficulty of achieving the full transformation of central office design and practices that we have outlined here, and, to date, our working examples are at best rough approximations of the ultimate goal. Part of the difficulty lies with the fact that conditions supportive of transformation efforts over time—among them, sufficient stability in top leadership, adequate resources, and a lack of churn in the policy environment—are often in short supply. What is more, the particular history and local context of each school district may make them more or less ready to tackle transformation.

What we have learned about central office transformation raises a number of questions that educational leaders might productively consider in the context of their own efforts to engage their central offices in improving teaching and learning district-wide. First, district leaders can ask themselves: *do we understand central office transformation as a distinct approach to reform?* As this chapter makes clear, transformation means far more than adding and removing units and reorganizing reporting lines within central office hierarchies. Rather, as a distinct approach to reform, central office transformation demands that central office leaders dig down to the level of the day-to-day work practices of *all* central office administrators, and to the ways these administrators understand the nature of their work and their relationships with schools—what Elmore, Fullan, and others have distinguished as "core" or fundamental change. Central office administrators who fail to understand the intensity of what this reform approach entails risk misappropriating reform ideas and otherwise incompletely engaging in implementation.

Second: *is our central office staff ready for the fundamental changes that central office transformation involves?* All three of our study districts began their central office transformation efforts with significant direct or indirect pilot periods during which time central office leaders came to terms with the importance of their central offices to district-wide teaching and learning improvements, established and elaborated a basic design and initial underlying theory of action to guide the reform effort, and made strategic hires—which also called for some strategic firing of certain central office staff and school principals. Accordingly, central office leaders interested in central office transformation might investigate their basic level of readiness for this reform approach by asking themselves about the extent to which they understand that central offices are important main participants in district-wide teaching and learning improvement, whether they have begun to develop an initial design and underlying theory of action for the work, if they can identify sensible starting points, and if they have the right people in the system for the work (or failing that, can imagine steps to recruiting or retraining current staff).

Third: *how can we prepare key stakeholders and other political supporters for engaging in this work over the long haul?* As the examples of New York City, Atlanta, and Oakland revealed, and as we have found in various other contexts that are beginning to engage with this work, central office transformation is highly complex and unfolds over time. Not all important reform partners—including school board members, community members, and representatives of external support organizations—come to reform with the stomachs or staying-power that complex, long-term work demands. Recognizing that, district leaders serious about transformation would do well to consider engaging those stakeholders in strategic discussions that would help prepare them to support the work over the long term, especially during periods when results from the work are inconclusive at best.

Despite the challenges and the scale of the effort that transformation requires, at the very least, school district leaders would do well to ask themselves these questions. The time has come to stop tinkering with central offices and more fundamentally transform their core work to meet the performance demands of supporting high-quality teaching and learning at scale. The efforts of pioneering districts provide some initial images of possibility from which districts of all sizes can visualize and design their own strategies. These strategies start with innovating central office leaders' willingness to set aside central office business-as-usual and reimagine a system of support for schools oriented toward results. Policymakers can support such work by moving beyond simple performance mandates to invest in school districts that are serious about transformation.

Notes

1 This chapter represents an expanded version of an American Enterprise Institute publication by Meredith Honig, entitled, *From Tinkering to Transformation: Strengthening School District Central Office Performance—AEI Education Outlook, 4* (June 2013). Washington DC: American Enterprise Institute. See also the original study report and subsequent journal article publications for further details (Honig et al., 2010; Honig, 2012; Honig & Rainey, in press).

2 As explained in the Methodological Appendix, as part of their overall central office transformation process in 2007, the New York City Department of Education radically reorganized its central office into distinct "School Support Organizations" (SSOs), each of which functioned, in effect, as the "central office" for schools that chose to affiliate with it. Since it was not feasible for us to study all 14 SSOs, particularly given our emphasis on understanding the work practices of central office administrators across the central office, we chose to focus on the Empowerment School Organization (ESO). All 14 SSOs were charged with raising student achievement, but the ESO, at the start of our study, seemed particularly focused on strengthening the day-to-day work practices of central office administrators to support schools' capacity for improved teaching and learning.

5

CONDITIONS SUPPORTING CENTRAL OFFICE LEADERSHIP FOR INSTRUCTIONAL IMPROVEMENT

Meredith I. Honig and Michael A. Copland
With the assistance of Lydia Rainey, Juli Anna Lorton, and Morena Newton

As we have argued elsewhere, a promising direction for educational reforms places the spotlight on the school district central office and how it can support the improvement of teaching and learning system-wide (Honig et al., 2010; see also Chapter 3 in this volume). In a nutshell, this view holds that, while the central office can play an important role in school improvement efforts as many contemporary reform policies and its constituents increasingly expect, its origins, traditions, and typical capacity make it challenging for many central offices to engage in such a role (e.g., Spillane & Thompson, 1997; Bryk et al., 1998; Berends, Bodilly, & Kirby, 2002). In our research, we found that central offices come to serve as catalysts and supports for better teaching and improved student learning when they fundamentally transform their long-standing ways of doing business. As described in Chapter 3, such transformations involve: learning-focused partnerships with principals focused on principals' growth as instructional leaders; the redesign of each and every central office function to perform in ways that provide high-quality, differentiated, and relevant support services to schools; and new forms of leadership throughout the central office that support such processes. But given the challenges that implementing such changes present, what conditions support central offices in engaging in such radical improvement strategies?

The experiences of the three, very different school systems we studied——Oakland, CA; the Atlanta Public Schools; and the New York City/Empowerment Schools Organization—supplemented by what we have found in working with other districts of varying sizes and contexts, point to a set of identifiable conditions that lie within the reach of many sites. District leaders can use these conditions as starting points for building out the kinds of supports their staff will need to be successful at this work.

This chapter highlights conditions that are helpful (or in their absence, act as hindrances) to the implementation of central office transformation. We first briefly review the basic design and premises of a transformed central office, and then walk through five key actions that central offices took to build their capacity for designing and realizing central office transformation. These actions represent a subset of what central office leaders will need to do to launch their central office transformation initiatives in earnest; but without at least these steps, central office transformation is unlikely to advance to even early stages of implementation:

- Getting the right people into the right roles, and clarifying the work to be done.
- Anchoring the work to an explicit theory of action.
- Continuously supporting the professional learning of leaders, as well as others, at both the central office and school levels.
- Protecting people's work so it can stay focused on learning improvement.
- Developing and using evidence through and about central office practice to support continuous improvement in the performance of the central office.

Features and Premises of Central Office Transformation

In our study districts, leaders recognized that just setting out to make the central office more efficient would not help schools build their capacity for significantly improved teaching and learning at scale. These leaders understood what decades of experience and research have shown: that districts generally do not sustain district-wide improvements in teaching and learning without substantial engagement by their central offices in helping all schools build their capacity for improvement (for a more extended discussion of this research base, see Honig et al., 2010). The districts we studied were attempting to heed those lessons by engaging in what is a far cry from central-office-administration-as-usual. Instead, their approach rests on four basic premises.

First, the approach assumes *the main focus of central office reform is teaching and learning improvement*. Other reforms aim to increase the efficiency with which the central office provides basic services to schools, and often refer to these services rhetorically as support for teaching and learning. In transforming central offices, by contrast, staff are able to demonstrate *how* their work matters in concrete terms to teaching and learning improvement. What is more, they act, not just talk about it, and actually change their work to leverage specific supports for teaching and learning improvement.

Second, *leaders engage the entire central office in reform*. Many, perhaps most central office change strategies demand that certain departments, such as those focused on curriculum and instruction, work with schools in new ways. By contrast, central office transformation involves remaking how *all* central office administrators work with schools and with each other—everyone from the entire central office, no matter what department, unit, or function, participates in the transformation.

Third, in the course of transformation, *central office administrators fundamentally remake their work practices and their relationships with schools, to support teaching and learning improvements for all schools*. In more typical instances of reform, central offices routinely attempt to reform themselves by restructuring formal reporting relationships within central office hierarchies, adding or removing units, or revising their standard operating procedures. While structural changes such as these can be helpful, a transformation strategy is fundamentally about remaking what the people in central offices *do*—their daily work and relationships with schools.

Finally, *leaders assume that the central office itself constitutes an important focus for reform in its own right*. Some districts aim to remake central office work practices and relationships with schools in service of implementing a particular program or initiative. For example, as part of new small autonomous schools initiatives in some districts, central office administrators aimed to change the relationship between the central office and schools participating in that specific reform effort (Honig, 2009). Portfolio management reforms seem headed in a similar direction (Honig & Dearmond, 2010). By contrast, districts engaged in central office transformation are working to change their central offices regardless of the particular programs or initiatives in which they may be participating at a given time.

The central office transformation efforts we have studied were taking action on these premises by pursuing specific reform strategies that we organized into three main strands (explained more fully elsewhere, see Honig, 2013 and Chapter 3 in this volume):

- *Create and carry on learning-focused partnership relationships between school principals and central office staff,* aimed at helping principals build their capacity to lead for improved instruction in every classroom. Districts pursue this goal by assigning to this task executive-level, dedicated staff with appropriate skills— whom we refer to as "Instructional Leadership Directors" (ILDs)[1]—and protecting their time so that they can be spending most of every day in schools with principals.
- *Prioritize, develop, and align all central office services,* so that they maximize support for the learning-focused partnerships and, more generally, for improved teaching and learning in all schools. Districts realize this goal through the development of new performance-oriented services—those likely to support schools in realizing improved teaching in every classroom. In the process, staff work ably with data to identify and continuously revisit their service menus

and focus on solving performance problems rather than on working within traditional central office "silos."

- *Approach leadership as "teaching and learning,"* and thereby engage in forms of central office leadership that help all staff seek continuous improvement. Rather than lead in ways that, in effect, "tell" people what to do or try to compel their performance, this leadership approach anchors action to continuous inquiry into current practice and results, and creates continual opportunities to teach participants throughout the system how to perform more effectively.

Such efforts were hardly a rehash of old efforts at "restructuring" the district organizational chart. Nor were these instances of a top-down or bottom-up approach to change. Rather, the strategies went right to the heart of practice—what people in central offices actually do day in and day out—to help improve teaching and learning for all students. But what enables and sustains an approach such as this that seeks such fundamental change in a long-established institution?

Conditions That Support Central Office Transformation

Our research and partnership work suggests that it takes a special set of conditions to realize the vision of central office as a support system for instructional improvement. While we identified various conditions as important to enabling these reforms, five stood out as essential across all three districts. Three conditions set the new practices in motion: finding the "right" people to assume or grow into the various roles that transformation calls for, while clarifying what the roles entailed; offering a clear rationale for working in these ways, embedded in a "theory of action" that all participants understand and accept; and engaging all relevant players in the ongoing professional learning that new forms of practice necessitate. A fourth condition clarifies central office staffs' roles and protects their time so they can engage in the right work in support of schools, and a fifth ensures that they receive and seek regular feedback on their work. We discuss and illustrate each, drawing on examples from the three districts we studied.

Getting the "Right" People Into the Right Roles and Clarifying the Work to Be Done

Not all people are equally suited to the new work that central office transformation entails. So an initial challenge for the district that is serious about central office transformation is finding—and growing—the "right" people, and clarifying the work to be done in their new roles.

Finding the "right" people. Initially, this means some new hiring, some repurposing of existing staff, and also letting some staff go. In the case of the Instructional Leadership Director (ILD) role, the experience of the three districts we studied closely underscores how important it was to find people with a particular orientation to their work. The most successful ILDs we studied consistently thought of their leadership as "teaching," based in work experience in which they had extensively supported adult professional learning (Honig, 2012). Others, such as those who understood their position as that of a traditional "area superintendent" in a mid-sized to large system tended not to take a teaching approach to their role and not to be associated with positive results in terms of increased supports for principals' professional growth.

Our study districts also worked to fit the right people to the right roles by casting a broad net for staff, sometimes tapping those with nontraditional backgrounds for certain central office roles. For example, a cadre of Broad Fellows worked on a number of special projects throughout the Oakland central office, many of them eventually taking on more permanent positions related to community accountability and the oversight of over 28 "workstreams" or projects to help ensure that they operated in "project management" fashion—that is, in cross-functional, coordinated teams devoted to meeting school needs more effectively. Many of these Fellows had limited educational background but some experience with organizational development and fiscal management generally unavailable in the central office. Oakland's central office leaders also brought on McKinsey & Company, a consulting firm, to conduct a "clean sheet" process of fundamentally rethinking the number and nature of central office positions, which led in some units to the removal of a significant number of staff. As a result, some of the new project and department directors found they had up to 50 to 60 percent of their positions vacant.

Central office administrators saw removing staff to free up positions for new personnel as essential to executing the central office work. In the words of one, some people saw turnover in a system as negative, but "I just think it's kind of the shake-out that goes on when you're trying to put the right people in the right seats." Another added that getting some staff to change their work in the ways the reform demanded was like trying to "teach a dog to meow" and that no amount of retraining was going to change their practice. An Atlanta staff member argued that being able to bring in new staff was essential to realizing the goals of central office transformation. One colleague coming into a director's role had over 10 vacancies, which provided that person with considerable room for maneuver in setting up the kind of unit the transformation process called for. As he put it, "Having those vacancies gives you a lot more room to operate and get the skill set that you need to do what you need to do."

Because the Atlanta district is in a right-to-work state, leaders there had more flexibility for firing and hiring personnel than their counterparts in the New York City/Empowerment Schools Organization (ESO) and Oakland, who were bound by union agreements and, in some cases, state mandates that constrained certain positions. Nonetheless, leaders in those other systems generally worked creatively within union agreements and state law to increase their ability to restaff certain positions. For example, in New York City, state law required principals be evaluated by "community school superintendents"—individuals who under a preceding district structure had overseen sub-districts clustered into geographically defined "regions" (the regional offices had essentially functioned as the central office for the schools in those geographic areas). Under transformation, system leaders disbanded the regions and replaced them with "school support organizations," each of which represented for affiliated schools the "central office" (more than 500 of the city's schools were affiliated with the ESO). To comply with state law, the community school superintendents retained responsibility for principal evaluation but otherwise had their other prior responsibilities shifted to other staff or eliminated. In both New York City and Oakland, when central office leaders were unable to remove staff who seemed unable or unwilling to work with the new project-management focus, they generally moved them to positions that required discrete tasks or "transactions" which did not require some of the advanced skills demanded to execute the new work.

Clarifying the roles. Along with identifying the "right" people, districts have to get clear what the (new) work is, what the positions are—and aren't—responsible for, and where mutual or shared responsibilities lie. Some transforming district leaders discovered this the hard way, as an Atlanta administrator reflected about his district's launch into project management:

> My mistake [early on] was thinking that with that vague direction about "Go forth and . . . figure out the 'what is' and the 'to be'" was going to get it . . . and to have them do it on their own—you know, identify a leader in the group and go forth. No. No. They started meeting. Now . . . to give the team credit . . . they jumped into it. . . . Even when it's not crystal clear, you know because they know I'm saying, "You are very smart people or you wouldn't be on this team, so I don't expect you to come to me with just questions, questions, questions. I expect you to come to me with solutions." So that's the reason why they said "Okay, we can do this." But I didn't think anything about the human side of that—what I was really asking them to do. I didn't think about the skill set either for them to do it other than that they were smart and they knew something had to be done. . . . [I overestimated their] understanding of project management methodology, so you could do the "what is'" and the "to be"—even a good understanding of the system as a whole.

Getting really clear about the nature of the work for staff to be doing was an essential, though it could take time and a process of learning to get there.

Anchoring the Work to an Explicit Theory of Action

Part of clarifying the work to be done lay in developing and articulating a larger rationale for the transformation effort as a whole. In this regard, district leaders supported their central office transformation process when they developed clear theories of action. The idea of a *theory of action*, derived from studies of individual and organizational learning (Argyris & Schön, 1974, 1996), posits that for fundamental reform efforts to be successful, participants need to understand not simply what the reform entails but also the rationale for the reform—the underlying problem the reform aims to address, the rationale for the different reform pieces, and how the pieces add up to a coherent effort likely to impact desired results. Theories of action for transforming the central office in each district were different from strategic plans, which are more formal policy documents that might be revisited, vetted, and decided upon once every three to five years in an organization. By contrast, theories of action in the districts we studied were living documents that leaders actively used to anchor the work and the work of their systems. Unlike some strategic plans that simply list goals and actions a district will take, these theories of action articulated the through-line connecting different central office actions to school-level changes and to results for students. By showing such a through-line, leaders aimed to help central office staff understand that their work mattered substantially to results for students. The theories of action also provided not just the *what* of the work but also the *why*—based on learning research that shows practitioners are more likely to deeply engage with new ideas and transfer those ideas to new settings when they understand not simply what the ideas are but their underlying rationales.

Leaders in transforming central offices supported the implementation process when they continuously communicated their theory of action, teaching people inside and outside the system what the process involved and its underlying rationale. For instance, in Atlanta, various executive central office staff made formal and informal presentations on the central office transformation effort at various stages of its development. The superintendent was the most frequent, and most public, presenter, taking advantage of opportunities in various forums to discuss how the work was evolving and lessons that she and others had learned about how to help schools improve their performance. Such forums included meetings of all Atlanta administrators as well as community recognition ceremonies and speeches to other groups in the community. As the superintendent repeatedly pointed out, her role in the central office transformation effort meant not only developing the theory of action for change over time, but continually engaging her staff in understanding the history and evolution of the effort and the underlying rationale for changes in support of teaching and learning improvement. In her words,

> I must be able to articulate [what we're doing and why] to every group of stakeholders. So I'm giving speech after speech, meeting after meeting, I go to everything from Rotary, Kiwanis, coalition of big business, to living room chats, to School Reform Team cluster meetings of PTA—and I think people like for me to do that. They come out, they want to hear it.

Confirming the value of such communications, we found remarkable consistency between how the superintendent framed the importance of transformation in central office practice, and the learning improvement that actually occurred in schools. This foundational rationale ran counter to the way business had been done in Atlanta, and required major changes in how people in the central office thought about their work, as we have described elsewhere in this chapter (see also Chapter 3 in this volume; Honig et al., 2010). The essential message that supporting schools was the paramount duty of the central office was captured in a refrain we heard consistently from multiple central office leaders, that their work involved "flipping the script." Reflecting the theory of action that redefined the central office as a service organization meant to support the work in schools, "flipping the script" was this district's common phrase for a sea change in how the central office–school relationship was understood, and why the central office existed.

Similarly, in New York City, executive staff of the ESO frequently communicated internally and externally about shifts in how their central office transformation effort was evolving to reflect new learning, as the ESO worked to scale up their initial efforts to dozens, then hundreds, of schools. In support of the value of such communications, Network Leaders offered remarkably consistent accounts of the history of the central office transformation effort and reasons for its growth in particular directions. Some pointed out that, while they did not necessarily agree with some developments, particularly in the area of accountability, they were well aware of what those developments were and how the various leaders of the system expected them to participate in implementation. Where this kind of communication regularly occurred, it helped to reinforce the importance of everyone tying what they were doing to the overarching efforts to improve teaching and learning; it seemed to help various internal and external participants in implementation engage more fully in understanding the work and how they contributed to the work. Evidence from Oakland, too, confirmed the importance of such ongoing communication, particularly with regard to how the transformation effort addressed teaching and learning improvement goals, by both positive and negative example, as one central office administrator described,

> I spend a lot of time with principals talking to them . . . about their budgets, their concerns, the services. . . . I've been going out to these staff meetings where we go as a strategy team to talk to principals and staff. And I've been purposely talking about [the budgeting system] more because I want to hear what people are saying. And what I've realized is most people, including principals, like when I really explain what was the theory of action behind [the budget system] . . . and how it was an equity strategy because it redistributed the wealth from the highland to the lowland schools. . . . And [if] you're a flatland school you'd get more money, but you were supposed

to use that money to hire more coaches and things to support your new teachers so that eventually . . . you would get a more and more seasoned staff. That was the way it was supposed to work. And the reality is . . . a lot of people didn't do that. Instead of hiring a coach they said, 'Well, let's do reduced class size.' Well sure, reduced class size is good, but if you're all new teachers and you have reduced class size and there's no one to coach you, guess what, those teachers are going to leave. You're going to have a higher attrition rate because people are going to be frustrated.

Despite the efforts of this one speaker to communicate the theory of action of the central office transformation efforts, some central office administrators struggled to understand aspects of the central office transformation process and their underlying rationale. And at the school level, the message was not always clearly heard or accepted. Their lack of clarity or understanding, coupled with a vacuum of leadership at the superintendent's level, had potentially negative consequences for implementation. Clear articulation of the theory alone, by some leaders and not others, was no guarantee that it would be understood and internalized by a critical mass of the leadership cadre or the intended recipients at school level.

Continuously Supporting the Professional Learning of Leaders and Other Central Office Staff

Even when they restaffed certain positions, clarified the work to be done, and articulated the overarching rationale for transformation, leaders in transforming systems found that ongoing professional development for central office staff was central to their success. Accordingly, these leaders invested in professional development of central office staff as a key strategy for supporting the design and implementation of their central office transformation effort. In so doing, these district leaders charted new territory. As many respondents reported, prior to the transformation effort, professional development opportunities for central office personnel were few and far between, and may have included, at best, attendance at annual conferences or participation in doctoral programs at universities alongside other educators. By contrast, as part of the transformation effort, the central office professional development efforts aimed at providing each individual central office administrator with multiple opportunities—some whole district, others unit-specific or individualized and job-embedded—for improving their practice in alignment with transformation goals.

Supporting professional learning of Instructional Leadership Directors. For example, central office administrators in all three districts brought ILDs together in meetings ostensibly to help strengthen the ILDs' work with individual school principals. In Atlanta these occasions happened as part of weekly meetings with the deputy superintendent, and in New York City and Oakland, ILDs came together twice each month in meetings at least partially dedicated to support for their practice. These meetings, among other forms of professional development, gave ILDs a forum for examining their work with principals, and considering how to improve it. However, the time other central office administrators actually dedicated to ILDs' professional development was sometimes shortened or completely interrupted when meeting agendas were shifted to address other, usually operational issues. Nor did all the professional development opportunities engage the ILDs in challenging conversations about the quality of their work with school principals and how to improve it. Not surprisingly, when their professional development time was shortened or not characterized by such challenging conversations, ILDs tended to report that the professional development they received did not help them improve the quality of their work with school principals.

The New York City/Empowerment Schools Organization (ESO) stood out among our three sites for the amount and quality of time actually dedicated to the professional development of Network Leaders (that district's equivalent of an "Instructional Leadership Director") and specifically to challenging conversations among them about how to improve the quality of their work with individual school principals. We observed almost 100 hours of twice-monthly Network Leader meetings that typically featured a significant amount of attention to what some referred to as Network Leaders' "inquiry." Sometimes these inquiry sessions focused on ideas senior central office administrators brought in from the outside. More frequently, the staff provided Network Leaders with a prompt related to how they were handling certain situations, such as making accountability demands meaningful to principals or getting principals to trust their feedback.

For example, in the following exchange, a small group of Network Leaders responded to instructions from the facilitator to share one challenge they were facing in their work with school principals and how to address it. Network Leader 1 introduced the problem of how to help principals truly understand what it means to exercise instructional leadership.

NETWORK LEADER 1: How can I make that [focus on principals' instructional leadership] actionable?

NETWORK LEADER 3: [What I look at is] what are the different opportunities I can have with [principals] that will gain their trust, so I can have some influence? If that's what your goal is. I think you almost have to go backward and have a set of experiences that aren't so high stakes, so that when high stakes experiences arise, [the principals] trust you.

NETWORK LEADER 2: But there's no guarantee. But I hear underneath what you're saying that you want some assurance [that the principal is going to engage in work with you on improving their instructional leadership]. The desire to be influential is partly rooted in belief that when we are confronted with situations we offer what we know is right, and when [principals] don't take [our] advice, we are hurt.

NETWORK LEADER 1: ... I'm worried about [principal's name] and his school ...

NETWORK LEADER 3: What's the work with this person? Because it seems to me this is someone who needs to feel he comes to decisions himself. How can you frame this so he feels he is coming to decisions on his own. ... You have to take a tack ... so you can meet [principals where they are] ...

NETWORK LEADER 1: Have you gained that respect from your principals in a year and three months?

NETWORK LEADER 3: The goal is not so much about us gaining credibility, but about their development. It's not really about us.

This exchange is typical of the conversations we observed in its focus on a specific challenge these ILDs were facing and their grappling with how they might take action on those challenges. To cultivate this kind of conversation, the ESO had staff specifically dedicated to professional learning for the Network Leaders. One of the staff reported that the job included continually protecting the space in these meetings for the Network Leaders to talk about their own learning, a stream of conversation that the participants much appreciated.

This professional learning was as much driven by the ILDs themselves as by other facilitators. Half the Network Leaders we interviewed in New York City reported that they facilitated such conversations for themselves by meeting with their colleagues either during or outside of network meetings. Similarly, in Atlanta at the time of our data collection, School Reform Team Executive Directors, a counterpart to the New York Network Leaders, came together monthly to share ideas and materials that they found useful in their work with principals. As one reflected, "We all meet and talk about issues that are common to us and we share some ideas, so that's helpful. ... I always need some learning supports [like those]." These Executive Directors emphasized that occasionally these meetings involved not simply the sharing of materials but extended conversations about how they were actually working with their principals.

By contrast, weekly meetings in Oakland of ILDs (called "Network Executive Officers" or NExOs) infrequently focused directly on ILDs' work with principals on their instructional leadership. On a few occasions, the meeting facilitator led the participants through a "consultancy protocol" that prompted a NExO to present the case of one school for feedback from ILD colleagues. However, those presentations tended to focus on the performance of the school, with only some discussion of the performance of the principal, and remarkably little discussion of how the NExO might support the principal. The short time for conversation allowed in that particular consultancy protocol curtailed critical conversations about the ILDs' work with their schools, a sharp contrast to the more flexible, open-ended discussions among Network Leaders in New York City.

The process whereby NExOs received annual performance evaluation feedback was hardly a substitute, and ultimately the ILDs who worked with elementary principals met on their own to share their work and plan jointly together. Likewise, they convened themselves with an outside facilitator to receive some professional support.

Supporting the professional learning of other central office staff. Beyond the ILDs, in all three districts, executive central office staff launched significant efforts to provide ongoing professional development for staff throughout the central office to help them adopt the new orientation to their work that central office transformation demanded. For example, in Oakland, executive central office staff organized a series of professional development retreats, mid-year workshops, and ongoing unit-specific conversations to help central office staff come to see their work as providing high-quality services to schools, specifically to strengthen schools' teaching and learning improvement efforts. As one executive-level staff person described the hands-on, ongoing involvement in central office professional development,

> ...in the beginning, I created a...boot camp and I just got different resources from around the district to train people on different systems and procedures.... Since then...I spent time with each person on...some different systems stuff, and then what we've done is break down the various areas of things that people should know. So the new operations support coach spends time with each operations support coach learning those kinds of skills, and also about being an operations support coach. So part of that person's training assignment is to teach them not only about those things but to take them on at least one school visit, so you see...what does that actually mean to be at a school and how do you approach that relationship and all of that. And so then they get that perspective from a number of people.

Reports from participants indicated that these large-group meetings and job-embedded supports focused on basic central office procedures and how staff could come to know schools better to trouble-shoot nonroutine problems in ways that promised to be optimally responsive to schools. In addition, central office leaders created a new partnership with a local community college to increase some staff members' access to associate degrees and other educational opportunities to increase their readiness for jobs requiring more skills.

Within the New York City Empowerment Schools Organization (ESO), just as they did with the Network Leaders, central office staff regularly convened the Network Team members—four to six experienced administrators who worked with each Network Leader, together serving approximately 25 schools in the network—for professional development on central office systems and how they might work with schools in ways that supported teaching and learning improvement. Beyond the ESO, system leaders relied, in part, on market mechanisms to drive improvement in the rest of the central office—in broad terms, the strategy of redirecting a significant amount of funds to the schools and "selling" central office services to them on an as-needed basis, and in competition with similar resources they could buy from other parts of the public system or outside the system. New York City leaders did not simply create a market. They also launched a professional development group called the Market Maker, to help prepare staff to work effectively within the district's internal "market economy" and thereby increase the chances that central office administrators would actually provide services to schools that schools would want to purchase. As one central office administrator described,

> So, Market Maker was developed to sort of catalyze that market, meaning both build an infrastructure so that the sellers could actually package the services and market them and sell them. . . . You've got people [in the central office] who are sort of accustomed to providing [various services to schools with a] take-it-or-leave-it kind of mentality. [With the Market Maker we] . . . say to them . . . "Why is this service that you're wanting people to buy valuable? "Why would a school want that?"

Multiple respondents described the importance of these professional development opportunities to helping staff throughout the central office successfully participate in their work with a project-management, customer-service focus. For example, several commented that they believed the Market Maker and other professional development efforts were essential to realizing the goals of central office transformation, so that staff within the new structure did not revert back to the old ways of doing business.

Protecting People's Work So That It Can Stay Focused on Learning Improvement

Learning new practices accomplishes little if other matters crowd out the time and energy needed for the new work. The pattern is all too familiar at the school level, where principals intending to engage in instructional leadership can easily get sucked into other administrative and operational matters (e.g., Portin, DeArmond, Gundlach, & Schneider, 2003). The same is true in central offices. Recognizing this reality, districts serious about transforming central office practice to improve teaching and learning make intentional efforts to "keep people's plates clear" of work that is not instructionally related, or less essential to improvement purposes.

This essential piece of the support system for instructional improvement was especially obvious in the way the central offices protected ILDs' work. Though they were supposed to focus their energies on supporting principals' instructional leadership, many other matters competed for the ILDs' time that could take them out of schools and away from work with principals. To forestall this possibility, or cope with it when it happened, various central office administrators, including ILDs themselves, took steps to remove responsibilities or tasks that would make it harder for them to maximize the time they spent helping principals exercise instructional leadership. In Atlanta, the School Reform Team Executive Directors frequently credited various central office staff, including their deputy superintendent, with helping them in this regard. As one recounted,

> . . . We had blackout days, right, and the blackout days were equivalent to one and a half days a week. And the blackout means that you don't pull principals, you don't pull school Executive Directors . . . because people are in schools working. And so . . . the school Executive Directors asked for that time to be increased and it was increased to two and a half [blackout days per week], and basically our position was it's a very poor commentary if this is our core business and we are only having blackout for less than half of the time [in the workweek]. And so [the deputy] was like, "You're absolutely right. Two and a half days."

Senior central office administrators were particularly instrumental in protecting ILDs' time for work with principals by reducing demands on ILDs that either threatened to consume too much time or that otherwise did not promise to strengthen ILDs' support for principals' instructional leadership. For example, one such central office administrator in Atlanta reported making a special effort when ILDs called him, or when an ILD had a principal call him: "I try to make sure they get what they need as quickly as they can, because the bottom line is providing service to schools. That's it. That's it."

We found the same kind of support system in place in another district, but noticeably absent in the third. Strikingly, every single Network Leader we interviewed in New York City repeatedly reported that any time they brought a challenging issue to the attention of senior staff people in the Empowerment Schools Organization, these staff either provided information that was needed to expedite the issue or handled the issue themselves. All these ILDs reported that these efforts on the part of senior staff helped them increase the time they spent working with school principals on their instructional leadership. By contrast, some Oakland NExOs reported canceling meetings with individual principals, especially in the spring, due to personnel hearings or "fire drills"—urgent meetings back at the main central office building generally not related to their efforts to support principals' instructional leadership. NExOs also reported having much of their time consumed by "homework assignments" from the senior central office staff, such as using templates to record all their schools' assessment data or data on professional learning communities and family engagement, among others. One reported that, as a required part of the new accountability system, they had to give multiple presentations on their schools to executive staff during the fall of our data collection period because so many of these schools were listed as low performing. When asked how, if at all, such "red school presentations" related to their own work with principals on instructional leadership, NExOs generally reported that the presentations kept them in compliance with the accountability system but did not contribute to their work with principals.

Relying on central office colleagues or supervisors was not the only way ILDs managed to keep themselves focused on instructional leadership support work. They also exercised initiative on their own, by learning to say "No," delegating tasks to others, and even by collective resistance to what they saw as unreasonable demands from some part of the central office that was less tuned to their work, as in Oakland, where NExOs committed to spending at least 75 percent of their time working with school principals, while opposing attempts by district senior staff to load them up with other responsibilities or take over too much of their twice-monthly meeting time for issues not related to improving principals' instructional leadership.

Using Evidence for Continuous Improvement of Professional Practice

The continual gathering and use of evidence of various kinds appeared essential to supporting the transformation effort. Such efforts, sometimes called "performance management," typically focused on monitoring progress, assessing results, and providing feedback, not just for schools but for each and every central office employee.

In New York, for example, senior central office staff intentionally used evidence to inform and continuously improve how they worked to support ILDs' practice. That is, rather than using this evidence mainly to *evaluate* ILD effectiveness, these central office administrators used various data *to inform their own practice* in supporting the ILDs. To illustrate, a central office staff person in New York reflected publicly that, in examining feedback from Network Leaders about their experience working with him/her,

> I often found myself stretched too thin. I know I was giving short shrift to things that must be done more thoroughly, from certain people who could benefit from more support. I didn't make the time to work closely with them. As I learned and got deep into operations issues, I wasn't being as focused on instructional issues for a period this year. In general my weakness in terms of supporting folks is I'm not that good . . . at positive feedback. I display my sense of respect usually by critique [rather] than by applause. That usually doesn't work for everyone.

This comment, to which Network Leaders responded with applause and praise, captures how those assisting the central office–principal partnerships were using evidence from experience, including feedback, to improve their own practice in providing such assistance.

Those providing professional support to ILDs routinely solicited and used evidence from various sources to inform their assistance for ILDs. Particularly in New York, feedback from ILDs significantly shaped how other central office administrators designed and implemented opportunities for Network Leaders to improve their practice. For instance, executive central office staff in New York routinely facilitated extended discussions during their twice-monthly network leader meetings about how well the meetings and central office staff were working for participants and how both might be improved. At several of these meetings, central office staff used data from written end-of-meeting reflections and evaluations to kick off and otherwise ground those discussions.

Multiple staff people within the ESO described and demonstrated that their professional responsibilities specifically included capturing input from Network Leaders and translating it into terms that others throughout the ESO and central office system might use to inform and improve their supports for network leaders. For example, one of these staff people jumped into a conversation and reminded the group,

> I'm working hard to capture a lot of rich and useful conversation, and trying to distill it into three large strands. The broad stroke is we talked about how we need to differentiate our work, and do that in [a] way that builds capacity at the network level, school leadership, and classroom level. How do we find ways to identify strengths . . . within networks . . . and between schools? Second, how do we provide collegial resources, in that, making sure network teams recognize the needs they have, and have the time to go deeper to come up with multiple grouping strategies to figure out areas of needs and strengths. Collect tools so schools don't have to replicate. This could be housed electronically and include inside tools, best practices in teaching and learning and operations. . . . Others talk about the importance of [having the time for] sharing best practices . . . Anything else?

Beyond informing their own practice, district leaders gathered extensive evidence from the school level to shed light on how well the central office as a whole was doing its job. One key strategy for collecting feedback from principals related to changes in central office work was to convene principals for discussions of their interactions with the central office. In one district, the superintendent met regularly with small groups of principals to discuss their experience with various aspects of the central office, including those aspects that reflected the district's transformation efforts. These conversations provided either the feedback or direct recommendations back to central office units to inform their change efforts. Sometimes, the superintendent asked staff from other central office units to sit in on these principal meetings to hear the feedback directly. Similar arrangements in the other two districts, supplemented by regular surveys to the principals about the quality of central office services, had the effect of providing specific information about ways the central office was or wasn't supporting learning improvement, and led quickly to adjustments, sometimes substantial ones.

As the above examples show, central office administrators in these systems not only collected data, they also intentionally used those data to change how the central office operated. Central office administrators in Oakland used findings from the conversations in the principal advisory groups, as well as the Use Your Voice survey, to develop a "Service Scorecard" for each central office unit. As its main architect described, the Scorecard "highlights their key services and the standard to which those services will be delivered, and progress toward those goals." This administrator then used the Scorecards in meetings with central office staff to engage them in challenging conversations about their progress with improving their service to schools. Data from the Scorecards was the starting point for productive retreat conversations, among other instances, that identified and set in motion projects aimed at improving the functioning of central office units concerned with facilities maintenance, management of teacher substitutes, and payroll accuracy, among other targets. In subsequent work on these projects, staff continued to use evidence to monitor their progress.

Respondents throughout the central offices generally reported that these efforts to systematically and regularly collect and use multiple forms of evidence to inform their efforts were fundamental to their progress. As one central office administrator in Oakland explained, one of the problems with the old central office was its lack of being data-driven. He went on to explain,

> And the more we have data to tell our story about, well here's how we're really doing, and you can perceive it however you want. But actually what happens is when you start using data, you start changing your perceptions of people. So that's why I'm training my managers on how to do that and be very data-driven. And be almost like a coach of a baseball team that's using their stats all the time. . .

As the above comment suggests, use of evidence strengthened the central office transformation efforts not only by infusing the change process with input and new ideas, but also by helping create a feeling among central office staff that they were being listened to and acknowledged for their work—a key resource for reculturing in organizations where staff may have felt unrecognized, criticized, or outright demoralized.

Such evidence use processes were ongoing and fundamental to the work of transforming the central office, even nine years into the work in Atlanta, in part because the nature of the reform was not to implement a fixed model but to continuously improve work practices across the system. As one central office administrator noted, he continually consults with evidence of how well the transformation process is working, to inform his own participation in the process. The administrator reflected, "That really was part of *my* learning."

By gathering, interpreting, and using data of many kinds as a routine part of central office practice, the districts we studied created a different kind of culture, within which new forms of central office practice could emerge. In a sense, evidence use by central office staff and about their work was a counterpart to the data-based practice of instructional leaders, not to mention teachers themselves, at the school level (see Chapter 2 in this volume).

Concluding Remarks

The conditions supporting central office transformation described in this chapter reflect a straightforward logic: put the right people in place, give them a clear sense of what they are doing and why to support learning improvement, teach them what they need to know and help them continue to learn as they proceed, keep them from getting distracted, and provide them regular feedback. The logic is all the more powerful because it emphasizes an essential feature of central office transformation—that the actual daily work of central office staff must change in substantial ways and must be sustained over time. These conditions are not about *structural* changes; they are about ensuring that, within whatever new structures are created, the people doing the work of the central office are enabled and motivated to visualize and carry out these practices.

That said, realizing these conditions is often a tall order. For example, "getting the right people in place" poses great challenges for some district leaders who struggle with understanding what should count as the right work and who are the right personnel for those roles, especially in diverse systems with various schools that have different challenges and strengths. For various legal, personal, and other reasons, leaders in districts with which we work often display great reluctance to let staff go.

Understandably, the five conditions described here are not *preconditions* for transformation to take place, but rather ongoing actions that accompany what is a long process of change. In fact, the actions that establish and sustain these conditions take vigilance and continual attention to what people need to do their work well. In other words, trying to create and maintain these conditions is a dynamic effort.

Other conditions that appeared in only one or two of our three study districts may also require sustained attention for central office transformation to be successful in other contexts. The downturn in funding support for public schools that the nation has witnessed in years since our data collection concluded can obviously hamper some aspects of any transformation effort. Furthermore, unexpected exits and entrances within the district or its immediate surroundings—turnover in the Superintendent's office, for one thing, or in the mayor's office or the teacher's union leadership—can substantially change the line-up of participants and stakeholders, not to mention the stakes, in the transformation process.

Districts that are serious about central office transformation must be realistic about these matters and acknowledge many of them lie somewhat or completely out of district leaders' control. But as our study districts show, these matters need not completely frustrate transformation efforts. One was taken over by the state in the midst of the transformation process. Others faced substantial lawsuits, pointed criticism from advocacy groups, and other distractions, and all faced the loss of funding. But they persevered by paying careful attention to the ongoing supports people needed throughout their central offices to be successful.

Note

1 The actual position titles varied considerably across districts. We use the term "Instructional Leadership Directors" as it captures most descriptively what these staff were actually doing and their common responsibility.

PART III

Investing in Learning-Focused Leadership

In this Part, we refocus on the allocation of resources at the school and district levels—especially, time, people, and money, but also more elusive social resources—to further the goal of learning improvement. More specifically, we explore what it means for leaders to treat resource allocation as an *investment*—that is, an attempt to align resources dynamically and strategically with learning improvement goals, with the expectation of a "return" over the long term. As we unfold these ideas in the context of learning-focused leadership, we highlight how investments—and especially investments in staff—aim at instructional leadership itself, in addition to whatever is done to direct resources towards teachers and teaching. Finally, we pay close attention to what it means for leaders to seek and sustain an *equitable* allocation of resources, in the face of predictable pressures and pushback from various interests across the system.

The chapters in this Part 3 draw on the third strand of the *Study of Leadership for Learning Improvement*—the strand which examined the resource dimensions of learning-focused leadership at both the school and district levels. The strand team studied investment dynamics in four districts, two of which were also used as sites in the other two study strands (the Atlanta Public Schools and the New York City/Empowerment Schools Organization), and the other two, Portland (OR) Public Schools and Lane Country District 4J (in Eugene, OR), used only in this strand, to offer complementary investment stories in contrasting urban and exurban sites. Across the four districts, the study team collected data in a total of 15 schools, each chosen for evidence of progress (as locally defined) on improving student learning and for evidence of experimenting with the allocation of resources to maximize the equitable improvement of student learning. The four districts were similarly selected to reflect overall evidence of learning improvement at the time of the study's inception, as with all district sites chosen for the *Study of Leadership for Learning Improvement*.

This strand's mixed methods design emphasized qualitative sources and close-up, case-based understanding of investment dynamics, combined with attention to the countable evidence about actual resource allocations (budgetary dollars, staff FTE, etc.). As we explain more fully in the Methodological Appendix, we used these sources to find out how staffing resources were allocated at the district and school levels, how key decision makers at each level approached the decisions they made about these resources, and how the context for allocation decisions figured into the process. Throughout, we noted how equity was or was not considered in the allocation process, and what consequences allocations decisions had (or might have) for the *equitable* improvement of learning opportunities or outcomes. Our investigation was anchored to ideas in the school finance literature and to the ways that broader school and district reform literatures approach resources.

This part offers two chapters, the first of which (Chapter 6) lays out the ways the districts under study created investment frameworks that guided districts and school-level decisions about staffing resources, and then, within those frameworks, directed resources to address enduring and emerging staffing challenges. Our analysis includes the ways leaders subsumed within the investment equation the cultivation of a supply of suitable staff, the reallocation and repurposing of existing staff, and the strengthening of staff capacity and performance. Of particular interest to these districts was the idea of funneling resources into the support of instructional leadership. Chapter 7 then explores the idea of investing for equity. Based in a set of notions concerning equity and adequacy of resource investment, the analysis examines how the challenge of investing equitably poses for leaders a set of technical issues and at the same time invokes political dynamics that are inescapable. Drawing on examples from across our school and district cases (and probing one exemplary case deeply), we create a typology of possible responses to the equity puzzle and a set of principles that can guide learning-focused leaders' efforts in this regard.

6

FRAMEWORKS AND STRATEGIES FOR INVESTING IN INSTRUCTIONAL LEADERSHIP

Margaret L. Plecki and Michael S. Knapp
With the assistance of Tino Castañeda, Thomas Halverson, and Chad Lochmiller

In an interview midway through the school year, the principal of a very large elementary school in New York City explains why he has rearranged his budget to support team teaching arrangements in his first and second grades, resulting in classrooms of approximately 28 children taught all day by two certificated teachers:

> A lot of people think I'm crazy and ask "How can you possibly afford it?" It's a long-term investment. I really believe strongly that this is going to help those kids—that I don't have to have after-school programs and Saturday programs and test prep programs and this or that program for third-, fourth-, and fifth-graders, which is really not going to merit much gain. . . . I think by making the investment in the early grades, I'm making an investment that's going to payoff in the long run and I think I'll see it on the other end. There may come a time though, and I'm aware of it, but I may have to look out to other organizations to help fund and support it—foundations that will fund and support that kind of work because we're heading towards some real tough, difficult economic times not just in the city but throughout the country. . . . I just hope the Chancellor and the Mayor don't pull out all my money before I can prove it.

This principal made this choice after having gone through a careful and difficult process of aligning his budget with a learning improvement agenda he established with his staff. There are other worthy things he could have done with the money needed to pay for the team teaching arrangement—among them reducing class sizes across all grades (though by less than the radical reduction in the early-grade classrooms), mounting an array of remedial programs for older struggling students, creating targeted test-preparation classes, and the like. But he has opted to substantially change class size and instructional attention for a particular segment of the nearly 1,000 students in the school, and to bring to those first- and second-graders instructional resources that may actually be more than the sum of two teachers. The early returns suggest his hunch may be working, not only in student learning but in the quality of the teachers' work as a team; he has observed from classroom walk-throughs, or other observations of his staff (e.g., during prep periods), "The teachers that are team teaching are working twice as hard, maybe three times as hard because they challenge each other, they question each other."

This staffing decision prompts various questions, concerning what enabled this principal to visualize the possibilities and the trade-offs, to imagine this move as a long-term *investment*, and what empowered him to actually make this somewhat unorthodox staffing arrangement. In addition, his actions raise issues of how he can persist in the face of resistance, both from within and outside his school, if not his own self-doubt, and how he (or others) might figure out whether the investment is paying off. At the same time, the principal's decision is a microcosm of a larger set of issues confronting the district as a whole. To begin with, how does the district in which the principal works funnel sufficient resources to him and others like him to enable this kind of staffing arrangement, especially at a time of economic downturn? Furthermore, how is the district investing in him, his efforts, and those of his leadership team to guide learning improvement efforts in his school, and indeed all schools in the district? These kinds of questions could be asked of hundreds of leaders, at both the school and district levels in school systems across the country, who are serious about improving the quality of teaching and learning.

A number of school reform efforts call for or presume that resources are directed to activities that align with instructional improvement priorities and build a long-term basis for equitable learning improvement. Strategies for enabling leaders to direct resources to these purposes are gaining popularity—among them weighted student funding, greater flexibility for schools' use of funds (a condition that enabled the scenario above), greater choice for parents in selecting schools, increased autonomy for principals to hire and assign staff, and greater accountability for principals regarding their schools' performance, particularly in larger district settings. Most such proposals aim to close persistent achievement gaps, and the logic is simple: if more or different things need to be done to close achievement gaps, or if certain groups need more help for this goal to be achieved, then directing resources to these purposes is essential.

Yet, despite examples such as the one above, resources often are neither well aligned with reform goals or student needs, nor directed to long-term, sustainable changes. Across diverse settings, staff are deployed in remarkably similar ways (Chambers, Shambaugh, Levin, Muraki, & Poland, 2008; Kimball, Milanowski, & Heneman, 2010; Miles, 1995; Monk, 1994; Odden & Picus, 2008), with only small adjustments made, often to honor staff preferences or requests for a change. Typically, last year's budget predicts this year's, with only incremental adjustments (Erlichson & Goertz, 2002; Hartman, 1999; Odden & Archibald, 2001; Rubenstein, Schwartz, Stiefel, & Amor, 2007). Or, when substantial cuts are required, all units' budgets are reduced by the same percentage, leaving current priorities intact and unexamined. In a similar way, the master schedule for the coming year—the principle vehicle for allocating time resources in a school building—often closely mirrors the current year's allocation of time and course offerings. Leaders avoid redirecting funding from one purpose to another lest they unleash a howl of protest from those whose budgets are shrinking the most. Put simply, how resources are distributed and used in a district or school is often remarkably resistant to change, despite the call for a substantial shift in the way the district does business (Adams, 2008; Miles, 2001; Thompson, Crampton, & Wood, 2012).

Learning-focused leaders can do better. In particular, like the principal with whom this chapter began, they can start visualizing resources—and especially staffing resources—as essential parts of a long-term strategy for changing how the school or district works to support learning. In addition, they can ensure that these investments point directly not only at student learning, but also the learning of professionals and the system as a whole. Finally, they can recognize that *leadership itself* is a worthy investment target if they want other investments (in teachers, professional development, new math curriculum, etc.) to develop roots in local practice and yield results over the long-term.

This chapter explores these matters by assembling what we learned, as part of the third strand in the *Study of Leadership for Learning Improvement* (Plecki et al., 2009), from intensive study of four urban and exurban districts, and within them 15 schools. Both the districts and schools were chosen as examples of making progress on locally determined learning improvement goals (see Methodological Appendix for details on study design). In short, the chapter considers what it means for such leaders to go beyond the traditional pattern of incrementally adjusting funding, time, or staffing allocations to address salient needs in ways that are coherent, equitable, and sustainable, and that appear to be contributing to improvement in student learning.

Investing Resources as a Problem of Learning-Focused Leadership Practice

Investing resources in districts and schools, as in other contexts outside education, implies decisions aimed at maximizing goals, with an expectation that the investment will yield a *return over time,* though not necessarily immediately. It also implies that investors take calculated risks and monitor and adjust investments on a regular cycle, in light of changing conditions and accumulating evidence regarding the effectiveness of particular investment strategies.

Our analysis considers a range of resources, chiefly human capital (people), time, and money, which have been widely recognized as the most central resources at educators' disposal (City, 2010; Plecki et al., 2006). But this simple way of describing resources that count the most in leadership for learning improvement masks several important complexities. First, the three interact with each other and each is instrumental in the effective use of the others. Put simply, these three are regularly transformed into the others, and used in combination to achieve results. Money "buys" people (e.g., through salary and other forms of compensation) and it also "buys" time (e.g., by enabling programs and activities to be sustained over defined periods of time). In combination, money, time, and people are the where-withal for building the *capacity* of people (as evident in professional development efforts), not to mention the basic instructional work of a school. Thus, each resource affects the others, and even depends on the others in order to achieve the intended purpose.

Second, though essential, these three do not reflect the full range of resources that matter for learning improvement (Grubb, 2009; Rice & Schwartz, 2008). As one observer reflects, "People, time, and money are not enough" when one focuses on how resources are *used* to advance improvement goals (City, 2010, pp. 19–20). Rather, a series of more intangible *social* resources, including relational trust, hope, vision, and energy, play additional and critical roles in the translation of "raw" resources (staff expertise, time allocations, and the use of funding) into actual results (e.g., Bryk et al., 2010; Bryk & Schneider, 2002; City, 2010). Fur-thermore, these tangible and more intangible social resources combine and inter-act within a system in dynamic ways to form what has been noted as *professional capital* (Hargreaves & Fullan, 2012). The upshot is that wise investment decisions need to anticipate, as best they can, the dynamics of resource use and to activate the full range of relevant resources. In this respect, leadership plays a crucial role—not only are leaders investment decision makers, but they are also trust-builders, articulators of guiding visions, mobilizers of energy, and developers of professional capital in pursuit of a learning improvement agenda.

Staffing resources, on which this chapter focuses, are especially important to think about as investments. Salaries and benefits account for 90 percent of yearly education budgets (National Center for Education Statistics, 2013). Furthermore, and perhaps more importantly, the people who are its focus can grow in expertise, capacity, and longevity, yielding many times the return on original investments. In this sense, the investment decision is potentially more than a *quantitative* allocation of so many dollars, FTE, or minutes to a particular instructional improvement goal. Ultimately and necessarily, it is concerned with the *quality* of the resources and how they are used (City, 2010). We already know that the quality of teaching staff is a hugely important factor affecting student achievement in the classroom (e.g., Clotfelter, Vigdor, & Ladd, 2010; Hanushek, 2011; Rice, 2003). The same can be said concerning the quality of school principals' leadership and its reciprocal, if indirect, effects on student learning (e.g., Hallinger & Heck, 2009; Leithwood & Louis, 2012; Leithwood & Riehl, 2005). For this reason, the scope of discussion in this chapter encompasses staff investments not only in recruitment, hiring, distribution, and (re)assignment, but also in the deployment and structuring of time, professional learning opportunities, evaluation, supervision, and other forms of support. All these matters are potentially part of the investment equation.

We bring an additional lens to understanding investment in staffing resources that of "learning-focused leadership," explained more fully in the Introductory Chapter of this book and in other writings (see Copland & Knapp, 2006; Portin, Knapp, Plecki, & Copland, 2008). Given the premise of this lens—that, to be learning-focused, school and district leadership targets not only student learning, but also the learning of professionals and the system as a whole—we looked especially closely at how investments targeted professional learning and also the collective changes in thinking, actions, and routines (among adult participants in an educational organization) that constitute "system learning." There are good reasons for this emphasis, as reformers have long recognized the steep learning curve that ambitious reforms imply for all adults in the system (Thompson & Zeuli, 1999; Drago-Severson, 2009). An important consequence is often overlooked by reformers and analysts alike: investments must also be made in leaders and leadership, alongside teachers and others who work most directly and continuously with students. This makes sense: leaders not only make resource investment decisions; they are also intimately connected to the translation of resources into the tangible and intangible conditions supporting the learning of students and professionals at all levels of the education system.

Hence, potential investment questions, large and small, become a regular part of the work of a learning-focused leader, even though the questions may initially be raised with short-term needs in mind. Who teaches whom this year? How do we fill the recently vacated position? Can we rearrange the staff we have or what they do to make headway on the low levels of math performance? Which schools need new professional development resources, and if so, what kinds? The questions are endless, and the daily pressures of leadership work often push leaders to react to the immediate crisis, particularly in an atmosphere of economic downturn and shrinking budgets. In all of these areas and more, learning-focused leaders take on the task of getting their investment decisions to match—and hopefully maximize—both short- and long-term instructional improvement priorities and values (Calvo & Miles, 2012; Odden & Picus, 2011; Sorenson & Goldsmith, 2013). Leaders also play a role in determining how human resources are developed and supported to take on the responsibilities to which they are assigned (Boyd, Lankford, & Wyckoff, 2008; Kimball, Milanowski, & Heneman, 2010). If powerful and equitable learning opportunities are to be provided for students at every school, then the way staffing and other resources are directed to, and within, schools, and the discretion leaders have to configure these resources, need immediate attention.

Confronting Staffing Challenges in Demanding Contexts: The Nature of Leaders' Investment Work

Learning-focused leaders in the districts we studied faced a set of staffing challenges that prompted their investment work. To appreciate their ways of addressing these challenges, it helps to acknowledge the challenges confronting them, with an eye on what it implied for investment in leadership resources; then, to consider the types of staffing decisions and frameworks they could use to address these challenges; and finally to note other conditions in their local contexts that could shape their investment decisions. We illustrate the discussion with examples from the four districts.

Enduring and Emerging Staffing Challenges

If they are serious about learning improvement, district leaders quickly recognize two overarching staffing challenges: first, recruiting, retaining, and developing a well-qualified, diverse teacher and administrator workforce, and, second, strengthening and supporting the practice of leadership, especially at the school level, but also in the district central office (as more fully described in Chapters 4 and 5 of this volume). At the intersection of these two lies a third that is only beginning to be recognized: building and supporting an *instructional leadership cadre* across levels in the district that complements and augments the capacity of school leaders to carry out this function. Satisfactorily addressing these challenges raises an array of investment issues, including finding the right people and defining their work in relation to a learning improvement agenda; reallocating and repurposing existing staff, as necessary, to pursue the agenda; and building the professional capacity and performance of all staff (see Chapter 5 for the discussion of these as conditions for transforming central office practice). Without a successful approach to these matters, efforts to achieve system-wide learning improvement are bound to fail.

Recruiting and retaining a well-qualified, diverse workforce. The quality of the educator workforce has long been recognized as the backbone of the public school system and efforts to improve schooling. Some of the biggest challenges concern the teaching ranks—like the difficulty of staffing high-needs schools, the high-mobility of teaching staff, and large numbers of novice teachers—and are well known in settings such as the ones we studied. So are the consequences: in many districts, schools with the highest proportions of poor, nonwhite, and low-scoring students are more likely to have teachers who are inexperienced, lack appropriate credentials, and have lower test scores, as well as higher rates of teacher and principal mobility and attrition (Clotfelter, Ladd, & Vigdor, 2006; Feng, 2010; Kalogrides, Loeb, & Beteille 2011). Add to that, first-year teachers tend to produce student achievement gains that are significantly lower than similar teachers with 10 to 15 years of experience (Rockoff, 2004; Harris & Sass, 2011; Ronfeldt, Lankford, Loeb, & Wyckoff, 2013).

These staffing patterns were apparent in the districts we studied. For example, across our case study districts, one quarter (on average) of first-year teachers who were at a given school in 2006–07 were no longer there the following year. The reasons for such turnover are many, but the often cited reasons of low compensation and a difficult-to-teach clientele are not the only ones. In addition, in urban settings, other conditions are also implicated, among them: a lack of resources, support, and recognition from the school administration; a lack of teacher influence over school and classroom decision making; too many intrusions on classroom teaching time; and inadequate time to prepare (Ingersoll, 2004; Borman & Dowling, 2008; Boyd et al., 2011; Brown & Wynn, 2009; Guarino, Santibanez, & Daley, 2006).

Strengthening and supporting school leadership. In ways that are both obvious and subtle, the quality of leadership figures prominently in the teacher staffing patterns just described. School leaders, in particular, are in a position to provide support, acknowledge teachers' needs, direct resources to them (within limits), involve them in decision making, and otherwise create environments that can help struggling teachers survive. Yet school leaders, too, exhibit high turnover rates, as in New York City, where district leaders estimated that, to serve its approximately 1,500 schools, 300 new principals would be needed every year. This fact begs the question of how the district can ensure a capable and stable cadre of school leaders to carry forward the work of learning improvement.

The roots of this staffing challenge are also numerous, but they implicate the ways a large district cultivates school administrators, what it expects of them, and how they are supported to meet expectations—all dimensions of the investment problem facing the system. The difficulty of the school leadership job in urban areas, for example, and its relation to principal turnover has been well established (Farkas, Johnson, Duffett, Syat, & Vine, 2003; Loeb, Kalogrides, & Horng, 2010), along with a series of conditions that include uncompromising politics and bureaucracy, complaining parents, complicated special education laws, and threats of litigation, on top of other administrative responsibilities required to keep a school or district running smoothly. But beyond these generic hazards of such working environments, a specific set of expectations comes with the territory that directly implicate how the district supports its school leaders, configures their roles and responsibilities, and sets expectations for their performance.

New expectations for school leadership roles in particular school settings mean that school leaders have much to learn, and need help doing so—such as developing cultural competency (as in Eugene, OR, which made this a central reform theme), entrepreneurial capacity and resourcefulness to thrive in an educational "marketplace" (as in New York City, which devolved new authority to the school level, in a system emphasizing competition), and the ability to use disaggregated data to help school staff differentiate instruction to meet learning needs of subgroups such as English language learners, students with disabilities, and racial and ethnic minority groups (as in all the districts we studied). Perhaps the greatest need is developing principals' capacity for engaging in instructional leadership—a clear expectation of these districts—not to mention protecting their time for this work, which is often compromised (Hallinger, 2011; Portin, DeArmond, Gundlach, & Schneider, 2003).

Strengthening the instructional leadership cadre across levels in the system. Alongside the need to strengthen school principals, and in part because of it, a third staffing need has arisen: how to grow and manage an *instructional leadership cadre* within and across schools. Even with sufficient time and expertise, principals cannot shoulder the full load of supporting instructional improvement. Yet many other school staff can offer this kind of assistance to teachers and are beginning to appear in larger numbers and greater variety in school districts across the nation (Leithwood, Mascall, & Strauss, 2009; Supovitz, Sirinides, & May, 2010). This development was evident in the districts we studied, where educational reforms prompted the development of new roles within schools such as achievement coordinators, instructional coaches, teacher leaders, data specialists, assessment coordinators, and others, as we will explore later in the chapter (see also Chapter 2 in this volume).

Beyond school walls, members of a district-wide instructional leadership cadre, typically home-based in the district central office, or in regionalized support units, assist teachers in multiple schools, work in "learning partnerships" with school principals to develop their instructional leadership skills (see Chapter 4 in this volume), or occupy other positions working across schools. These staff offer another level of instructional leadership support, often to front-line instructional leaders. Noticeably, as discussed later in this chapter and elsewhere in this volume (see Chapters 5 and 6) the instructional leadership cadre can offer guidance and support not only to teachers, but also to individuals in leadership positions.

Types of Staffing Investments and Investment Frameworks

As they made investment decisions about staffing resources aimed at the staffing challenges described above, the district and school leaders we studied took action on one or more of three types of investments: *cultivating the supply of staff relevant to the learning improvement agenda* (e.g., by judicious use of new funding to acquire staff with particular skills, or by developing "pipeline" or "pathway" approaches to in-house leadership development), *reallocating or repurposing current staffing resources* (e.g., by aligning staff work and position descriptions more closely with learning improvement priorities), and *strengthening staff capacity and performance* (e.g., by investing in professional development, guidance, and feedback systems).

Table 6.1 illustrates the way leaders might be addressing the three challenges at different levels of the system, with an explicit goal of improving the quality of leadership and its focus on learning improvement.

TABLE 6.1 Three Types of Staffing Resource Investments Aimed at Leadership for Learning Improvement

	Cultivating Supply of Staff Relevant to Learning Improvement Agenda	*Reallocating and Repurposing Existing Staff*	*Strengthening Staff Capacity and Performance*
District	• Developing targeted recruitment mechanisms • Strengthening support for new teachers • Creating new instructional leadership or support positions • Establishing "pipeline" or "pathway" routes to leadership roles for staff to develop their careers toward leadership	• Redefining administrative positions to emphasize instructional support • Improving human resource functions and support for schools	• Requiring and supporting data-based forms of leadership practice • Investing in school-based professional learning support for teachers • Creating better assessment and feedback systems that offer leaders evidence about their work
School	• Creating new teacher leadership positions in the school • Serving as a host school for teacher candidates • Recruiting new staff who exhibit potential for teacher leadership	• Changing teacher leadership assignments • Developing instructional support teams • Matching talents with leadership tasks • Reallocating time to enable regular staff conversation about their practice	• Restructuring professional learning time to increase collaborative efforts • Improving instructional coaching in response to evidence about performance • Engaging with community resources to advance improvement agenda

To enable leaders' efforts to imagine and pursue these kinds of actions, the districts we studied created *investment frameworks* that determined the rules governing decisions—especially the decisions made at the school level—regarding the allocation, assignment, distribution, and ongoing support of staff. In effect, the frameworks specified where initiative for improvement activity lay and specifically what flexibility, autonomy, responsibility, or discretion was expected or allowed at different levels of the school system. Four types of investment frameworks emerged from our analyses:

• *Mandated investment frameworks* imposed on district and school leaders the ways in which a particular staffing resource should or might be used. For example, the district might require a principal to use FTE or a position for a specific purpose or role in their building as part of a district-wide reform strategy.

- *Negotiated investment frameworks,* unlike mandates, offered leaders latitude to choose among options. For example, the district might limit, but not specify, the types of staffing expenditures that a principal can make with the Title I budget or other categorical resources. Negotiated investments sometimes result from an external partnership, grant, or other discretionary source, and may allow principals greater latitude in deciding how to invest staffing resources.
- *Incentive-based frameworks* created mechanisms for rewarding or sanctioning leaders' as well as other staff's performance in response to particular school-level outcomes. For example, a district might incentivize improved instructional leadership by rewarding school principals who met student performance goals, or widely and publically disseminate results from individual schools that allowed comparisons of relative improvement among similarly situated schools.
- *Market-based (or market-like) investment frameworks* encouraged staffing resource decisions that responded to the demand for particular services, generally through choice arrangements (e.g., parents' choosing schools or programs, schools' choosing support services). For example, a district might make centralized services available on a fee-for-service basis and eliminate those services that were not "bought," while simultaneously increasing others that were in greater demand.

Each framework makes assumptions about the way school and district leaders understand their role and their responsibilities for investing staffing resources. In our four districts, these assumptions varied, reflecting differences in the districts' approaches to learning improvement and how to support school leadership. As shown in Table 6.2 below, no district employed a single framework, but instead combined frameworks in ways that emphasized certain arrangements over others.

The New York City Empowerment Schools Organization (ESO) employed a combination of market-based and incentive-based frameworks, with rewards for principal and school performance. The system of "School Support Organizations"

TABLE 6.2 Configuration of Investment Frameworks in Case Study Districts

District	Mandated	Negotiated	Incentive-Based	Market-Based
New York, NY	X	X	XX	XXX
Atlanta, GA	XX	XXX	XX	—
Lane County 4J (Eugene, OR)	X	XXX	—	XX
Portland, OR	XX	XX	X	—

XXX = Major district emphasis; XX = Moderate emphasis; X = Minor emphasis; — = No emphasis at all.

of which the ESO was a part (central office support arrangements that schools chose to associate with and, in fact, paid for) presumed that market forces would prominently influence resource and other decisions made at the school and district levels. However, paralleling these market-based strategies, the district's accountability system rewarded or sanctioned the work of principals and school staff, particularly through an annual School Progress Report and School Quality Review for each school. To a lesser degree, mandated and negotiated frameworks also influenced school staffing allocations.

In contrast, Atlanta set parameters around investment activity through a combination of mandated and negotiated frameworks, coupled with a system that offered some rewards and sanctions. Staffing resources in Atlanta were invested in a uniform way across schools, with both the number and types of positions determined by the central office. While allowing for some discretion at the school level, available choices were restricted to a menu of options articulated by the district.

In Lane County District 4J (Eugene), a different configuration of investment frameworks was in place, in part, due to the district's history of decentralization and the long-standing practice of allowing parents to send their children to various schools of choice. Thus, resource investment activity was framed by a combination of negotiated and market-like arrangements. The district provided additional resources to targeted schools, and principals had some decision making discretion regarding how these staffing resources were utilized, based on data that identified strategies aimed at addressing learning priorities. At the same time, principals of some neighborhood schools felt the impact of the "market" as parents opted to send their children to one of the district's schools of choice.

Portland established yet another arrangement, in which negotiated and mandated frameworks shaped the deployment and use of staffing resources, along with a limited use of sanctions. While the district allowed school-level discretion in the use of staffing resources, tight budgets had restricted staffing levels, even as student needs had increased. The district's shift towards common curriculums in the year or two before we visited added mandates that influenced how staffing resources were used. In addition, a decision to create K–8 schools by merging elementary and middle schools, driven in part by underperformance in the middle schools, had significant implications for the merging and reallocation of staffing resources to serve the varying needs of both elementary and middle school students, staff, parents, and community.

Other Conditions That Frame Investment Decisions

As the brief review of the districts' investment frameworks has hinted, school and district leaders' investment work takes place in demanding environments. Five conditions in these environments—partially resulting from district policy or organizational decisions, and in part a reflection of other events or contingencies—are an important consideration in leaders' decision making about resources.

First, the *ebb and flow of fiscal resources* directly influences what kinds of staffing investments are possible. New money permits the creation of new positions, funds more extensive staff development, and underwrites other support activities, while shrinking budgets require the consideration of quite different actions, such as employee layoffs, increases in class size, or the reallocation or repurposing of existing human resources. The four districts we studied had different histories in this regard, though all were facing the prospect of substantial budget cuts due to the economic downturn at the close of our data collection period. Both of the Oregon districts, for example, had weathered a significant budget shortfall in the years immediately preceding our data collection window due to state tax limitation measures and enrollment decline, whereas New York City and Atlanta had been relatively prosperous during the same time frame. Districts can be proactive in seeking ways to generate additional revenue, and the four we studied are no exception, as multimillion dollar corporate and philanthropic grants were secured by three of the districts during our study time frame. But these sources are episodic and do not greatly alter the fundamental facts of fiscal life determined by state finance systems, local tax levies, and enrollment patterns.

Second, the *current and potential sources of staff supply*, residing in a local labor market and whatever talent pools the district is able to set up, offer potential personnel for the schools and central office, though these pools may be limited in certain ways. Limited pools and constrained labor markets may prompt the district or school to seek out or cultivate out new human resource pools, including through in-house or closely linked alternative leadership preparation programs (as several of our districts did).

Third, the *arrangement of the district's human resource function* handles the hiring of staff or some aspects of their ongoing work. Often overlooked, the human resource department in large school systems can play a pivotal role in the ability of the district to populate the schools with capable staff (e.g., Campbell, DeArmond, & Schumwinger, 2004; Odden, 2011). Not surprisingly, district leaders in the sites we studied were reconsidering how to improve and reconfigure the human resource function, so as to provide services that were more connected, responsive, and tailored to the individual needs of schools, while at the same time building policies and processes that attract sufficient numbers of appropriately trained individuals to fill positions. New York City's effort to split the function between a Talent Development Office and a set of regionally located "Integrated Services Centers" handling routine personnel matters was a case in point.

Fourth, *collective bargaining agreements and the culture that surrounds employment relationships* impact how staff are or can be deployed, how they do their work, and how they are supported. Investment strategies that seek out nontraditional forms of staffing may require additional negotiations between labor and management. Unions were active players in several of our sites, as both collaborators and critics, of district efforts to revamp how staff, both teachers and administrators, would be evaluated.

Finally, *the district's accountability system* (subsuming that of the state and federal government, as well) directly or indirectly frames staff performance and intimately shapes investments aimed at further developing staff capacity. All these systems were likely to call for demonstrable levels of school performance, thus shaping what school administrators would be expected to accomplish, often within a limited time frame (e.g., in both Portland and New York City schools, principals were expected to show some progress within two years, or risk losing their jobs).

Investing in Instructional Leadership: Positioning People, Developing Capacity, and Enabling Their Work

The districts we studied sought to address the staffing challenges described above in several ways that aimed at their teacher workforce directly, among them, through professional development aimed at teachers, recruitment and talent development schemes, and teacher evaluation. But one additional aspect of their investment strategies was striking: they were actively *investing in instructional leadership itself,* by creating positions, structures, and arrangements dedicated to this purpose within and across schools, as well as investing in capacity building (especially concerning the leadership of data-based practice), or other forms of support that enabled the school-level leaders to work more productively.

By seeking to increase and improve instructional leadership activity inside or across schools, these districts were moving in a direction that has begun to be noticed by scholars (Mangin, 2009; Miles & Frank, 2008; Robinson, 2010). Such a strategy echoes an expansive body of literature on the means and mechanisms by which organizations invest in human capital (Becker & Huselid, 2006; Cascio & Boudreau, 2008; Lawler, 2008; Pfeffer, 1998; Odden, 2011; Odden & Kelly, 2008; Smylie & Wenzel, 2006). As such, these investments simultaneously raise questions about staffing *supply* (Do we have the right people in place to do this work? If not, how can we find them or grow them?), *capacity of staff* (Can staff achieve the desired goals? If not, what supports are needed?), and also *performance* (How will we—and they—know when staff are doing their jobs well?). A central part of our analysis concerns how leaders considered and addressed these matters—that is, ensured supply, allocated or repurposed staffing resources in productive and equitable ways, further developed staff capacity, and motivated as well as demonstrated performance—as they identified and implemented investment strategies. They did so by putting resources into district-based staff working across schools, other staff located inside of schools, and building leaders' capacity to work in data-based ways.

Investment in Instructional Leadership Staff Across Schools

Sometimes as part of a larger attempt to reconfigure the central office and its relationship to schools, districts invested in support of cross-school instructional leadership by creating and filling new positions, or reassigning supervisory central office staff (e.g., assistant superintendents, executive directors) or nonsupervisory staff (e.g., curriculum coordinators, professional development specialists) into new roles more closely aligned with the needs of principals and their schools. These staff might operate out of a traditional central office unit or be reassigned to (or recruited for) an intermediary unit located between the district office and the schools that provided direct, more accessible support to schools. These staff were often assigned to, or supervised by, district administrators who also worked directly with schools and their principals. Such intermediary roles can act as a catalyst for reform (McLaughlin & Talbert, 2002) and become part of a central office "transformation strategy" aimed at improving student learning—a matter examined elsewhere in this volume (see Chapter 4) and related publications (Honig & Copland, 2008; Honig, Copland, et al., 2010).

Two cross-school investment patterns appeared in the districts we studied: (1) orchestrating instructional leadership activity through mandated or negotiated investments in central office staff who served multiple schools and (2) developing a "market" for central office instructional leadership, driven by school needs, preferences, and choices.

Orchestrating cross-school instructional support through mandated or negotiated investments. A common strategy in each of our districts—perhaps the most straightforward way of investing in instructional leadership—was to create and fund district-level instructional leadership positions that served multiple schools. One simple way was to make individuals with subject-specific expertise available to schools. Portland Public Schools' experience highlights both the potential and early implementation issues that such a strategy can encounter. To improve support for classroom teachers, the district invested $3.6 million annually to create and maintain a cadre of 60 Teachers on Special Assignment (TOSAs) housed within the central office and assigned to specific content areas. The TOSAs were expected to work directly with individual teachers, teacher teams, or entire school staff on the delivery of the district's common curriculum or specialized education services (e.g., special education, gifted, English as a second language). Given their curricular focus, the TOSAs reported directly to the director of curriculum.

According to district leaders, this investment had yet to realize its potential, and they pointed to several factors that might be limiting its value. First, the TOSAs' ability to work directly with classroom teachers was often delayed, due to the multistep process of requesting support, though the process could sometimes be facilitated by prior relationships among the parties. Second, TOSAs were often confused about whether they reported to the school principal, the principal's supervisor, or the directors of central office instructional departments. Third, given the many demands placed on them by multiple schools, TOSAs had difficulty distributing their time and support adequately and fairly to all requesting schools. As senior district administrators and school principals readily admitted, budget restrictions and other fiscal constraints had compounded these difficulties.

Atlanta also invested in a new role for teacher leaders, but conceptualized it differently from the approach used in Portland. Atlanta maintained a cadre of 42 "Model Teacher Leaders" (MTLs) at a comparable level of investment ($3.1 million annually). Like the TOSAs in Portland, these staff were intended to provide direct support to classroom teachers and teacher teams in schools that requested their services. Atlanta had more time to develop this strategy and had taken the concept of a district-level instructional support system a step further than Portland, largely in response to many of the same challenges that Portland had been encountering. As one senior district official noted, when the district's MTL model was first developed, it lacked systems to manage the demands placed on the district-level instructional support staff and bring continuity to the support they provided. In response, the district changed the reporting structure for the MTLs, so that they reported directly to the principal's supervisors, the Executive Directors for each "School Reform Team" (a network of 20–25 schools linked to groups of dedicated central office staff serving their improvement needs most directly). Additionally, the district then allowed classroom teachers to request support directly from the MTLs; alternatively, principals could also call upon the MTLs when assistance was needed. Moreover, the district relocated the MTLs to the School Reform Team office—thereby placing them closer to the schools they served.

In the Atlanta schools involved in our study, classroom teachers and principals signaled that the MTLs were an indispensable source of support on a host of matters related to instruction and their work as instructional leaders.

- According to one classroom teacher, "I can go to the Model Teacher Leaders with any question I have or any concern, and they have always been able to help me."
- A senior administrator observed: "The Model Teacher Leaders know the school achievement plans at each [of their] schools, they know their comprehensive school reform designs . . . they begin to own those schools and build strong professional relationships with those teachers so that the teachers trust them."
- Another senior administrator noted, "When the Model Teacher Leaders enter a school, it's not uncommon for teachers to run toward them asking them questions or inviting them into their classroom."

Senior district leaders saw the Model Teacher Leaders as a significant component of the district's instructional reform agenda, offering support that overlapped with supports provided by school principals, helping teachers "deliver instruction at a deeper level."

Atlanta's teacher leader investment strategy was coupled with one other initiative—that created the "Executive Director" position for School Reform Teams. This individual, referred to as an Instructional Leadership Director (ILD) in analyses carried out in the second strand investigation (see Honig, 2012; Honig & Rainey, in press; and Chapter 4 within this volume), concentrated time on building the school principal's instructional leadership capacity.

Related workload, supervisory, and organizational changes, not to mention a stable overall stance towards reform, appeared to enhance or inhibit the prospects for a more vital and continuous connection between these instructional leaders and both principals and classroom teachers. All together, the strategy approximates what has been characterized as an "infrastructure for learning" (Darling-Hammond et al., 2005). However, it takes more than organizational positioning, supervision, and communication pathways for cross-school instructional leadership to provide effective instructional support to schools. Evolving the appropriate organizational conditions is clearly an important part of the story, as is the development of new practices (see Chapters 4 and 5).

Building a market for cross-school instructional support driven by school needs, preferences, and choice. The version of New York City school reform that was in place at the time of our study depended on both district- *and* school-level resource decisions in a "market-like" arrangement, thereby providing a radically different image of district investment in cross-school instructional leadership support. Unlike Portland or Atlanta, this reform theory redirected resources from some central office functions to schools, thereby augmenting their discretionary funds, and then required school principals to select one of 14 "School Support Organizations" (SSOs) that occupied an intermediate niche in the system. (One such SSO, the Empowerment Schools Organization, embracing approximately a third of all schools in the city, was the principal focus of our investigations in New York City.) Once under the umbrella of an SSO, schools allied themselves with a network of 20–25 schools, clustered around a Network Leader and a team of four Network administrators; schools paid an annual fee for this membership ($29,500 per year within the Empowerment Schools Organization). Reflecting market-like forces, networks came into being only if a sufficient number of schools wanted to join them; otherwise, almost literally, they would go out of business. At the same time, the district limited the market by preapproving a slate of SSOs, some of which were created by the district and others that were external organizations approved by the district.[1]

Instructional leadership support was a central, though not sole, focus of the Network Team's work. The Network Leader, acting as an "Instructional Leadership Director" (see Chapter 4, this volume), concentrated time on instructional leadership issues. Two other positions within the Network Team, one called

Achievement Coach and the other Lead Instructional Mentor, were primarily concerned with helping schools boost achievement and the quality of instruction, especially for novice teachers.[2] Achievement Coaches responded to whatever the school deemed necessary to boost student performance, including helping to develop more data-based modes of practice and designing professional development around school-identified instructional improvement needs. Lead Instructional Mentors offered support to whomever the school had designated as mentors for novice teachers. In the 2007–08 school year, 500 or so schools were supported through 22 Networks set up through the Empowerment Schools Organization, each with one (or in a few cases more than one) Achievement Coach and one Lead Instructional Mentor.

As an investment strategy, the New York City/Empowerment Schools arrangement departs from more traditional practice in three ways. First, it separated the link between central office support functions and the formal supervision of school principals. Second, the arrangement made the *school* the primary investor in instructional leadership support. Third, it enabled the school, as investor, to radically differentiate the forms of instructional leadership support in which it invested: schools within the ESO did not *have to* seek out Network Team staff for help developing their instructional leadership capacity; instead, they could go elsewhere for instructional leadership support (e.g., to external partners, the city's Office of Teaching and Learning, or local university programs) or could internally organize and implement their own professional development.

While the Network Team arrangement represents a departure from standard practice, it also comes with a significant risk. Whether or not the Achievement Coach—or any members of the Network Team, for that matter—engaged in instructional leadership or instructional leadership support depended on what schools asked for. In the 2007–08 school year, school leaders, especially inexperienced ones, typically asked for assistance with matters not closely related to instruction—budgeting, personnel actions, responding to irate parents or community members, handling procurement issues, meeting compliance requirements, and navigating the placement of special education students, to mention only a few of the matters that prompted a call to Network Team administrators. And given the introduction of an ambitious new set of accountability tools during the 2007–08 year, school requests were often directed at the Achievement Coach or others to assist with the deployment of these tools or the use of data they yielded.

Thus, as an investment in support of instructional leadership, the Network Team arrangement could fall short of providing sustained, expert attention to the various instructional improvement issues facing a school's staff. That said, several related actions could mitigate this fact. First, schools could and often did go elsewhere for particular kinds of instructional leadership, especially to universities and external partner groups, and also to other schools in the peer networks that began to develop in the Empowerment Schools arrangement. Second, the relationship between Network Teams and school leaders could evolve so that, once more pressing needs were met, school staff would turn more to instructional support matters. Third, the Network Teams could seed requests for instructional assistance by engaging school leaders in an ongoing conversation about instructional matters, as they started to do in 2008–09 with the introduction of an instructional framework tool developed by the Empowerment Schools Organization. Network Teams started using this tool to prompt school leaders' consideration of their instructional improvement needs and the ways the Network Teams could be helpful. Finally, as alluded to in Chapter 4 (this volume) and described in greater detail in other writings (see Honig, Copland, Rainey, Lorton, & Newton, 2010), Network Team Leaders and other Network Team members often had clear and focused agendas around improving school principals' instructional leadership, and in various ways engaged principals in assistance relationships that strengthened this aspect of principals' practice.

In the short-term, building a school-driven market for instructional leadership support appeared to increase responsiveness to the school's expressed preferences for assistance, not all of which were directly related to instructional improvement. It also allowed for a variety of sources of support. However, the long-term success of this strategy depends on other resources, policies, conditions, and incentives that are coupled with the initial investment decision.

Investments in Instructional Leadership Within Individual Schools

Investments in instructional leadership *within* schools often accompanied efforts by districts to strengthen the cross-school activities described above. The within-school investments we observed, made by district officials, school principals, or both, generally reflected three approaches to budgetary management and control.

The default: Leave it up to the principal. Some districts assumed a less directive or active role regarding in-school investment in instructional leadership support, leaving it largely up to principals to do so, if they wished, as in one school we studied in Portland. In this example, unprompted by the district and without a dedicated budget source, the principal enlisted selected classroom teachers as co-leaders of the school's instructional improvement agenda. Referred to as "facilitators," these teachers participated on the school's leadership team and acted as liaisons between the principal and grade-level teams. While retaining full-time classroom teaching responsibilities, facilitators regularly participated in meetings focused on administrative and instructional issues. The principal made these roles possible by collaborating with the teachers' union to arrange for extended duty pay and by cultivating support for this model among the teachers in the building.

This familiar form of teacher leadership development in the school reveals several challenges for districts seeking to create a coherent instructional reform agenda. For one thing, principals varied in their capacity to imagine and carry out such arrangements, let alone their desire to do so, leaving the possibility that instructional leadership in some schools would be in short supply, while well developed in others. Furthermore, simply creating these roles in particular schools, without capacity building and leadership support activities (see Chapter 3 in this volume), did little to ensure that the school was adopting practices that supported the instructional improvement agenda.

A reallocation alternative: Funding particular positions for within-school instructional leadership. Alternatively, districts invested dedicated resources to be used for installing or strengthening the within-school instructional leadership cadre in all schools. Atlanta Public Schools did so by funding, in addition to the Model Teacher Leader roles discussed above, within-school "Instructional Liaison Specialists" who worked collaboratively with the principal and classroom teachers to facilitate instructional change aimed at meeting district-derived performance targets.[3] This investment was made possible by modifying the existing allocation formula for assistant principals, in effect, repurposing some Assistant Principal positions (beyond the single position that all schools above a certain size are allocated) with one Specialist per school. In doing so, the district created 70 such positions through reallocation of existing funds. The Specialist had no classroom teaching responsibilities and spent the majority of his or her time working with teachers or teacher teams, planning or facilitating professional development, working individually with students, and otherwise supporting the principal and school leadership team.

Through these means, the district institutionalized a new addition to the within-school instructional leadership capacity. The Specialists participated as regular school staff members under the principal's leadership. However, unlike the facilitators in the Portland school, the Specialists were required school-level positions. Consequently, even while the principals could reconfigure or add to Specialists' predefined duties, their ability to redirect the resource for other purposes was substantially limited.

As with the district-level investments discussed earlier (and echoing the more extended discussion in Chapter 2 of this volume), the following appear to play an important role in creating conditions that maximize the potential of the original investment:

- Investing sufficient time for those in instructional leadership roles to work regularly with teachers (in and out of the classroom).
- Creating team structures for those exercising instructional leadership to coordinate instructional support efforts within the school.
- Investing in professional learning opportunities specifically designed for those exercising instructional leadership.
- Devoting sufficient time and energy to recruiting, orienting, and preparing the individuals who occupy these roles, on the premise that not everyone is

right for the job and few are fully prepared for the demands of working in such roles.

Attending to these matters was largely up to the school principal, though the central office sometimes played a role as well. Creating and filling mandated, school-level instructional leadership positions alone is no guarantee that instructional leadership will be exercised effectively. Investments of other resources—some under district control, others controlled by the school—combined with other organizational changes are key to realizing the potential of this instructional support.

A negotiated investment alternative: Enabling schools to expand their instructional support cadre. A wider range of within-school instructional leadership arrangements was possible when the district transferred to the school both the resources and the discretionary authority to create instructional support positions to suit particular school needs. This alternative seeks to maximize the flexibility that districts grant to principals to invest resources and provide support to principals as they consider resource investment decisions and strategies (within this approach, the district could also specify the types of staffing resources over which flexibility extends). In effect, the districts allocated three types of resource: *authority* for school leaders to act on particular kinds of staffing (or other resource) decisions, *actual resources* over which the school leaders can legitimately exercise discretion, and *assistance* to enable school leaders to take good advantage of these discretionary opportunities.

This alternative can be understood as a recent addition to decades-long experimentation with granting greater autonomy to schools, on the premise that those closest to the classroom are best positioned to make good decisions on behalf of children's education. A wave of site-based management experiments in the 1980s (Beck & Murphy, 1998; Brown & Saks, 1987), more recent expansion of charter schools (Farrell, Wohlstetter, & Smith, 2012), the small school movement (e.g., Raywid, 1996), and a continuing movement toward creating systems of autonomous and differentiated schools (Honig, 2009) have tried to make good on the premise. Yet the evidence is not clear that, by itself, freedom to maneuver prompts appropriate investments that support better outcomes. Principals who have more options often default to familiar allocation strategies (Mayer, Donaldson, Le Chasseur, Welton, & Cobb, 2013; Monk, 1987), especially in the area of staffing roles and assignments.

Reminiscent of the argument for combining bottom-up change with top-down support (Fullan, 1994), coupling increased flexibility with focused support may enable principals to successfully examine and rethink their resource investment approaches and strategies.[4] While decentralizing authority and resources, the district retained a distinct, even strong, presence in the way these resources were used, a pattern noted in reforming districts, in which "significant authority and responsibility are assigned to the schools" at the same time that the district maintains "a strong presence" (McLaughlin & Talbert, 2002, p. 188). More appears to be at work in the districts we studied than a simple swing of the pendulum between a largely decentralized approach to reform and a more centralized one, or vice versa. Instead, we encountered an intentional effort to couple increased flexibility with more centralized capacity-building and guidance.

At the root of attempts to maximize school-level flexibility in investing staffing resources was a calculation about how much support school principals needed and how best to get it to them. District officials were well aware that, as one noted, "Just because principals have been granted more freedom doesn't mean that they'll know what to do with it." The matter of how to help principals know—and learn—how to make good use of the new authority was resolved differently. The district could approach this question by restricting the range of school-level decision making, as in Atlanta, where only a limited number of investment options were available to principals, guided by specific frameworks. Principals had come to accept these restrictions and guidance as a source of support for their decision making. One principal commented,

> At first the district's approach really bothered me because I thought [the district] hired me to run this school . . . so my thought was, let me run it . . . but I learned a lot from the protocols that they provided . . . sometimes I've resisted . . . but I've realized that I can make it work. . . . I've been a principal now 15 years . . . and there are some things that sometimes you're in the rut, you're doing the same thing over and over.

From this principal's perspective, the district protocols provided fresh ideas and alternatives to practices that she had relied on but never fully assessed in terms of their effectiveness.

Alternatively, the district could offer principals far greater latitude, including freedom to choose their preferred form and degree of central office support, as in New York City's Empowerment Schools Organization, which granted school leaders considerable autonomy and control over many aspects of their budgets, raising the possibility that principals might not ask for help when they might have really needed it. The Network Team's support was there to be called on if needed, but at the school leader's discretion. And initially the schools we visited, mostly run by experienced principals, tended to be selective in asking for assistance. However, in the following school year, the relationships between Network Teams and the principals seemed to be deepening, involving more interaction around a greater range of issues, with more openings for district staff to encourage what it judged to be wise use of the school's resources.

Principals responded in various ways to the flexibility granted to them over the configuration of staffing resources, arrangement of instructional time, and

TABLE 6.3 How Principals Used Flexibility to Focus Staffing-Related Resources on Instructional Improvement

	Staffing Resources	*Instructional Time*	*Discretionary Dollars*
Elementary School	Principal "departmentalized" grades 2–5 requiring teachers to prepare for fewer lessons and to specialize in specific content areas.	Principal created passing periods within a departmentalized staffing plan to prepare upper elementary students for middle school.	Principal used discretionary funding to allow staff to visit schools serving low-income students to observe effective instructional practices.
K–8 School	Principal enlisted classroom teachers with special interests as elective teachers when additional resources for elective courses were unavailable.	Principal created a schedule to allow classroom teachers in grade-level teams to collaborate for 180 minutes per week. During collaborative time, students are in elective courses.	Principal compensates facilitators for extra duty using discretionary funds. The facilitators serve as teacher leaders in the building connecting the school's leadership team with each grade-level team.
Middle School	Principal revised student–teacher ratios to create five instructional coaches in subject areas. Coaches provide increased support to classroom teachers and increased adult presence in hallways during passing periods and lunch periods.	Principal and staff created a new master schedule that allows classroom teachers to "loop" with their students in an attempt to enhance student–teacher relationships (and also separates students during passing periods to reduce behavioral problems).	Principal used discretionary funds to provide before- and after-school tutorials (including transportation) for students struggling in math.
High School	Principal used resources intended for assistant principals to create academy leader positions that extended instructional support into each small learning community.	Principal created a Professional Activity period for teachers, used to address instructional priorities for that day. Activities included one-on-one tutoring with students and contacting parents.	Principal changed budget process by dividing the discretionary budget among three small learning communities and allowed teacher leaders to make decisions regarding expenditures.

allocation of discretionary dollars. Four examples in Table 6.3 illustrate a range that was common across the schools we visited.

As the examples show, most of the schools put some or all of their discretionary resources into instructional leadership itself, for example, by compensating teacher leaders and increasing their facilitation roles, revising student teacher ratios to create part-time subject area coaches, or by creating "academy leader" positions. (The elementary school, which used its resources to encourage a more specialized teaching configuration and to support intervisitation with other schools, already had a robust teacher leader cadre in place by the time we visited it.)

By all accounts, the allocation of increased authority and discretionary resources to the school, coupled with formal or informal supports, sat well with the principals we studied, especially in the New York City/Empowerment Schools Organization, where principals chose to operate within a system of enhanced discretion (see Portin et al., 2009; Portin & Knapp, 2011). One of these elementary principals noted:

> Normally, [the money I have put into partnerships] would have been . . . spent by the district before I even saw it, in staff developers. You know, the staffing, the support personnel, having more control over having the mentor that I want on staff, and not the district sending me a mentor—I can hire one of my own people to do that role, and make sure that mentor really matches the teachers.

This principal did not speak for all his colleagues across the city. Not all opted to be a part of the Empowerment Schools arrangement, nor did they necessarily want as much control over professional development or instructional support resources as the individual above. But the system allowed for this variation.

Whether backed by strong principal leadership as in the Portland case, supported by a common instructional framework as in Atlanta, or guided by a demanding accountability system as in New York City, the success of investments in the instructional leadership cadre at the school level appeared to depend on many things: staff chemistry, whether and how school leaders laid the groundwork for team-based instructional leadership, capacity to create a supportive school culture, and persistence by school staff in working through the ambiguities of these instructional support roles (see Chapter 2 in this volume; Portin et al., 2009; Portin & Knapp, 2011).

Related Investments: Building Capacity for Data-Based Leadership

As noted above, investing in instructional leadership and leadership support meant more than acquiring and assigning staffing resources. In addition to ensuring a broader more varied supply of people to exercise instructional leadership, districts put resources into building leaders' capacity, and also into related conditions necessary to translate supply and capacity into performance (e.g., by arranging conditions, incentives, and relationships to bring sustained instructional leadership support to classrooms).

Especially prominent among these supportive investments were resources devoted to building leaders' (and others') capacity for data-based practice. While ultimately aimed at teachers, this kind of investment concentrated in the short-term on individuals in leadership positions (e.g., central office staff, principals, instructional coaches, and others who worked with teachers). These arrangements were typically linked to federal, state, or district accountability systems, but not exclusively. Though accountability-focused investments can prompt compliance or generate feedback that is used in limited or punitive ways, the press for data-based practice evident in the districts we studied seemed to be encouraging a wider array of responses.

Learning-focused leadership depends upon the use of data to inform decisions and leadership actions related to instructional improvement (Copland & Knapp, 2006; Knapp, Copland, & Swinnerton, 2007). Recent discussions of district reform have increasingly focused on the use of data as a primary lever for systemic instructional improvement (Darling-Hammond et al., 2005; Murnane, City, & Singleton, 2008; Supovitz, 2006). Districts that use data effectively often do so as part of an "inquiry cycle" (Copland, 2003), a potentially valuable tool for making resource investment decisions in schools, districts, or states (Knapp, Copland, & Swinnerton, 2007; Plecki, Alejano, Lochmiller, & Knapp, 2006). While research is emerging on the way district decision makers use evidence in their work (Earl & Katz, 2006; Honig & Coburn, 2008; Murray, 2013), scholars have little to say about how data are informing or facilitating changes in existing resource allocation patterns, or else underscore the lack of data use for these purposes. More to the point, research has yet to consider how resources are invested in the development and use of data and that leaders do to build and use an evidence base for instructional leadership.

Our data highlight three related areas of investment in data-based practice, all of which were directed in multiple ways at the leadership cadre. The first, focused on the effort to *develop data infrastructure* (e.g., data systems, software, and protocols), sought to make data use possible and information accessible to staff at all levels of the system. A second investment attempted to *promote data literacy and use,* and thereby to increase the leaders' ability to make use of data to inform their own and others' practice. This strategy sought to install specialized district or school staff roles (e.g., variously named, "senior achievement facilitators," "student achievement coordinators," or "data coaches"), support professional development about data use, and create regular occasions for making sense of data. Third, to realize either or both of these investments in terms that were meaningful to their local context, district or school leaders often *generated new forms of data,* along with the occasions that invited or compelled people to make sense of the data. As Table 6.4 summarizes, these investments took many different forms.

In a curious way, these investments resembled the pattern of investing in instructional leadership described earlier in this chapter. While some of these resources went into equipment—such as the hardware and software necessary to mount Atlanta's data warehouse for integrating information from the Georgia On-Line Assessment System (GOAS) or New York City's Achievement Reporting and Innovation System (ARIS)—more of it went to creating or repurposing district- or school-level positions that addressed the leadership of data-based practice. It was also important to dedicate time and attention to training individuals in these newly crafted positions and provide them the wherewithal to train others to act as resources to people across the district. Thus, within the overarching support system for instructional leadership each district created, the activities and expertise of these people formed a supportive subsystem.

The subsystem for supporting data-based leadership practice could be fairly simple, as in Eugene, which made sure each principal had a part-time Student Achievement Coordinator, ostensibly to augment the principal's ability to monitor student learning and to help craft data analyses and displays in forms that were more accessible to teachers. The Coordinator job description referred to keeping "the school focused on what can be done to improve student achievement and close the achievement gap," which might include "leading systematic inquiry into the achievement gap or facilitating professional development on how to understand data and on how to take action" in light of what the data represented. In practice, however, the Coordinators took on various other responsibilities, including coordinating Title I activities or leading an intervention team for students struggling with behavioral issues.

At the other end of the continuum, in a school district as large as New York City, the support system for data-based leadership practice was much more elaborate. First of all, specialized central office staff called Senior Achievement Facilitators worked with schools in one or more of the school networks affiliated with a particular School Support Organization on the implementation and use of the accountability tools. Reporting directly to the district's Assessment & Accountability Office, these Facilitators often assumed a teaching role vis-à-vis school staff who were not so sure what they could and should be doing with data, or who did not grasp a larger vision of data-based practice. Other staff were positioned to provide data-related assistance to the schools. Network Achievement Coaches often spent time helping school staff make sense of periodic assessment information, prepare for a School Quality Review, or engage in a cycle of inquiry to address instructional improvement issues. Together and separately, Senior Achievement Facilitators, Achievement Coaches, and even Network Leaders offered various forms of assistance for expanding the school staff's data literacy or use—all within the parameters of what schools asked for.

TABLE 6.4 Illustrative District and School Efforts to Invest in Data-Based Leadership Practice

	NYC / ESO	Atlanta	Portland	Eugene
Investments in Data Infrastructure (e.g., data systems, computer software, data warehouses, etc.)	• Development of Achievement Reporting & Innovation System (ARIS)	• Warehouse to facilitate utilization of Georgia Online Assessment System (GOAS) • Infinite Campus	• System for helping leaders to utilize the Oregon Assessment of Knowledge & Skills (OAKS) system • Access to eSIS, statewide student information data system • Investment in "PPS Data Mart" and data warehouse	• System for helping leaders to utilize the Oregon Assessment of Knowledge & Skills (OAKS) system • Access to eSIS, statewide student information data system • Investment in data warehouse
Investments in Data Literacy and Data Use (e.g., through specialized data support roles or team structures, and related professional development)	• Creation of school-based Inquiry Teams • Establishing district data support roles (e.g., Senior Achievement Facilitators) • School-by-school creation of data support roles (e.g., Achievement Coordinators)	• Support for professional learning opportunities at the district and SRT level • Support for Model Teacher Leaders (MTLs) as data analysts serving multiple schools • Creation of Instructional Liaison Specialists (ILSs) within the school	• Provision of professional learning opportunities • Selection of data protocols and other analytic tools • Funding for research staff to work with school principals	• Regional principals' meetings • Participation in external professional development (e.g., Wallace LEAD Initiative) • Provision of FTE for the Student Achievement Coordinator position in high-needs neighborhood schools

Efforts to Generate New Forms of Data (e.g., by collecting data from internal and external stakeholders)			
• Regular surveys of school staff concerning support from ESO • School Quality Reviews (SQRs) conducted by outside teams • "Environmental Surveys" regarding school climate • Protocols that guide observations, interviews, and other sources of information about performance of struggling students targeted by school Inquiry Teams	• Regular surveys of school staff concerning support from the SRT and other central departments • District-wide instructional observation protocols and evaluation procedures • Quarterly "Fireside Chats" with members of the community • Frequent meetings with community leaders and business executives	• Surveys of school principals and school-level staff concerning support from central departments • District-level Performance Audits • Frequent meetings with community leaders and business executives	• Surveys of school principals, school-level staff, and community members (e.g., as part of strategic planning, budget process)

The latter example highlights a final dynamic of the leadership investment story in these districts. Because the districts' investment strategies often generated new kinds of data, the districts needed to put resources into capacity building efforts (e.g., professional development, coaching, help-lines and other on-call services) that would introduce people to these data and what could be done with them. In addition, they needed to create occasions for people to make use of the data. They did so by allocating time, establishing incentives, creating requirements and routines—for example, through data use protocols, advisory visits focused on data use, regular team structures (e.g., "inquiry teams" in each New York City school), reporting cycles, and other means that brought particular kinds of data to leaders' (and others') attention.

A great deal of new learning was involved in moving from the initial investment stage to a stage of secure practice, and districts had made varying degrees of progress toward that destination (see Chapter 4 in this volume regarding progress of the central office). While many of these investments were relatively new at the time of our study, with no guarantee they would be sustained until more robust data literacy prevailed in schools, the effort was already penetrating instructional leadership practice in the case study schools. As detailed more fully elsewhere (Portin et al., 2009; Knapp & Feldman, 2012), school leaders and other staff in these schools were paying close attention to data (especially from testing) and developing a language for talking about instructional improvement that was fully oriented to systematic data sources.

Conclusions

This chapter has offered a portrait of a particular form of resource investment that was a central part of the learning improvement strategies undertaken in the four districts and 15 schools we studied. Specifically, leaders in these systems found ways to invest resources *in instructional leadership itself,* at the same time and in close connection with their attempts to funnel resources into instruction and the quality of the teacher workforce. In so doing, they were taking a long-term view of the situation, and recognizing that, absent a robust leadership support system, many of their attempts to improve teaching and learning would yield less, if anything.

These investments were noteworthy in several ways. First of all, they directed resources to both the district and school level, in recognition that resource-related decisions needed to be made at both levels if learning improvement goals were to be met. However, decisions about the degree to which each level was involved, and with what discretion, was shaped by an "investment framework" created by the district that identified where initiative lay within the system, and who had authority to act regarding what resources. Each of the four districts we studied varied in their approach to an investment framework, and each choice represented particular assumptions that the district leaders made about principals and their leadership capacity. This, in turn, impacted the kind and amount of support that principals were given or received in order to effectively lead a learning improvement agenda.

Furthermore, these districts' investments in instructional leadership recognized that much more was involved than getting "good people" into designated positions, either on a school's staff or serving multiple schools. Rather, in addition to taking action to stimulate or cultivate the supply of people who were positioned to exercise instructional leadership, they put resources into building staff capacity and into improving their performance, as noted in Chapter 5 of this volume. Notably, they created what amounted to a "system of support" for instructional leaders, to help them learn to lead in a data-based way, and enable them to help others engage in practice that was anchored to data and evidence. As such, these investment strategies presumed that leaders needed a sophisticated grasp of data use, a variety of data to draw upon, and access to a fully developed informational infrastructure.

Our analysis does not exhaust the ways that these districts and schools could or did invest in instructional leadership. Beyond building, activating, and supporting an instructional leadership cadre within and among schools, these districts did other things to draw a potentially better prepared set of staff into leadership roles. In particular, several of the districts had set about cultivating from within or external sources new generations of future leaders to fill either long-established positions such as school principal or the more recently created ones such as Model Teacher Leader or Senior Achievement Facilitator. Within-district principal preparation programs in Atlanta and New York City are one example of such efforts (e.g., the Superintendents Academy for Building Leaders in Education program in Atlanta and the New York City Leadership Academy and New Leaders for New Schools in New York). Over the long-term, these attempts are likely to contribute to the overall investment purpose in important ways that our analysis has not begun to trace.

In closing, we need to remember that the instructional leadership investment story we have presented is not necessarily typical of districts or schools across the nation facing the challenge of learning improvement in challenging circumstances. After all, we chose these districts as sites that were demonstrably making progress toward learning improvement goals. As such, their progress was no doubt attributable in part to the relative stability of executive-level leadership (in all but one case) and somewhat favorable funding situations at the time we began our study (in three out of four sites), among other conditions. That said, the issues and constraints facing these districts are the same as those that many others must contend with, and these sites offer images of what is possible when educators enact a more learning-focused approach to leadership.

Notes

1 The New York City Department of Education did allow schools to "opt out" of district-approved support, provided the school met certain performance criteria and paid a modest fee to the district for administrative activities (e.g., payroll, custodial services, etc.).

2 Other positions in the Network Team included a Business Services Manager (who assisted schools with a variety of matters related to budgets, personnel, hiring, procurement, and fiscal or facilities compliance); a Student Services Manager (who assisted with matters related to the placement of special needs students, related compliance reporting, and other matters concerning services for such students); and the Network Leader (who provided overall leadership support of many kinds).

3 Though not part of the sample for the third strand of the *Study of Leadership for Learning Improvement*, other districts included in other study strands exhibited a similar strategy. Springfield, MA, for example, created "Instructional Leadership Specialist" positions for all of its schools, as described in Chapter 2 of this volume.

4 In this instance, the nature of the supportive relationship itself is likely to matter a good deal—specifically, how the district central office establishes and evolves its "assistance relationships" with schools. See analyses of these relationships in Honig, Copland, Rainey, Lorton, and Newton, 2010.

7

INVESTING FOR EQUITY IN INSTRUCTIONAL IMPROVEMENT

Margaret L. Plecki, Thomas J. Halverson, and Michael S. Knapp
With the assistance of Tino Castañeda and Chad Lochmiller

The idea of *investing* resources (people, money, time) in learning improvement presumes that resources are targeted to particular purposes—and not others—within the district and its schools (see Chapter 6 in this volume). In so doing, the investor is likely to be asked: Why not use the resources for X or Y or Z? Why favor *that* school, unit, or program and not this one? How *fair* is this allocation? How will *this* specific group of students (or teachers) benefit? Will all students (or teachers) benefit equally? Why or why not? The answers to these questions invoke the delicate politics of making investments in the context of scarce resources and competing interests. The questions also confront a basic premise of learning-focused leadership, and indeed the broad policy movement that seeks to "leave no child behind": that leadership and reform aim at providing *all* young people with education that is both powerful *and equitable* (Clune, 1994; Copland & Knapp, 2006; Ladd, 2008; Organisation for Economic Co-operation & Development [OECD], 2007; Scheurich & Skrla, 2003).

While the tug of war over scarce resources can be seen as a process of negotiating among competing interests, it is also a central occasion for district and school leaders to consider notions of *equity and fairness.* Based in some compelling vision of what is equitable and fair, the leadership challenge is to invest resources in ways that respond to the unique needs of students, teachers, and schools while maximizing these goals and developing economically and politically sustainable strategies for doing so.

Either explicitly or implicitly, these matters were a central concern in the districts and schools we investigated in the third strand of the *Study of Leadership for Learning Improvement* (Knapp et al., 2010; Plecki et al., 2009), and their experiences in investing resources bring to light the core issues at stake and some possible ways they can be addressed. Their attempt to grapple with equity concerns while investing resources to support learning improvement highlights the complexity of this facet of leadership work in two ways. First, it highlights the conceptual challenges of dealing with this fundamental but difficult idea. Put most simply, as various scholarly literatures have long recognized (Baker & Green, 2008; Berne & Stiefel, 1999; Grubb, 2009; Ladd, 2008), the conceptual problem resides in the fact that *what is equal is not always "equitable."* Despite the natural leadership tendency to make sure all parties have equal resources—thereby "leveling the playing field"—educators and their constituencies know intuitively that not all students need the same supports for learning, and that some students who face significant economic, linguistic, or other disadvantages are likely to require much *greater* support, to ensure an "equal" opportunity to succeed, no less to ensure success itself (Downes & Stiefel, 2008; Harris, 2008; Ladson-Billings, 2006). Leaders struggle to address historical and persistent inequities that are all too common within schools and classrooms across the nation, despite numerous federal, state, and local efforts to reduce them (Baker & Corcoran, 2012; Ladd, 2012).

Second, the attempt to invest resources equitably and effectively within districts and schools highlights the fact that achieving equity goals is not only a *technical* or *structural* problem, it is also a *political* challenge in which diverse views of what constitutes "fairness" must be adjudicated (Oakes, 2005). In broad strokes, the more that equitable solutions diverge from equal allocations, these political dynamics are likely to become all the more acute—because certain interests get an increasingly disproportionate share of a given resource (staffing, funding, time, expertise, materials), while others get less. Retrenchment conditions are also likely to surface political dynamics in more acute form, as leaders are forced to do the same (or more) with less, and the stakeholders view the resource distribution equation in stark, zero-sum terms.

Contextual factors may also contribute to the political dynamics and leadership challenges in developing more equitable responses to address the learning needs of all students. These factors include the nature of the relationships among school administrators, school boards, and labor unions and the specific policies that result from collective bargaining agreements. These labor arrangements can impact the types of staffing resource allocation strategies available for consideration in both productive and unproductive ways (Strunk & Grissom, 2010).

Thus, an explicit focus on equity brings a new dimension to the investment equation, as suggested in Figure 7.1. We explore this dimension in this chapter as follows. After a brief discussion of the central leadership challenges and concepts at play, we distinguish different types of resource decisions that invite the *differential* investment of staffing and other resources in activities aimed at particular schools, classrooms, programs, or students, and show how these actions attempted to realize the goals of learning-focused leadership that prioritizes equity. We

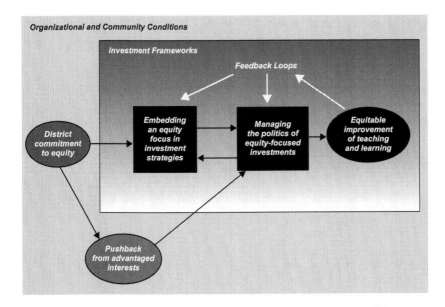

FIGURE 7.1 Embedding and Sustaining an Equity Focus in Investment Strategies

explore each of these with district and school examples across our sites. Then, drawing from one particularly instructive case, we explore how leaders can manage the political dimensions of leading for equity. We conclude the chapter with a few observations about the leadership actions leaders may consider as they move through stages of an equity agenda.

The Leadership Challenge

Public school leaders are increasingly being asked to do more with less, and to provide an opportunity for more of their students to experience school as an "equalizing" social and economic vehicle. Accountability initiatives like No Child Left Behind have shifted the focus of attention toward measurable outcomes in schools and across districts, and the corresponding wealth of published data about student performance has brought issues of difference and disparity to the forefront of school leaders' attention (Lee & Wong, 2004; Oakes, 2008). The four districts we studied (Atlanta Public Schools, New York City/Empowerment Schools Organization, Portland, OR, Public Schools, and Lane County District 4J in Eugene, OR) resemble a range of large and mid-sized districts across the country; they were wrestling with the complex and dynamic challenge of trying to raise the academic performance of all students, close the achievement gap, and distribute educational access and opportunity more equitably to every student. These objectives can at times compete for both attention and resources, and leave school leaders struggling to find adequate or useful decision making models and resource allocation strategies. Adding to this challenge is the growing realization by many school leaders that creating new funding formulas is not enough.

Specifically, leaders face some common problems of practice with respect to resource allocation, four of which are central to the task of equitably allocating resources based on differential needs (Plecki et al., 2006):

1. *Targeting achievement gaps.* Here, the cumulative disadvantages affecting some groups of students relative to others almost inevitably imply directing more and different resources to less advantaged students, to help them catch up with more advantaged peers. The key leadership act is to "put the money where the rhetoric is," by making achievement gaps a basic reference point for resource-related decisions, based on clear evidence (which accountability systems can help provide) on the nature of achievement gaps and progress on addressing those gaps.
2. *Organizing schools to enable the alignment of resources with equity-focused learning improvement.* Formula-driven approaches to allocating human resources to schools, coupled with the typically egalitarian culture of schools, often push them to be organized to be "equal" (e.g., same number of students in each class, same teaching assignments), and as such, typically not well aligned with an equity agenda. The leadership challenge is to structure time, staff roles, staff and student assignment, particular programs, funding formulas, and other organizational conditions that enable resources to be used in a more flexible and purposeful way, so as to maximize equity goals.
3. *Developing and distributing "human capital" equitably, among schools, programs, and classrooms.* The lines of least resistance are often for capable staff to be distributed inequitably among schools and programs (e.g., put the best teachers in the most advanced classes). Fully accomplished teachers are also typically in short supply. To counter these tendencies, leaders can provide supports, incentives, and opportunities for professional learning that build motivation and expertise, thereby fostering higher performance among all teachers, while also encouraging or directing the greatest talent to serve the greatest need.
4. *Managing the politics of equitable, learning-focused leadership.* All steps taken to allocate resources equitably, which almost always means unequally, will generate political pressures, due to competing demands from actors both inside and outside the education system. Leaders are often on the receiving end of these pressures, but also in a good position to mediate them.

All four challenges articulated above were present in our district cases, and responses to any one of them either interacted with, or were dependent upon, strategies to address the other three. In this chapter, we explore all four, while paying particular attention to understanding the fourth challenge regarding the successful management of political tensions associated with equity-focused leadership.

Clarifying Conceptions of Fairness and Equity

To pursue these challenges, leaders immediately confront the complex and politically charged determination of what is "fair." Ask any group of educators (as we did our informants) about equity as a concern or principle of their leadership action, and a range of responses is likely: from equity as the equal distribution of workload across teaching staff, to the reduction of achievement gaps, to equalizing access to selective programs, to the attention paid to special needs students as compared with others, to the pursuit of social justice in communities of poverty. The educators are likely to talk about—or around—issues of equity in their work in a variety of ways, but often with difficulty, or in ways that indicate they struggle to reconcile competing ideas (Marshall & Ward, 2004). At the root of their struggle are some notions of fairness and equality (e.g., equality of opportunity), coupled with heightened concern for the circumstances of less advantaged individuals or groups.

Beneath what people say or think are three notions that have been articulated by the school finance literature across the past several decades: equality, equity, and adequacy (Corcoran & Evans, 2008; Hanushek & Lindseth, 2009; National Research Council, 1999; Springer, Houck, & Guthrie, 2008). Of particular concern are the multiple and evolving meanings for the term *equity*, for they highlight the source of many struggles in this realm of leadership work (Bulkley, 2013).

In operational terms, the answer in many districts to this question of what constitutes a fair funding system has often been a distribution of dollars (e.g., funds for instructional materials) and human resources (e.g., principals, librarians, instructional assistants) to schools based simply on the number of students enrolled. On the face of it, this arrangement is clearly equal, and in certain situations would be considered equitable, as in cases where distributions are blatantly unequal. For example, in response to the "savage inequalities" that have often been described in urban schooling (e.g., Kozol, 1991), *more equal* treatment of all parties is an easily agreed upon goal. Yet even this goal is not easily met: the material, intellectual, and social resources of schooling remain stubbornly unequal, even when attempts are made to equalize the availability of books, technology, adequate facilities, literacy coaches, and other such resources (Baker & Corcoran, 2012; OECD, 2007; Rothstein, 2004). Confronted by these basic inequalities, the first impulse of reformers is to try to equalize available resources. The underlying assumption is this: *When parties (districts, schools, teachers, classrooms, etc.) are themselves considered equivalent, then treating them equally is generally viewed as the "equitable" thing to do*—this principle is described as "horizontal equity" in the language of school finance scholars (Berne & Stiefel, 1999).

However, a substantial body of research has established that not all students' needs are equal, and those with economic, social, or language challenges bring to school an increased need for support that might not be met solely by the additional support that categorical funds such as federal Title 1 dollars provide

(Harris, 2008; Jimenez-Castellanos & Topper, 2012; Jordan, 2010). Therefore, a funding formula that doesn't recognize these need-based differences not only fails to adequately support its students, but in fact, may be exacerbating the achievement gap within the district (Baker & Corcoran, 2012; Reardon & Robinson, 2008). Unfortunately, this realization often leaves district leaders with the complex and perplexing question: If an equal distribution to students and to schools (in proportion to enrollment) doesn't work as an effective and equitable funding formula, how do we determine (and justify) giving some more, and others less?

Central to this question is a complicated debate about the differences and distinctions between equality and equity. The equal treatment of equals, or horizontal equity, may not pertain, especially where students are not equally situated and bring varying abilities and needs to their school. In this circumstance, the unequal nature of the playing field creates the need for the differential treatment of unequals, or what is known as *vertical equity* (Berne & Stiefel, 1999).

The first level of "equity testing" within a district is often to determine whether or not horizontal equity has been established through the existing funding formulas; that is, are equals being treated equally? But equal resources don't necessarily result in a lessening of the achievement gap or the equal distribution of access and opportunities across districts or schools. This prompts leaders to examine the second level of equity testing: "an assessment of the 'appropriate unequal treatment of unequals' or the desired relationship of resources to needs" (Rodriguez, 2004, p. 8).

However, even if a need for vertical equity can be established, defining and operationalizing "student need" can be a difficult task, as one scholar has noted:

> Vertical equity is a concept that continues to be among the most difficult to clarify. . . . Although principles that underlie it are commonly understood, due to so much attention in the sociological and economic literature on the impact of schooling on student achievement, what is less available are standard definitions and measures of educational need (Rodriguez, 2004, p. 17).

Again, as the quote illustrates, the fundamental leadership challenge rests both in the recognition that unequal resource needs exist among students within a district, and in accurately and consistently identifying and measuring these needs.

Further complicating this challenge is understanding the important distinction between equity among students and equity among taxpayers within the district. As many state school finance systems are dependent on property tax revenues and/or the passing of supplemental bonds or levies, considering the fairness to the taxpayer within the community is often an important part of the equity equation within a district (Rodriguez, 2004). At the heart of the matter here is a concept that is fundamental to vertical equity—the *appropriate* treatment of unequals (Berne & Stiefel, 1999; King, Swanson, & Sweetland, 2005; Ladd, 2008;

Underwood, 1994). Reasonable people may differ on what constitutes an "appropriate" response to the differences among students within the system that may warrant differential support, and what allocating resources "in direct relation" to the educational needs or presumed disadvantages of these students may imply (Chambers, Levin, & Shambaugh, 2010).

A further dimension of the funding formula for district leaders to confront is the concept of *adequacy* or sufficiency, and its relationship to equity. Establishing an equitable distribution of inputs to students and schools across a district is only half of the challenge; there is also the question of educational *outputs*—in particular, student learning outcomes—to consider. Districts may determine that an average test score or level of proficiency is an outcome standard to be met by all students, and thus an equality of outcomes may require an inequality of inputs, providing further justification for the concept of vertical equity (Ladd, 2008). And the greater attention in recent years to results, coupled with the persistent patterns of low performance for some segments of the student population (even when inputs disproportionately favor the least advantaged), have led educators and scholars to focus more on equality of outcomes, and specifically on allocating the level of resources that are presumed *adequate* to the task—that is, sufficient to support equitable outcomes for all students (Clune, 1994; Downes & Shay, 2006; National Research Council, 1999; Odden, 2003). Rather than focus on relative inputs, this conception focuses on "an absolute threshold. . . . An education system meets an adequacy standard if all schools have sufficient resources to achieve a specified outcome standard, given the particular set of students they serve" (Ladd, 2008, p. 404). Once again, judgments of what is adequate to this purpose may differ, and rest on different philosophical premises (e.g., is our job to provide equitable opportunities to succeed, or to ensure success?).

Though they have been most fully developed to understand the allocation of funding in education, the principles of horizontal and vertical equity and adequacy apply just as well to other resources with which educational leaders are concerned, among them, time, staff FTE, expertise, space, and materials, to mention several that are likely to figure prominently in the leaders' decision making, and may not reflect money per se (City, 2010).

These conceptions of equity and adequacy help to clarify why and how the task confronting the districts and school leaders we studied was complex. As the persistence of achievement gaps in their settings suggests, it was not enough for these leaders to provide equivalent inputs for schools. Rather, resource investment strategies that differentially target specific groups of students as well as the schools that served high concentrations of these students were called for (Henry, Fortner, & Thompson, 2010). While the strategies appeared to show promise, these technical solutions were not without political challenges, which we will explore as the chapter unfolds. But first, we clarify the range of different solutions these leaders devised.

A Range of Technical Solutions: Differential Investment Toward Increasing Equity

Various staffing investment decisions can address equity concerns by differentiating the resources that go to different units (classrooms, schools, teacher groups or teams, programs) in proportion to perceived need. The districts we studied used the investment of resources as a central tool in seeking to enhance equity. Some of these investment decisions concentrated on increasing the supply of staff who could address particular learning improvement needs, others focused more on reconfiguring roles for staff, while still others were more centrally concerned with improving staff capacity and performance. We discuss and illustrate these approaches with examples drawn from two of the districts that, at first glance, represent nearly opposite conditions. On the one hand, the Lane County 4J District in Eugene, OR, encountered long-standing equity issues that had escaped notice and serious attention for years. On the other hand, the New York City Department

TABLE 7.1 Types of Differential Investment Decisions to Enhance Equity

Type of Differential Investment Decision	Focus of Equity Concern	Level of Decision Making
1. Allocating funds or staffing FTE (full-time equivalents) differentially in proportion to need	Schools experiencing the greatest need or that are hardest to staff	District
2. Investing most heavily in building capacity of staff, based on need and challenges	Concerns within or across schools about weaknesses in staff knowledge, skill, and commitment	District, school
3. Improving the match between students and staff through changes in classroom or school assignment	Mismatch between staff capacities and particular student learning needs	District, school
4. Augmenting the allocation of instructional time for underserved or underperforming students	Insufficient instructional time (that can be addressed through alterations of the master schedule, repurposing of particular time blocks, teaching assignments within time blocks, or additions to the normal school day)	School
5. Pooling and concentrating existing resources to maximize assistance to struggling students	Insufficient concentration of resources (e.g., dollars, FTE, or even students, treated as a resource), brought to bear on students exhibiting the greatest need	District, school

of Education presented district and school leaders with every imaginable equity issue in stark terms. Yet despite the differences in these settings, many if not most of the underlying approaches to investing staffing resources differentially to improve learning more equitably were similar. In these cases, five types of differential investment strategies are readily apparent, summarized in Table 7.1, occurring at district and school levels (and sometimes at both levels simultaneously):

Solution 1: Staffing or Funding Schools Differentially

Perhaps the most obvious form of investing resources differentially to promote equity occurs when district leaders *change the amount of staffing resources that they allocate to each school* in an attempt to offer more dollars or staff to schools that face greater challenges in educating their student populations. This straightforward approach to realizing vertical equity typically offers schools some combination of (1) specific staff positions or (2) an additional funding amount, much of which may (or must) be used to pay for staffing resources. To accomplish this purpose, districts either redesign their base allocation formula so that it integrates some notion of vertical equity—e.g., by weighting the funding formula so that more intensive learning needs are reflected in the budget—or maintain a base allocation formula that *equally* distributes resources to schools, while supplementing that base with additional resources designed to bring about more equity (Chambers, Levin, & Shambaugh, 2010).

Among our study sites, the New York City Department of Education went the furthest in redesigning its base school resource allocation formula in an attempt to increase equity. According to the district's official communications in 2007, the reason for developing this new way to allocate money to schools, which they termed Fair Student Funding (FSF), was that

> Every child deserves the same opportunity for a great education. And that means every school deserves fair funding. For years, our school budgeting has fallen short of that promise. It's time to change that. Under Fair Student Funding we will begin to fund schools based on the needs of the children at each school. Because that's what matters most. (*Fair Student Funding: Making It Work for Your School and Your Student*, May 2007)

Under these reforms, a weighted student funding formula determined the amount that each school *should* be funded based on student enrollment demographics, so as to create more equitable conditions. Under the new formula, some schools gained, while others received proportionally fewer resources. The weighting could be done with a more targeted purpose, as in Eugene, which offered all schools a special literacy fund over and above the basic allocation, based on a formula that took into account the proportion of students in poverty, the number of English language learners, and the number of special education students. The difference in what a school received could be substantial: In the 2004–05 school year, literacy funding augmented school budgets by amounts ranging from $5,600 to $28,900 per elementary school. For middle schools that same year, the amounts ranged from $30,600 to $47,300 per school; and at the high school level, from $62,700 to $108,000.

Alternatively, the additional resources could come as a grant or lump sum, as in New York City, where schools with high poverty numbers got a special allocation of "Contract for Excellence" money (originating from the state), earmarked for class-size reduction and several other purposes presumed to enhance the instructional program in these schools (Schwartz, Rubenstein, & Stiefel, 2009). In Eugene, equity grants were made to schools with the highest minority and poverty counts, starting in 2002. Eligible schools submitted proposals to the district for how they would spend the grant money, and the amount allocated to each school depended on the proposed uses (sometimes adding staff, in other instances aimed at improving staff capacity). Therefore, the amount each school received through this program would vary.

Alternatively, the district could invest in particular staff positions directly, in proportion to assumed need. The role of the allocated Student Achievement Coordinator position in Eugene was defined by the district to be assessing the progress of students and supporting school staff in analyzing and using those data to improve instruction. This additional half-time staff person was made available to a small number of schools with declining enrollments and low performance that had been negatively impacted by a school choice policy, and where the remaining student populations reflected higher-than-typical concentrations of students from low-income backgrounds.

Solution 2: Investing in Building Staff Capacity to Increase Equity

Beyond making resources available to schools that typically increased the supply of staff, districts could *direct resources differentially toward increasing staff capacity,* typically through one or another form of professional development investment. Most obviously, these investments could concentrate on particular groups of teachers or even individuals whose skills seemed most in need of support or who were working with underserved groups of students. But in a more subtle way, professional development funds could also be targeted to *all* staff to help them *differentiate* their teaching work more effectively, thereby allocating the resource of their instructional attention and energy more equitably among their students.

In Eugene, targeted literacy funds and "academy grant" funding offered an obvious resource for this kind of capacity-building work, and many schools opted to take advantage of it for this purpose. In this respect, the district's investment simply provided school decision makers with a flexible resource that could be directed to purposes that were explicitly intended to enhance equity, but could be used in a number of ways. More often than not, in situations where school leaders have substantial amounts of discretionary funding available for professional development, as in New York City/Empowerment Schools, the funds were used to support a variety of professional learning needs, all of which were loosely related to improving school performance, but often without an explicit equity justification.

But given a clear equity agenda on the part of the school leader, with or without similar expectations from the district, discretionary, capacity-building funds could serve a focused equity-oriented purpose, as in an elementary school in Eugene where the principal invested time and resources to have his staff visit and observe two elementary schools in a nearby district. While the district allowed schools such as this one the freedom to use their academy funds for a variety of professional development and school redesign purposes, the district had suggested that schools use the money to visit other schools. This school's principal responded accordingly, largely to raise his staff's expectations for how the minority, low-income, and English language learner students of their school could achieve academically. The principal described his staff's reaction to visiting schools with similar demographics in which a high percentage of students were achieving state standards:

> . . . We did school visits as a staff four years ago when we were trying to find places that looked like us that were successful, and we were the best staff, the most resources of any—hands down—anywhere we went. [But this time] it was like . . . these people are getting 90 percent of their kids reading at benchmark and they look exactly like us and they're operating with like a third less resources.

The principal pointed to these visitations as key turning points in changing the expectations of his staff for how they as a school could get their particular student population to achieve. In a related way, the investment by a New York City elementary school principal in a year-long professional development series focused on differentiated instruction was meant to help his staff visualize more concretely how to align instruction more responsively to their students' strengths and needs. Though aimed at all staff in the building, this investment in capacity building concentrated on differentiation of teaching time and attention, such that the most needy students would get a more powerful learning experience.

Solution 3: Altering Student, Teacher, or School Assignment Policy

Beyond the gross distribution of staff FTE or dollars and the systematic differences in staff capacity that disadvantage some schools or students over others, significant inequities often exist in the ways staff and students are assigned to each other and to schools (Adamson & Darling-Hammond, 2012; Clotfelter, Ladd, & Vigdor, 2006; Yamasaki & Goes, 2009). Especially at the school level, but also through district-level action, leaders face the puzzle of matching students to the settings and people who can help them learn most effectively. Attempts at doing this matching more equitably sometimes involve *altering the assignment of students or teachers to schools,* or within schools, *searching for a more equitable assignment of students among programs, classrooms, instructional experiences, and teachers.*

Assigning students more equitably to schools. Student assignment policies can enhance equity in several ways. First, school assignment can increase certain students' access to programs they may need and in which they were formerly unable to participate. Second, the reassignment may change overall enrollment distributions, thereby ensuring that enrollment shifts do not erode certain schools' capacity to mount high-quality programs. In the extreme cases, reassignment can mitigate against or forestall precipitous enrollment declines, which can have a devastating effect on a school's staff capacity, not to mention morale, particularly in cases where the decline is due to larger economic and demographic shifts occurring throughout the community.

To return to the Eugene case, the flow of students out of neighborhood schools and into alternative schools under the district's choice plan had generated some serious inequities that prompted several reassignment policies. The first policy, to forestall the tendency for middle-class students to leave neighborhood schools, created an "alternating pick" lottery system to increase the probability that low-income applicants would have access to these schools. The second policy capped enrollments in secondary schools, slowing a trend for certain more affluent schools to increase enrollment and thereby accelerate the extent to which the student populations in other schools were increasingly segregated by social class. Third, the district ended the co-location of alternative schools and neighborhood schools, as this practice seemed to encourage the migration of students from the neighborhood school to the alternative provided under the same roof. Together, these reassignment policies were meant to prevent the growing separation and concentration of student needs by social class, with its natural tendencies to exacerbate inequities. These moves were not without controversy, a matter we take up later in the chapter.

Assigning teachers more equitably to schools. Either by guiding the movement of teachers among schools, or simply recruiting and hiring in a targeted way, districts and schools together could seek to *assemble a staff that better matched student needs,* a matter most dramatically seen in schools that served a large English language learner (ELL) population, generally Spanish-speaking. In one New York City Empowerment School, the principal made a concerted effort over a period of years to recruit and retain Spanish-speaking staff, especially those who had grown up in or resided in the school's community. The principal's efforts in this regard were in large measure successful, in part, a reflection of the discretion granted to schools in hiring and configuring staff. One of the Eugene elementary schools, serving a similar population, engaged in a parallel effort, this time through active collaboration with the district central office and the teachers' union, to increase the number of Spanish-speaking staff in the school. This school was also one of the district's targeted schools. When developing the district policies regarding designation as a targeted school, district leaders recognized that the shift in status and focus in the targeted schools would potentially be problematic for some teachers who had worked in those schools for years. Consequently, the district negotiated an arrangement with the teachers' union to allow teachers in targeted schools an earlier window to apply for other positions in the district. They also negotiated an arrangement that allowed the school to post their open English as a Second Language positions earlier than other schools in the district. These efforts changed the composition of the staff in these two schools in such a way that students, who often found school a foreign and unresponsive environment, encountered a more engaging set of learning environments.

Assigning students more equitably to teachers, programs, and tracks within schools. No matter what resources came to the school—in the form of increased dollars, staff with particular capabilities, or an appropriate mix of students—a finer-grained challenge resided within the school. Here, leaders confronted a range of inequities, some overt, some less visible, that meant that certain groups of students were systematically exposed to teachers without the capabilities needed to meet their needs, or some students clearly needed more and different kinds of help with their learning. To address within-school inequities, school leaders could take many steps—especially with the way particular teachers were asked to take on classroom assignments that played to their strengths or, conversely, were shifted to assignments that minimized the effects of their weaknesses—as in one New York City school in which struggling teachers who showed no sign of responding to feedback and instructional assistance were immediately removed from the regular classroom and given small pull-out assignments, while their classrooms were taken over by more competent specialists.

The pursuit of equity through within-school student assignment was nowhere more dramatically seen than in the grouping of students, and here differing notions of equity came into play. In one large elementary school in the New York City/Empowerment Schools Organization, students were clustered by their apparent profile of multiple intelligences into separate "academies" within the school, each designed to approach learning in ways that optimally matched particular learning profiles. Another principal, holding steadfastly to a principle of social equity, persisted in assigning students to classes heterogeneously, on the basis that this would prevent pernicious forms of social class segregation that he saw as corrosive to the learning of all students, and especially those from low-income backgrounds. In contrast, the principal of another school in the same district advocated regularly adjusting homogeneous grouping of students for literacy instruction, on the premise that this would most effectively lead to greater equity of academic outcomes.

However assignments were made, and whoever was officially assigned, the net effect was to alter the way staffing resources were deployed and used—and often with little or no change in the outlay of dollars or FTE. Where the reassignment enabled needy students to get better or more concentrated help with their learning, the reinvestment of staffing resources was differentially based on equity principles, whether or not they were so stated. A number of subtle possibilities arise here that are easily overlooked by educators seeking a structural, and often more expensive, solution to inequities in the schooling experiences or outcomes of those they serve.

Solution 4: Altering the Allocation of Instructional Time

Two kinds of time reallocation within the schools we studied were designed to give struggling learners a better chance at success, by enabling some learners to get more minutes of instructional time or more concentrated instructional attention (or both) than they otherwise would have, or more than other students experienced. The first approach simply added to the total hours of instruction for certain groups of students over and above what they would typically experience. Either outside the school day, as in after-school programs and Saturday school, or within the formal school days through additional intervention periods, these students spent additional time working on literacy or mathematics (and occasionally other subjects), sometimes with their regular classroom teachers and sometimes with other instructional staff. One district institutionalized this effort by selectively extending kindergarten from a half day to a full day in a small number of the schools serving the most impacted students. Other districts or schools increased the minutes of the school day, made resources available for Saturday classes, or used other devices that added time to the weekly or yearly instructional total.

A second kind of time reallocation came about by deploying staff in more concentrated arrangements that enabled teachers to spend intensive small-group or one-on-one time with particular students who needed it the most. For example:

- In one elementary school, supplementary funds intended to reduce class size were used to create team teaching arrangements in kindergarten through second-grade classrooms, on the supposition that early literacy was a fundamental foundation for subsequent school success.
- Intervention classrooms in another school replaced the 25-student classroom with one that focused on the same material with a classroom group of 6,

comprised of students who were experiencing difficulties, as indicated by their periodic assessment results.

These arrangements represent a way in which the deployment of additional staff in unusual roles (team teacher, intervention teacher), alongside or sometimes in place of a regular classroom teacher, effectively increased the total time and attention that particular students received. This provided for a focused and differential allocation of resources to assist specific students who needed additional support.

Solution 5: Pooling Resources to Create a Critical Mass of Support for Particular Needs

One final means of investing differentially in instructional support for particular groups of students occurred through school leaders' efforts to pool resources, so that, in the aggregate, they enabled an improved form of instructional service to be targeted to a particular learning need. We saw this most dramatically in ways that districts or school leaders clustered English language learners (ELLs) so that the special funds available to serve their needs could facilitate the hiring of staff with specialized skills. Without the clustering, these students would have been dispersed among a number of schools or classrooms that would not be able to create the specialized program. Two schools in New York City reflect this strategy:

- One school, created as a magnet for recent immigrants from Spanish-speaking countries, constructed a dual-language program that promoted fluency in both their native language and English.
- Another large school in the midst of a school-wide restructuring into four thematically defined academy programs set up one of the academies with a focus on "world studies." The great majority of the school's ELL students were clustered in this program, as were most of the bilingual teachers.

Schools in other districts reflected other variations on this theme, and in several instances, leaders were able to articulate a productive way of thinking about what they were doing with resources. Most notably, rather than approaching ELL students as a problem, they saw the students themselves as a social resource, whose cultural backgrounds could enrich the learning experience for other students, given the right kinds of conditions and support (Gonzalez, Moll, & Amanti, 2013).

Such pooling arrangements are not without potential drawbacks. Clustering of students who might otherwise be underserved by the school can create a kind of segregation that can have an isolating effect, with negative social and academic ramifications (Oakes, 2008). But our informants seemed to believe that such concerns were outweighed by the benefits that students would receive from a staff that had the skills and commitment to best meet their particular educational needs.

Managing the Political Dimensions of Equity-Focused Investments

In devising strategies for enhancing equity in learning improvement efforts, such as those just reviewed, district and school leaders are being asked to make judgments based on comparisons of the circumstances and needs of specific schools or groups of students, and ultimately develop resource plans that represent the district's or school's goals and objectives. Aside from their capacity to redirect resources to particular perceived needs, these decisions can, and often do, signal the way that specific schools and groups of students are valued within a district. These messages, unintentional or not, have profound political implications for leadership within the district and the community.

In attempting to manage the political dimensions of both introducing and sustaining investment practices that target equity within a district, three central strategies or practices appeared to show promise from the cases we explored for this study. Those strategies suggest three overlapping phases of equity-focused political work that play out across a long-term time frame.

- *Planning for equity.* In this phase, which can last years, leaders engage in groundwork that identifies the equity challenges facing a district or school and publicly build a community mission that prioritizes enhancing the equity of the educational system.
- *Shepherding the ongoing equity conversation while taking action.* During this phase, leaders engage stakeholders in continuing conversation leading up to, and implementing, specific decisions to invest resources disproportionately, and in so doing, try to craft coherence and foster deeper commitment among the various parties.
- *Anticipating, and persevering in the face of pushback.* During this phase, subsequent to one or more resource-related decisions, leaders anticipate and manage pushback from interests both inside and outside the education system who perceive their relative advantages to be severely reduced or eliminated and actively resist the proposed changes.

We elaborate on these stages by examining a particularly instructive case (Lane County District 4J in Eugene, OR)—the district in our sample with the longest chronology of efforts to invest in equitable learning improvement. The case helps to underscore the political dimensions of this investment story and how they can be addressed. While the dynamics revealed here are particular to district-level action, the same or similar dynamics play out in resource decisions within schools. In addition, though the specific conditions of this case story are not necessarily replicated in other school districts, the basic principles are likely to apply in many instances, as we indicate by references to equity-related resource allocation cases from our other sites.

An Instructive Case: Investing for Equity in Eugene

The Eugene school district serves approximately 17,500 students and is the fourth-largest school district in Oregon. Like many medium-sized, historically exurban or suburban districts in the country, the characteristics of the student population in this district's schools are changing, and estimates are that by 2015, close to a third of the district's students will be persons of color and approximately 40 percent will be students from low-income families. At the time of our study, affordable housing was becoming increasingly difficult to find within district boundaries, and as a result enrollments were increasing in surrounding communities and declining in Eugene. The school district was organized into four geographic regions, with each region serving as a feeder system of elementary and middle schools and one comprehensive high school. The district also had an extensive history of offering a number of small alternative schools, often housed adjacent to or in the same building as the traditional neighborhood school. Accompanying the history of alternative schools was a long-standing district school choice policy that allowed families to apply to and, if accepted, attend any school within the district.

The district had enjoyed significant stability in leadership and in its teaching corps. The superintendent who served during the time of our study had occupied that position for 10 years, and a number of the then current central office and school leaders had worked in the district for more than 20 years.

For a number of years, reducing the achievement gap had been the principal reform priority for the district—as indicated by a clear and resounding message from the school board, superintendent, district leadership, and principals. Due in large part to the superintendent's vision, determination, and leadership, cultural competence and issues of fairness and equity had been consistent themes within the district and central to its reform theory. There was little disagreement across the district that some schools had been disproportionally impacted by the changing demographics of the community, and that student performance had been tightly linked to poverty and racial/ethnic differences. The district's commitment to equitable outcomes for all students formed the basis for its reform strategy of improving access to strong programs in all neighborhoods and increasing staffing resources and support for those schools and programs most in need.

These themes and commitments are consistent threads running through the decade-long chronology of investing for equity, summarized in Table 7.2 below. Across this period district leaders took many steps to define, articulate, implement, and sustain their commitment to closing the achievement gap and improving learning for all students.

The case of Eugene underscores the fact that, in the early stages of the process, district leaders took deliberate steps to identify publicly the scope and nature of equity challenges facing the district. Specifically, they first invested resources in exploring what equity was (and was not) within the district. Defining the term

TABLE 7.2 Chronology of Equity Investment Strategies in Eugene, OR

Time Frame	Key Events	Central Equity Concerns	Outcomes
1999–2001	*Schools of the Future* planning process and follow-up	Surfacing inequities inherent in neighborhood schools versus alternative schools of choice How equal-per-pupil allocation process yielded inequitable resource distribution, especially in context of enrollment decline Consideration of potential school consolidation and closures, and their potential differential impacts	Public recognition of equity concerns Need for resolution of disparities in school resource/attendance situation
2001	Board discussion on establishing equity-related principles	Search for consensus among different stakeholders concerning school choice and its ramifications	Consensus statements on school choice that recognized equity principles
2002	Board retreats and follow-up actions	Continued discussion of the relation between school funding and school choice	Board forms a commitment to close achievement gap and enhance equity as central district goals Equity grants to the neediest Schools
2003–2004	*Access and Options Committee* planning process, and aftermath	Exploration of alternatives for realizing equity principles within a framework of school choice	Committee recommendations concerning school configuration alternatives and ways to enhance access and equity Differentiated literacy funding to all schools, based on weighted formula

Time Frame	Key Events	Central Equity Concerns	Outcomes
2004–2005	District outreach process (through surveys, focus groups, community forums, meetings with school staffs, principals, and union)	Assessing stakeholder views and commitments, in relation to *Access and Options* recommendations	Superintendent's recommendations to board—e.g., changing lottery system for alternative schools, redrawing attendance boundaries, designating neighborhood academy schools Extra funding to academy schools
2006–2008	*Shaping 4J's Future* planning process (focus groups, survey-driven deliberative process)	Imagining services and facilities for the next 5 years and more to support district's instructional program, to increase achievement of all students and reduce the achievement gap	Reaffirmation of equity, excellence, and choice as district values Limiting inter-school transfers (to limit drain from poorer schools) Movement toward differentiated staffing

equity was a critical leadership action that enabled participants to come to a shared, collective understanding of the differences between allocation policies designed to *equalize* resources across the district and those that *promote an equity agenda*. Doing so laid a critical foundation upon which district and school leaders could develop a broader program and curricular restructuring agenda focused on equity. From there on, successive cycles of planning and action, involving numerous committees (Schools of the Future, Access and Options) and district-sponsored initiatives (e.g., the Shaping 4J's Future initiative) built on the foundation.

Critical to this process was the inclusion and support of union representatives, school board members, parents, and members of the local business community. District leadership invested in a process that included these parties and built a broad-based network within the district and throughout the community. At each stage, district leaders invested heavily in the planning that surrounded both the process of trying to understand the differences between equality and equity, as well as in the deliberate move to include a broad cross-section of the community in the process of moving forward toward a shared policy goal for the district.

Another key element to the ability of this district to sustain an equity-focused investment agenda appears to be the deliberate transparency of the process.

Committees designed to explore issues of equity or inequity were broad-based and inclusive, and reports from these committees were openly discussed in school board meetings and in meetings the district leaders held with members of the public. In our conversations with union leaders, principals, faculty, and parents, it was clear that they knew what the district was up to with these committees and initiatives, and what the goal of all this work was—to increase access, opportunity, and achievement for all students within the district. The clear, consistent, and open message from district leaders appears to have helped build support among both district personnel and the community.

The process in which Eugene engaged resulted in the identification of particular schools that were targeted for additional resources and support. Virtually all of the main strategies described earlier in this chapter showed up at one time or another through the decade: differential investment in targeted schools, investing in staff capacity to increase equity (e.g., in efforts to both define and increase "cultural competence"), alterations to assignment policy (e.g., by capping the numbers of students who could attend certain oversubscribed, largely affluent schools), altering the allocation of instructional time within school programs, and pooling resources to amass supports for better serving critical needs.

An important aspect of the circumstances surrounding the initial granting of these targeted funds within this district was the fact that the district didn't "rob Peter to pay Paul." At certain times early in this investment cycle, the district had supplemental resources that it diverted to the specific (pilot) initiative of increasing literacy in underperforming schools, and so schools that were not receiving these additional funds were not losing any resources—they just weren't getting the "extra" funds these targeted schools were getting. Another important, and politically strategic factor, was the time limit put on this pilot. Selected schools were promised these targeted funds for only three years, and so non-targeted schools (and parents) viewed this additional support as temporary. As a result, there was very little initial "pushback" from principals of the non-targeted schools; how could they be against giving "extra" money to schools with a greater percentage of harder-to-serve students? The reception from parents within the non-targeted schools was much the same: as long as *our* school isn't getting less, why not give some of the district's "extra" resources to those schools or students who are falling behind academically?

What became increasingly complicated in this case was the emergence of a growing cadre of parents (from the non-targeted schools) who began to shift their position and withdraw their support, in reaction to the notion of differential funding for schools, and to question the "fairness" of a funding formula that was designed to be "unequal." For example, one of the district's popular alternative schools was attended primarily by students from affluent families. The district's open enrollment policy provided access to the alternative school for families across the district, but families needed to provide transportation to this school of choice. In an effort to provide opportunities for low-income families to attend this school, district leaders put forth a proposal to provide transportation for economically disadvantaged students who could not get there otherwise. Nearly immediately, parents with children already attending that school asked the district if transportation would now be provided for all students in the school. What incidents like this began to suggest is that parents in the "non-targeted" schools were comfortable with the targeted schools getting additional resources, if they were only used *within* those "targeted" schools, leaving "my kid's school" unaffected.

Planning for Equity

Revisiting the Eugene case chronology makes abundantly clear that investing in equity requires long, strategic, persistent, and patient planning, for many reasons, among them to air, recognize, appreciate, and adjudicate differing values, perceptions, and interests that come into play as leaders pursue an equity agenda. If equity principles are to guide the investment of staffing or other resources, a legitimized forum for these concerns to surface is helpful, along with multiple occasions for these issues to be given voice, and a process that develops both technical plans and broad-based, stakeholder support.

A look at equity-oriented planning by leaders in Eugene suggests a basic principle: to keep planning anchored to equity, leaders may find it useful to engage in a long-term, multistage planning process that continually revisits and builds a politically viable basis for equity-oriented investments. The decade-long process of planning and enacting an equity agenda underscores the point. This process reveals successive stages through which equity concerns became identified, explored, and embedded in a larger vision of the development of the district, often in the face of overt or potential resistance. At least three substantial planning periods took place—first, the *Schools of the Future* process in 1999–2001, followed by a more specific cycle of planning activity in 2003–2004 through the work of the *Access and Options Committee,* and following that, in 2006–2008, another comprehensive planning cycle in the *Shaping 4J's Future* initiative. Each planning cycle built on the last, and cumulatively across them all, a more specific and actionable program of equitable investments took shape and was enacted. No one of these planning processes by itself would have succeeded in addressing all or even most of the dimensions of the multifaceted planning problem.

Shepherding the Ongoing Equity Conversation While Taking Action

A second phase of investing for equity, paralleling and substantially overlapping the first, concerns the way participants become clear about what "equity" means and develop commitment to this idea, with full recognition of the trade-offs it may imply. In doing so, not all participants are equally committed, nor do they necessarily assess the trade-offs similarly, but across all, there is sufficient opportunity for awareness of differences and new thinking about equity to grow. Any time a school leader decides to diverge from the notion of equal being fair, a case must be made for why it is more fair to give one person or group more resources than others. At a district level, this conversation and debate is magnified, and conscious steps by leaders to "shepherd" this conversation over time appear to be helpful and probably necessary. Even with an extensive process of planning and an initial base of political support for equity-related actions, a continuing, proactively guided conversation offers a much needed way for participants to work though the inevitable distractions and disagreements. At the core of this conversation, concepts of equity and fairness need to be explicitly aired and shared, and leaders may well take a "teaching" stance in helping diverse constituents come to appreciate and accept the subtle differences between equal and equitable.

Our data point to four leadership actions that show promise for managing the political dynamics of this "shepherding" process over time:

- Being proactive rather than reactive
- Basing decision making and public discussion in data
- Investing in coalition building
- Translating equity principles into tangible investments

Being proactive rather than reactive. One of the clearest messages coming from the Eugene case is the significant advantage to getting out in front of this process. As noted in Table 7.2 above, the superintendent called for a process to assess the current state of the district shortly after assuming his position. The resulting *Schools of the Future* report highlighted a number of areas in which the district was deficient, with issues surrounding dimensions of equity at the forefront. The report and its conclusions acted as a springboard for further efforts to both better understand and meet these challenges. Clearly, being proactive and taking the lead on exploring, identifying, and articulating the district's equity challenges allowed district leaders to direct the initial conversation (both within the district and the community) surrounding issues of equity, as well as demonstrate the district's ability to critically assess its performance as a public sector institution.

Basing decision making and public discussion in data. One of the most significant and lingering benefits from the No Child Left Behind policies of the recent past may be the amount of school-level achievement data produced. These data have fueled conversations of many kinds among many stakeholder groups, and the conversations are often about equity. School leaders and other audiences can see very clearly that the gap exists, where it exists, and for whom. The increased transparency creates a yardstick for the public to measure and critique educators' work. It also provides a critical catalyst for creating new and innovative investment strategies that target underserved students.

In Eugene, as elsewhere, this wealth of specific performance data, which figured prominently in the planning cycles and other discussions, allowed district leaders to provide quantitative evidence of a difference in performance for specific populations of students across the district. Mining the data for insights, principals were able to identify students who were consistently falling behind academically. As a result, initiatives such as full-day kindergarten, before- and after-school programs, and additional, intensive reading and math instruction were developed. At the district level, the examination of data supported the creation of policies designed to reallocate resources for specific programs and students.

Investing in coalition building. What may be a by-product of all the planning and processing that occurred in Eugene is the way this investment resulted in the creation of a broad coalition of constituents having a shared interest in the process and the outcomes of equity policies within the district. The length and complexity of the processes at work are also an indication of the degree of coalition building that may be necessary to make an equity agenda a reality and to sustain it over time.

Not all our districts displayed such a continuous and persistent dialogue among stakeholders orchestrated by district leaders. That is not to say that an equity agenda was either absent or uncontested. In New York City, for example, a primary justification for the elaborate accountability system (fashioned by leaders with backgrounds in civil rights law, among other experiences) was to provide multiple streams of feedback to educators and other audiences in the hope of addressing established achievement gaps among the city's diverse student population. Under a mayoral control arrangement, and absent a viable school board, the city's then current reform arrangement did not create the same space or context for the public deliberation of value-based principles that the Eugene case exemplifies (Fruchter, 2007). Under such circumstances, coalition building to support an equity agenda must find other avenues of influence.

Translating equity principles into tangible investments. Finally, the fact that planning is punctuated by periodic actions that build incrementally on each other means that an equity agenda is more than just talk. These actions may not be, nor need to be, the most central, and perhaps controversial piece of an equity-oriented improvement plan, but rather practical, first and second steps that convey a sense of forward motion and hope—what some have called early "big wins" in the equity-focused investment process (City, 2010). The Eugene case illustrates one way that participants arrived at principles that embodied an aspiration to address inequities, resulting in specific decisions about the development and implementation of resource investment strategies. The resulting steps set the stage for the next round of agenda-building and deliberation.

Anticipating and Persevering in the Face of Pushback

As they shepherd the conversation, district leaders encounter a third and unavoidable phase of investing for equity. They will face pushback from constituencies who feel slighted by the impending or recent allocation decisions. Issues of equity and fairness as they relate to the investment of resources across a district can create pockets of tension both inside and outside schools and districts (Brantlinger, 2003). Challenges at times can be less about the actual amount of dollars going to a school and more about the ability of parents to control access to, and opportunities for gaining, social capital from schools or programs. One of the least understood and most complex dimensions of pursuing a district-wide equity agenda is in anticipating the types and degrees of staff, parental, and community pushback. Clearly, not everyone is going to consistently support district actions that invest resources differentially.

A growing cadre of parents in Eugene, for example, began to push back on the notion of differential funding for schools, and questioned the fairness of a funding formula that was designed to be unequal. The district's proposal, noted earlier in the chapter, to provide transportation to a school of choice for students who could not get to the school otherwise stimulated a vigorous counter response from parents with children already attending that school (who were providing their own transportation on a daily basis).

What incidents like this began to suggest was that parents in the (non-targeted) schools—those with fewer ELL students, students from low-income backgrounds, or students from single-parent households—were comfortable with the targeted schools getting additional resources if the resources were used *within* those targeted schools, but not when special resources were used to integrate those targeted students into other schools or programs across the district, thereby "saddling" a more advantaged school with new needs. A particularly troubling representation of this perspective was seen in the dismay expressed by some parents toward teachers who had decided to send their own children to a targeted school. "That's a good school for *those* students, but . . ." was the sentiment expressed by one parent.

The pressure to resist changes in resource reallocation practices can also come from school personnel who are impacted, especially when resources are limited or shrinking. In the Eugene case, early efforts to provide the targeted schools with additional resources came at a time when there was a modest increase in the size of the district budget. The district was able to supply all schools with an incremental increase while simultaneously directing proportionately more resources to the targeted schools to help meet the district's equity goals. Under those circumstances, educators throughout the district could readily understand and support the adjustments made in the district's resource allocation system. However, when resources became more limited (as in the subsequent fiscal environment), concerns mounted from those working in schools that were not targeted for additional supports, as they may have felt they were being asked to continue to improve performance with proportionately fewer resources than those schools identified as needing additional, equity-based supports.

For purposes of better understanding the nature of this kind of pushback, we locate it in relation to what we call *the margin of perceived competitive advantage*. A general summary of this pattern of behavior is that those who have historically held a competitive advantage within a society and school system have a dynamic, flexible threshold of acceptance or support for allowing others who have not held the same advantages to receive temporarily an unequal distribution of access to resources so that they can catch up. This acceptance and support usually lasts up until the point at which the historically advantaged people ("the haves") perceive their ability to maintain and perpetuate a margin of increased access to, and control of, information or resources (their "advantage") is threatened by others' progress ("the have-nots").

Looking at these episodes of inconsistent and conditional support from a school's or district leader's perspective, one can begin to anticipate how and when they might experience pushback from staff, families, or other community members. If superintendents or district leaders were trying to move forward with a targeted funding formula that treated schools disproportionately, they might expect both support and potential pushback at predictable points and, knowing that, take proactive steps to counter the pressures to back away from differential investments. As they do so, they will likely need to replicate the kinds of tactics discussed above to shepherd the equity conversation over time. As in the Eugene case, they will be getting out in front of the issue, naming it and framing it in the most productive way possible, engaging in broad-based conversation around data about what is and (to the extent data can be generated) around the likely effects of different scenarios and, as they do so, build coalitions of support.

Conclusions

As they seek to ensure the success of all children, educators in charge of allocating resources in the nation's schools and school districts face some of the most vexing issues in contemporary public education. Students who have been historically underserved generally need more than their more advantaged peers; hard-to-staff schools often require a greater investment in staffing than those that have little difficulty attracting staff; budgets are finite, and sometimes shrinking, while the policy environment and public aspirations for education are increasing; and so on. District and school leaders in the sites we studied were more than willing to take these challenges on. Both rhetorically and practically, these leaders placed a high value on achieving greater equities in schooling, especially through addressing both the opportunity gaps that were readily apparent and the resulting disparities in performance that collectively reflected the achievement gap. But in taking up this challenge, they predictably encountered some conceptual, technical, and political issues that needed to be addressed if an equity agenda was to be sustained over time. Three broad observations capture what we learned from these sites.

First, investing staffing resources equitably—which generally means in a differentiated and ostensibly unequal way—is difficult conceptual work. Leaders and other stakeholders have to come to grips with the slippery definitions of equality, equity, and adequacy, and the fact that more than one conception of fairness is at work within these terms. Since pursuing the goal of equitable learning improvement almost always means more than equalizing resources, opportunities, or treatments, leaders find themselves in the position of differentially investing resources to realize an equity agenda. But finding the "right" level of differential investment—the most *appropriately* unequal treatment of unequal circumstances—involves tricky judgments, weighing of trade-offs, and clarity about core values and one's philosophical grounds for action. This means that leaders must simultaneously engage all stakeholders in a conversation about what equity means and reach for consensus, while still adhering to core convictions about the need for action embedded in principles of social justice (Marshall & Ward, 2004).

Second, a variety of technical and structural solutions to this conceptual puzzle are possible and feasible to implement in many schools and districts. With careful attention to what current or projected resources are available, leaders can: reconsider how funding formulas take into account measureable factors associated with educational disadvantages; invest in staff capacity that helps support more equitable practices across a school and even within each classroom; alter how students, teachers, and schools are assigned to each other; change how instructional time is allocated; and pool existing resources to amass enough of them to enable particular needs to be met. These kinds of actions imply investment activity at both the district and school level, and can often be used in combination to fashion a multipronged approach to equitable learning improvement.

Third, leaders investing in equity in these ways are likely—almost certain—to encounter stiff resistance from stakeholders who have traditionally been advantaged by existing systems, and the leaders will need to adjudicate the inevitable contest over what is fair (Theoharis, 2007). At least the resistance is predictable: astute leaders can often anticipate where and under what circumstances advantaged interests are likely to feel their advantages are most threatened long before these concerns materialize and find public voice.

Our findings, especially well dramatized in the case of Eugene, point to three principles at work in situations where district leaders grapple constructively with the equity challenges in front of them. First, pursuing an equity agenda means a great deal of planning, undertaken across a long period of time and perhaps in multiple cycles of planning. These cycles do far more than establish goals, timelines, and steps forward; rather, they build awareness, offer many occasions to air differences, get equity issues and considerations into full view, articulate equity-related principles, and build sufficient working consensus around them—all as groundwork supporting the more specific plans and strategies that make teaching and learning more equitable.

In addition, leaders recognize that, accompanying the planning processes is a need to nurture an "equity conversation" over time—and in this conversation, help all participants learn, get clearer about each others' core values, and give voice in an inclusive way to *all* affected parties, not only those whose voices are most frequently heard. Such a conversation can be nurtured in various ways, especially by proactively getting out in front of the issue rather than reacting to an equity-related debate framed by events or other parties, and using data as a reference point for the conversation, so that it stays focused and minimizes conflict. Leaders also shepherd the equity conversation by building coalitions that broaden the base of support for decisions that could be unpopular. As the conversation proceeds, leaders also look for and seize opportunities to take practical steps forward, often small ones at first, but those with symbolic power and the capacity to build trust and hope in further steps.

Finally, leaders anticipate pushback from various quarters, and especially from those groups who are most advantaged by current arrangements. In the face of this resistance, leaders stay the course, making adjustments as needed to maintain forward motion, and once again, build alliances and use other devices to carry the day.

Our analysis found the overarching principle was that the pursuit of equity goals meant taking the long view—implied by the notion of *investment* itself (as discussed more fully in Chapter 6 within this volume)—and engaging in processes that unfolded over years. While there are strategic advantages to students' learning when educational leaders operate from a long-range, investment perspective, successful long-range investment planning depends upon incremental, short-term implementation successes and lessons, grounded in an ongoing inquiry process.

The leadership actions undertaken in our case study districts and schools were certainly influenced by the availability of resources, and the fiscal circumstances in which the cases were located clearly changed over the time period studied. However, it would be a mistake to assume that investing in learning improvement can only be contemplated in times of fiscal plenty. Quite the contrary: most of our sites had experienced severe retrenchment in recent years, and had used these times as occasions for creative improvisation on what they had been doing before.

In a similar spirit, the current or recent financial hard times also provide the opportunity for leaders to critically examine their investments in staffing resources and consider ways in which resources can be shifted, reallocated, or repurposed with a more strategic scope or focus (Calvo & Miles, 2012). The economic challenges further increase the tensions that leaders must negotiate when it comes to decision making about staffing resources, particularly with respect to the differential allocation of scarce resources among schools and students with varying needs. As at times of relative plenty, there are strong voices that assert that the only "fair" thing to do is to make sure everyone bears the burden "equally," a move that tends to reinforce any inequities in the current resource allocation system. So the challenge of finding the most equitable way of proceeding still remains, even if the main business of the day is making cuts. This challenge and the commitment to meet it lie at the heart of learning-focused leadership. Taken together, our case studies served to underscore the importance of investing for equity in learning improvement and to articulate the complexities involved when leaders work collaboratively with students, educators, and community members towards accomplishing the goal of creating an excellent education for all.

8

CONCLUSION

Practicing and Supporting Learning-Focused Leadership in Schools and Districts

Michael S. Knapp, Michael A. Copland, Meredith I. Honig, Margaret L. Plecki, and Bradley S. Portin

The argument presented in this book proceeds from a set of premises about leadership in relation to commitments made by educators, policymakers, and the public to improve the quality of teaching and learning in the nation's public schools. In short, we understand leaders' task as *joint learning work*, as daily interactions within larger and longer-term structures that makes everyone's learning—students, professionals, and even the system itself—the central business of schooling. Everything teachers, administrators, and others do can facilitate this purpose, but how to do so and what it means and looks like in practice is not so well understood, nor easy to realize. This book has taken on the task of illuminating that work, especially as it takes place in settings that have historically served our students least well.

What we learned from the three strands of the *Study of Leadership for Learning Improvement*, presented in the preceding seven chapters, offers complementary insights into the exercise of learning-focused leadership and how it is enabled and enacted in complex school districts. The result is a detailed picture of learning-focused leadership in action at multiple levels of the educational system.

Two sets of themes emerge concerning this way of envisioning leadership work in the context of a commitment to improve teaching and learning. In many respects, both concern one or more facets of what is often referred to as "instructional leadership" in the broadest sense, encompassing far more, at both the school and district levels, than the direct assistance and guidance to individual teachers. Here we add to a literature that has been preoccupied by principals, teacher leaders, and coaches as instructional leaders (Hallinger, 2011; Neumerski, 2013), by trying to capture a *system* of instructional leadership at work, including activities at multiple levels that concern instruction directly, and others that don't.

The first theme concerns the *practice* of learning-focused leadership and what it means to bring it to bear in a more compelling and equitable way on instructional improvement. In particular, our research highlights ways that educational systems can enable and, in effect, "reinvent" leadership practice so that it both addresses learning and embodies processes of learning for all. The second concerns the ways in which learning-focused leaders are themselves *supported*—in short, this theme spells out the attributes of a "leadership support system" that takes learning improvement as its central purpose. And leadership support is integrally connected to the practice of learning-focused leadership, and vice versa.

In this chapter, drawing on the preceding chapters and related publications we have produced, we review what we learned within these two themes, and then reflect on the new work and continuing challenges in districts and schools that seek to realize this approach to guiding and supporting learning improvement efforts.

Enabling and Reorienting Leadership Practice to Learning Improvement

In these districts and schools, focusing leadership on the improvement of learning—*everyone's* learning—meant several things at once. First of all, almost by definition, the improvement of teaching and learning became the central responsibility of the school and district central office, and those exercising leadership in central office positions or within the schools were relentless in communicating this message. Second, to make this message more than a rhetorical exercise, they purposefully invested resources—all kinds of resources—not just money (and often not much money), but also time, materials, expertise, and even autonomy in this pursuit, with a special emphasis on instructional leadership as a primary target of investment, and with a willingness to invest differentially, so varied learning needs could be better addressed. Third, they sought to adjust and even reinvent leadership work practice so that teaching and learning improvement stayed at the center of everyone's attention and efforts. Fourth, they created new kinds of relationships among staff, within and between levels, which resulted in better coordination of effort and attended to particular improvement needs that differed from school to school, teacher to teacher, or leader to leader. And finally, they made evidence of many kinds a medium of leadership work and a constant reference point in their interactions with teachers, each other, and stakeholders. We briefly describe these facets of leadership practice, highlighted in Figure 8.1 below, in light of what we learned from the study strands.

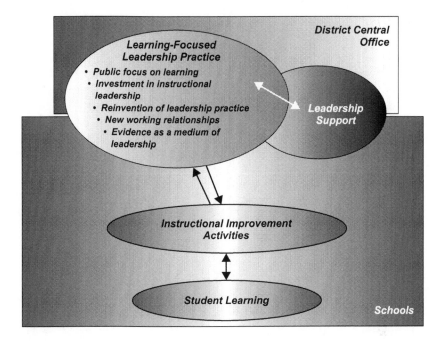

FIGURE 8.1 Central Practices of Learning-Focused Leadership

A Persistent, Public Focus at All Levels on Improving the Quality of Instruction

Not surprisingly, given the way we selected study sites, the districts and schools we studied made the improvement of teaching and learning a major emphasis, but the degree to which learning improvement goals were owned and internalized by educational leaders at various levels of the system was striking. In turn, these leaders projected a persistent, public focus on learning improvement, which reinforced the ownership of the message by participants throughout the system. What is more, this "persistent public focus on learning," a hallmark of learning-focused leadership (Copland & Knapp, 2006), was woven into daily practice in various ways, not just a matter of grand rhetoric or district mission statement.

First of all, it is understandable in an era of high-stakes accountability, that educators throughout the system would be paying close attention to measures of student achievement and to the consequences that flow from high and low performance on these measures. But doing so can easily become an exercise in compliance and regulation, more than a matter of professional commitment and daily practice, and educators can easily lose sight of learning goals. Here are some of the manifestations we saw of leaders communicating and internalizing a focus on learning improvement at the school and district levels:

- *District leaders were communicating clear expectations for learning improvement.* School leaders, on their part, were internalizing these messages, though often giving additional meaning to the call for learning improvements (e.g., by emphasizing much more than the test-score improvements that the accountability system might be seeking).
- *School leaders were making use of the district's (and state's) commitment to learning improvement as a lever for accomplishing improvement goals in the school.* Specifically, these leaders leveraged district or state accountability requirements as a tool in their pursuit of the school's learning improvement agenda.
- *Learning improvement messages from both district and school were being further internalized in <u>within-school</u> accountability systems,* in which school staff held themselves jointly responsible for student learning.
- Especially in the districts committed to central office transformation strategies, *district reform initiatives were developing a different working culture across the central office (and often a different organization of units, roles, and work) that placed primary emphasis on improving teaching and learning in schools.* On their part, district-level staff members in various positions were beginning to orient their daily work to this expectation.

In sum, across all levels in the sites we studied, it was clear that improving student learning—for the full range of students served by the system—was the main business of the school and district, and that to make that happen, the nature of instruction needed to become more powerful and equitable. School-based educators perceived the whole system, themselves included, to be about learning improvement. Recall the new third-grade teacher noted in the Introductory Chapter to this book: her understanding of the priorities for learning in her school, transmitted to her by her school leadership team and reinforced by district leaders' explicit expectations, was a natural consequence of a persistent, public focus on learning improvement.

Investing in Instructionally Focused People and Positions Within and Across Schools

A priority on learning improvement is one thing to assert, and another to enact. A central aspect of leaders' work practice at various levels of the systems we studied was making decisions about staffing resources, as well as related resources (e.g., money, time, expertise) that put people in position to carry out instructional leadership work.

As they allocated staffing and other resources for learning improvement, leaders approached the task of allocating resources differently than many of their counterparts in other districts, and even than they had in years past. They often thought of themselves as *investing* resources—that is, they took a long-term view of their efforts to support learning improvement and looked for "returns on their investment" over time. An elementary principal noted in Chapter 6, who had found a way to assign two certificated teachers to each of his kindergarten through second grade classrooms, articulated this idea clearly as a "long-term investment": "I think by making the investment in the early grades, I'm making an investment that's going to pay off in the long run, and I think I'll see it on the other end. . . ."

To facilitate investment in learning improvement, districts established "investment frameworks" that specified where initiative for improvement activity lay, and the degree of flexibility, responsibility, and discretion that resided at each level of the system. School leaders like the one speaking above operated within a framework that emphasized school-level autonomy; yet even his counterparts in other districts, operating under more centralizing investment frameworks, were nonetheless thinking and acting with a long-term approach to the resources at their command.

A broader set of investment decisions, made at the central office level, directed staffing and other resources to learning improvement goals and to the task of building human capacity for carrying out the district's educational program. Here they often singled out instructional leadership as an investment target. An especially common first step in this regard was to put in place a cadre of people engaged in instructional leadership within and also across schools. Here, some districts allocated a category of positions serving multiple schools—for example, the 42 "Model Teacher Leaders" in Atlanta, each of whom worked with a particular network of schools, or the 60 Teachers on Special Assignment in Portland, OR, to support classroom teachers in specific content areas. Alternatively, other districts invested more indirectly in instructional leadership by creating a "market" for cross-school instructional leadership support, as in the New York City/Empowerment Schools arrangement, where principals "purchased" the support services of a Network Team, experienced administrators on call to assist the school with instructional and operational matters. The net effect of this latter arrangement was to put in place a cadre of staff positioned to exercise instructional leadership across schools.

An underlying commitment to equity prompted district and school leaders on numerous occasions to make *differential* investments, allocating a proportionately greater—hence, an unequal—share of staffing or other resources to students, classrooms, schools, or other units that exhibited greater needs. These equity-focused investments were of different types, but regardless of type, they often generated a predictable "pushback" from internal or external stakeholders who saw their advantages eroding or somehow compromised. As we detailed in Chapter 7, to manage the politics of this pushback, leaders often needed to go to great lengths, engaging in equity-focused political work that played out across a long-term timeframe.

The net effect of these investments was to put in place staff who engaged solely or centrally in instructional leadership work, some within a single school, and others across schools. Two patterns were especially noteworthy.

The proliferation of individuals engaged in within-school instructional leadership.[1] Within schools, a striking number and variety of individuals exercised instructional leadership, in addition to the school principal or any assistant principals whose work was explicitly instructionally focused, under arrangements that allocated some portion of their assignment to leadership work. Sometimes arranged by the school through internal reallocation of responsibilities or judicious use of its own discretionary funds, and sometimes put in place by central office actions, these investments dedicated a significant portion of staff to the task of assisting with instructional improvement.

While titles varied (e.g., literacy, math, or technology coach; instructional liaison specialist; demonstration teacher; assessment coordinator or data specialist), as did the proportion of their assignment devoted to instructional leadership and classroom teaching or other duties, these "learning-focused teacher leaders" provided the bulk of the within-house professional development, offering one-on-one instructional coaching to classroom teachers, and engaging teachers with evidence and inquiry related to the school's improvement goals. Typically more than one such person exercised instructional leadership within each school, most often configured in one or more instructional leadership teams; and in the larger schools (e.g., elementary schools serving more than 1,000 students), eight or more individuals beside the principal might comprise the school's instructional leadership cadre. In this respect, instructional leadership work became team-based practice, as much as individual activity.

The dedication of specific central office staff, sometimes supplemented by staff from third-party organizations, to help school leaders strengthen their instructional leadership. Also present in most of the districts we studied, investment in a cross-school instructional leadership cadre took several forms. Under some arrangements, district central office staff (e.g., specialists from units concerned with curriculum or professional development) and an external organization working with the central office (e.g., consultants with expertise in particular subject areas such as literacy) offered group-based professional development for school administrators, teacher leaders, or classroom teachers, alongside some individual instructional coaching of teachers, often in demonstration mode, so that other teachers might learn, too.

Alternatively, and especially in the three districts seeking to transform their central offices, the district invested in new or repurposed central office positions that were dedicated to strengthening principals' instructional leadership though one-on-one "learning partnership" work with school principals, or interaction with them in networked groups. In two of the three transforming districts we studied, this cadre of central office staff (who we collectively referred to as "Instructional Leadership Directors"[2]) was supplemented by a small team of administrators (such as Atlanta's Model Teacher Leaders noted earlier) who helped with the instructional leadership work.

Reorienting Daily Leadership Practice to Learning Improvement

The work of an instructional leadership cadre, both within and across schools, is often new, ambiguous, and difficult. It calls on a knowledge base and skill set that many educators, no matter how accomplished in teaching and administrative or support roles, have not fully developed or even conceived. In a fundamental sense, the school and district educators we studied had to learn new forms of leadership practice, in varying degrees, that more specifically and continuously focused on learning improvement. This process was most visible in the work of school-based teacher leaders and the central office administrators who interfaced most directly with schools and school principals, but also for many principals and other supervisory leaders, who came to a new understanding of what "instructional leadership" meant for their daily work.

Team-based instructional leadership work. For both nonsupervisory teacher leaders (who held various position titles) and supervisory leaders like principals, the attempt to work in a learning-focused way brought new challenges, engaging each other as well as teaching staff across the school building. Teachers who came to exercise instructional leadership in schools were uniquely positioned for this work. Though some schools had a history of using content-area coaches, in few instances did a school staff have a template for understanding what the teacher leaders were supposed to do, and where they fit in the organization. Operating in between the school principal and the classrooms, in nonsupervisory roles, these teacher leaders developed their leadership practice on several fronts.

First of all, they became part of an instructional leadership team, and therein figured out how their different strengths might complement those of other team members in pursuit of the school's learning improvement agenda. In this context, they developed a set of team-based practices, as outlined in Chapter 2, new territory for many such staff. Then, in interaction with others in the school, they negotiated their "middle ground" position, in which they often acted as a bridge between the classroom and the school's supervisory leaders (though they were not part of the supervisory process), or even between the classroom and the larger learning improvement agenda of the district. Finally, assuming they were able to establish a good working relationship with classroom teachers—not a foregone conclusion, as they often faced resistance initially—they engaged classroom teachers in identifying and addressing problems of instructional practice. Therein lay problems of *leadership* practice, which they learned to identify and address, in ways that maximized learning improvement goals.

Working in collaboration with the teacher leaders but in different ways, the school principal and other supervisory leaders (e.g., assistant principals who took on instructional support as a central part of their practice) faced often unfamiliar aspects of their jobs as well, even though they might have engaged in instructional leadership in the past. In this regard, their leadership practice was exercised in somewhat different ways from the teacher leaders, in several arenas.

To begin with, supervisory leaders in the school had to lay the groundwork for learning improvement by assembling a high-quality staff, establishing and articulating a school-wide learning improvement agenda, and building school-wide trust and a staff culture that emphasized the need to join forces, work in teams, and develop collaborative solutions to the challenges facing the school. Though they did connect individually with teachers in a variety of ways, the capacity of supervisory leaders to "reach" classroom practice was greatly augmented to the extent they could forge, and *work through,* a viable instructional leadership *team,* rather than a collection of individuals who exercised instructional leadership without knowledge of, or coordination with, each others' efforts. Beyond that, however, many of these administrators worked on developing a new conception of individual "supervisory work" that departed from a traditional pattern of supervision through once-a-year visits to fill out the official performance evaluation form, to a pattern of multiple visits, often short and informal, designed to generate an ongoing conversation about practice with the teachers in question.

New practices for central office staff working directly with school principals. Though not positioned in the school, the central office staff whose purpose was to help school principals improve their instructional leadership (the "Instructional Leadership Directors") worked with a relatively small number of principals (between 20 and 25 principals, for example) one-on-one and in "networked" groups. Especially evident in the districts seeking to transform their central offices, the activities of these staff, in varying degrees, displayed leadership practices well established by theory and research in other sectors as likely to support professional learning, among them:[3]

- *Engaging the principals in instructional leadership as "joint work,"* so that principals felt their questions were heard, the new learning was jointly negotiated, and the Instructional Leadership Directors' talk and actions underscored that both were working *together* on a common task.
- *Modeling ways of thinking and acting as an instructional leader,* such as demonstrating how to have challenging conversations with teachers while also reflecting on the demonstrations, to help leaders see what was modeled and why.
- *Developing and using tools in one-on-one assistance relationships,* such as teaching and learning frameworks or protocols that guide the use of data and evidence in instructional improvement.

Not all participants came ready to do this work, but regardless of their backgrounds, central office staff spent a great deal of time, individually and collectively, figuring out how to allocate and spend their time productively with school leaders.

Others in the system, in a variety of central office roles, engaged in comparable efforts to discover or reinvent how their work could be oriented more specifically and directly toward the improvement of teaching and learning. Once again, in the districts emphasizing central office transformation, staff and units not involved in direct daily interaction with schools (e.g., the Human Resources department, units responsible for facilities) were mining the evidence emerging from the direct assistance relationships described above, as well as from other sources, for insights into how they could improve their performance in relation to instructional improvement goals.

Differentiating Leadership Relationships Within Schools, and Between Schools and the Central Office

The new forms of leadership practice just described imply a pattern of connection between district, school, and classroom that differs from typical practice in large school districts in two respects. First, most of the districts we studied placed emphasis on *differentiating* their approach to particular schools and school leaders to maximize their ability to help each school leader improve his or her practice. Similarly, within schools, supervisory leaders were often seeking a more informal and tailored way of interacting with particular teachers or other school staff than would normally occur in supervisory relations. Second, the relationships within schools, and between them and the central office, were intended to be more two-way and more responsive than is often the case in school systems. This showed up in our sites in several ways.

More differentiated and responsive central office–school relationships. Most dramatically seen in districts committed to fundamental transformation of the central office, both the design and the practice of the relations between central office administrators and school principals featured a differentiated approach to each school's unique needs, interests, and challenges, combined with increased access to central office resources. In the Atlanta Public Schools transformation design, for example, the newly created "School Reform Teams" offered a streamlined and accessible main point of first contact between a designated network of schools and the central office; the New York City Network Teams offered a parallel model. In both systems, the Network or Reform Team staff came to know a smaller number of schools well and to understand various aspects of their needs, to which they could respond more flexibly, or else broker the schools' relationship to whomever in the rest of the central office could handle a particular issue. Thus, these staff targeted particular and often different learning improvement needs within each of the schools in the network.

More responsive supervisor–teacher relationships inside the school. Within the school, the attempts by supervisory leaders to redefine supervision indicated a shift towards greater responsiveness, and away from a largely evaluative posture that organizational supervisions so often entails. This shift in relationship between the teacher and supervisor, noted earlier—from the annual formal, summative exercise to a more elaborated relationship involving various formal and informal interactions—meant that the supervisor could respond more often and in more varied ways to particular assistance or learning needs over time. In this way, the relationship became more formative than summative, and more likely to generate conversations about instruction, while also keeping supervisory leaders well informed about what was happening in classrooms.

Using Evidence as a Main Medium and Reference Point for Leadership Work

Data of various kinds, such as assessments, environmental surveys, student work, counts of work completion, or behavioral issues, occupied a prominent place in the leadership practice and working relationships described above. A series of intentional actions by leaders at all levels sought to make evidence about instruction, learning, leadership, or surrounding conditions a medium of conversation concerning learning improvement, as well as a device for improving instruction itself. Naturally enough, the test score data featured by state and district accountability systems were central to the data-use story, but the districts and schools we studied went beyond this evidence source to develop a far richer form of evidence-informed practice.

System-wide investment in evidence use. To actively encourage teaching and leadership that was informed by evidence, the states and districts we studied invested heavily in data infrastructure, data literacy, and new forms of data and evidence. Resources for this purpose were invested in various ways, among them, to set up online assessment systems that facilitated user access to assessment results, establish district- and school-level positions to help users learn how to understand and use data sources, institute survey measures for capturing feedback on school climate or leadership work, and create observational protocols and other data-focused tools to guide instructional leadership efforts in the schools.

The work of central office administrators with school principals both facilitated the principals' use of evidence and, at the same time, became an evidence source for improving practice in other parts of the central office. In a straightforward way, the central office staff who worked most directly with school principals to strengthen their instructional leadership were often in a good position to help school principals or others get smarter about what data might be saying about their schools' performance. A principal commented on how useful this could be:

> There's also benefit to the data work that we did in our network meetings that I immediately took . . . straight to my staff and had really meaningful conversations about data, about the benchmark assessments, about line item analysis, about looking at these data and how to use this data to inform what we're doing and make decisions. And a lot of that is . . . easier to do as a result of the work that we're doing in network meetings. We do it anyway, but it just helps get other protocols and other systems where they're analyzing it and just approaching it differently with our staff. So I get professional development there.

This kind of teaching about evidence use also happened in the context of one-on-one assistance relationships, in relation to any problem of leadership practice that data potentially informed. At the same time that school leaders were gaining facility with data through these encounters, the resulting information about each school's progress, struggles, and improvement work provided the rest of the central office with an important feedback source that it would not otherwise have.

Data as an anchor for school-based leadership interactions. On their part, principals made use of the data furnished to them by the districts (and the new learning about how to work with it) to both focus and anchor their improvement work. Furthermore, in many instances, they took the matter one step further, by creating within-school data systems that provided continual feedback loops to teachers, teacher leaders, and the school's supervisory leaders. A principal describes her version of such a system:

> We are a data-driven school. . . . The data are used to drive the instruction, to make sure that students who are not performing are receiving remediation in order to get to where they should be. Now [the facilitator] and [my instructional liaison specialist] look more at the "target tracker" and our "red alert" forms that are turned in weekly, which show student progress. . . . They're assessment documents documenting where the children are, what interventions are being used to help move them, if they are performing [low], where they should be on certain standards. . . . Red alerts alert us to see which students are having weaknesses, and as I stated, teachers are to provide interventions or strategies to help move them forward.

Not all schools created such elaborate data systems. In some instances, the "system" only consisted of a Scantron machine that enabled the school to get instant access to all the required assessments across the year, without having to wait for the sometime lengthy processing by the district central office or outside vendors. But whatever the arrangement and routines, school principals tried in various ways to have data become a medium of school-based educators' interactions over issues of learning improvement. That happened throughout the schools we studied, sometimes approximating an inquiry cycle (in some instances guided by central office staff), but other times consisting of an attempt to interrogate the data for clues about how to improve teaching and learning.

Teacher leaders found data to be a particularly useful entry point into instructional conversations with teachers who were often reluctant initially to accept or engage in a relationship with a person occupying a "middle-ground" position in the school. Teacher leaders often found they could redirect teachers' attention from a defensive posture or self-conscious worry about their inadequacies toward a problem solving process that took specific student learning issues or hard-to-teach curricular topics as the starting point for conversation. Teacher leaders were also in a position to decipher assessment data results for teachers who didn't understand what the district data system was sending them.

Building and Maintaining a Leadership Support System

We have reviewed above five sets of learning-focused leadership practices—concerning the embedding of learning improvement goals in daily work, the investment of resources, the reorientation of leadership practices to emphasize learning improvement, the shift in relationships to greater differentiation and responsiveness, and regular use of data in leadership work—that were evident in the schools and districts we studied. These practices took teachers, teaching, and student learning as their primary reference point; after all, instructional leadership is about improving instruction. But the route for reaching teachers and instruction often lay *through* other leaders' work. Because of this, school and district leaders in the systems we studied were simultaneously engaged in multiple forms of *leadership support*, alongside or as part of learning-focused leadership practice. In other words, they didn't take for granted that teacher leaders, school principals, or central office staff would know how to lead effectively or would have the means and legitimacy to engage others in learning improvement. Rather than assuming that only novice leaders need support, they recognized that *all* leaders need it. As a consequence, *explicit and focused support for leaders' work was intrinsic to learning-focused leadership.* Most important, the steps taken to support learning-focused leadership were themselves leadership acts, essential dimensions of a leadership system that guided the improvement of teaching and learning.

"Support" means different things to leaders who occupy varying positions within the educational system, and so the task of supporting learning-focused leadership reflects certain activities and arrangements, suggested schematically by Figure 8.2.

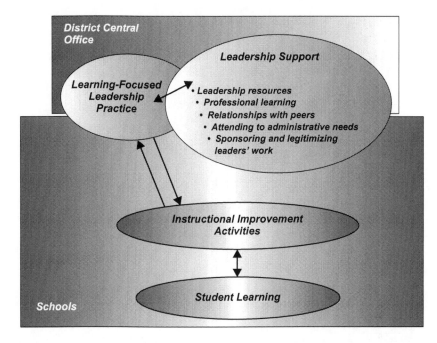

FIGURE 8.2 Activities and Arrangements for Supporting Learning-Focused Leadership

New teacher leaders in a school, for example, face challenges that are different from central office personnel managers; principals and instructional coaches, likewise, have different work to do, in the service of instructional improvement. That said, across the districts and schools we studied, some common sources and forms of leadership support were apparent, each attending to a different set of support needs. Five forms of leadership support, summarized in Table 8.1, were especially noticeable.

These leadership support activities and the forms of support they provide interrelate in many ways—regular professional development meetings can also serve as a location for fostering peer networks, crisis management assistance can turn into an occasion for new professional learning, and so on. Nonetheless, it is helpful to consider, one at a time, what these different facets of leadership support entail and the forms they can take in practice.

Providing Resources to Sustain Leadership Work

Supporting learning-focused leadership means, among other things, providing leaders with the resources that enable sustained attention to instructional improvement. The initial investment in staff engaged in instructional leadership,

TABLE 8.1 Range of Leadership Supports

Leadership Support Activities	Nature of Support
1. **Providing resources to enable leaders to sustain their instructional improvement work** (e.g., by making funds, expert consultants, or materials available to enable leaders to pursue their leadership agendas)	Material and financial support
2. **Creating and facilitating regular opportunities for leaders' professional learning** about their leadership work as well as about instructional improvement (e.g., by creating study groups, workshops, and regular meetings; also through mentoring arrangements)	Formal support for professional learning, intellectual support
3. **Brokering relations with leaders' peers and colleagues engaged in similar work** (e.g., by facilitating interactions among networks of principals, coaches, or central office staff engaged in similar work; and also in the interactions between leaders and mentors)	Social-emotional support, informal support for professional learning
4. **Responding in a coordinated and timely way to administrative, legal, political, or logistical issues facing the school administrators** (e.g., by creating one-stop-shopping systems for school principals to get help with management issues)	Operational support, trouble-shooting or crisis management
5. **Sponsoring and legitimizing learning-focused leadership** (e.g., by giving visible political support to staff occupying new and unfamiliar positions)	Political and organizational support, directional support

mentioned above, was only a first step. Beyond that, in the daily exercise of leadership, school and district leaders needed time, expertise related to particular problems of instructional practice, small amounts of funds for stipends or substitute teachers, and sufficient autonomy to experiment within a framework of agreed-upon expectations for results. The resource supports that our informants judged essential to their work varied by their positioning in the system, for example:

- *Resources provided to teacher leaders:* Scheduled time in the work week to interact with others in the school building's instructional leadership team, or for organized engagement with groups of teachers; funds to support participation in courses or other outside events; access to appropriate materials for coaching work.
- *Resources provided to supervisory leaders in schools:* Funds and/or FTE to use in hiring instructional support staff or others needed to support classroom teachers' work; autonomy or flexibility in using the school budget for instructional improvement purposes; data of various kinds on school performance, climate, participation; observational tools (like walk-through protocols) to help focus and expand instructional supervision work.
- *Resources provided to central office staff who work most directly with the schools:* Time for interaction among team members working with the same set of schools;

instructional frameworks, cycle-of-inquiry protocols, and other data-based tools used in interactions with school principals.

The districts and schools we studied differed in how much they were able to provide leaders; some were in better financial shape than others, and resource requests were not always met. But the important thing was that the sites we studied made special efforts to attend to individual leaders' varied resource needs at whatever level, and, where possible, to respond to those needs on a differentiated basis.

Supporting Leaders' Engagement in Their Own Professional Learning

The leaders we got to know in this study were learners, and they thought of themselves that way—in part, because the system in which they worked provided them with regular opportunities to enhance their learning about instruction itself and how it could be better, and simultaneously about instructional leadership work. For example:

- *Regular "learning walks."* Teacher leaders and supervisory administrators in several schools used regular classroom walk-throughs as a way of sharpening *each others'* capacity to grasp what was happening in classroom instruction and where it could be improved, in addition to offering teachers feedback.
- *One-on-one "learning partnerships."* In several districts, regular one-on-one sessions with central office staff provided principals with opportunities for feedback and modeling of good instructional leadership practice.
- *"Learning community" arrangements for leaders.* Weekly meetings of central office staff who worked directly with schools created a facilitated forum for examining their own work as district-based leaders and considering ways to improve it.

These kinds of activities, among many others, served as a source of ideas for approaching certain aspects of the leadership work, directly taught leadership techniques (e.g., through modeling of leadership practices and reflective debriefing of the observed modeling), and provided leaders with a regular opportunity to diagnose problems of their leadership practice. As we detail in Chapters 3 and 5, various kinds of people could facilitate these forms of professional learning support, including experienced administrators from the central office, external consultants, and expert colleagues or administrators within a school building.

Support for other leaders' professional learning occurred both formally and informally, through structured events and arrangements that were designated for professional learning, but also through less formal side-by-side working relationships. And efforts to support professional learning were not limited to those who worked most directly with teaching staff (e.g., principals, instructional coaches).

Professional learning was the responsibility of everyone, in much the same way that learning improvement was the reference point for everyone's work. Accordingly, at both the school and district levels, the sites we studied created regular occasions for everyone to learn new practices.

Facilitating Relationships Among Peers and Colleagues

The potential of relationships with peers to offer various kinds of support for learning-focused leadership was amply demonstrated in the schools and districts we studied. Here, while the support was often formally arranged or encouraged, it also occurred as a natural by-product of regular interaction among people who faced the same problems of practice and were eager to pick each others' brains, share frustrations, or otherwise stay in touch with new possibilities. Peer support through network arrangements in several districts linked sets of 20 to 25 schools together and convened principals, as well as other role-alike groupings (assistant principals, coaches) at regular intervals. Access to colleagues engaged in similar leadership work (specialists, coaches, instructionally oriented assistant principals) also happened within schools. In these instances, colleagues were often organized to provide a kind of mutual support system for each others' instructional improvement efforts—alternatively, as in many of the instructional leadership teams described in Chapter 2, peer support became a natural by-product of regular team work.

Participants in these support systems offered willing ears to listen to the issues that inevitably arose in the difficult work of instructional leadership—but also provided ideas, advice, and problem solving as trusted colleagues who were not in a position of authority over the leader seeking support. The team-based structures noted in Chapter 2 as well as the regular convening of network leaders and other groupings of role-alike central office staff described in Chapter 5 offered natural settings for this kind of support to be exercised, and it was much appreciated by the participants. In the most developed instances of this kind of arrangement, members of networked groups of principals were encouraged to see themselves as resources for each others' work, by making known and available to each other their differing expertise as a potential source for future assistance or advice. In this respect, the leaders' learning was as much driven by their own initiative and agendas as by facilitators.

Attending to Administrative or Management Issues in a Timely, Responsive Way

Especially for the administrative leaders in a school (principals and assistant principals) but for others as well, the daily urgencies of education in settings populated by historically underserved students entail an enormous number of practical and logistical issues that demand time, attention, diplomacy, and often specialized skill to handle. On one end of a continuum, these matters concerned the management of personnel, supply orders, procurement of vendor services, and maintenance of the school facility, and on the other end, the management of crises, staff conflict, delicate student placement issues, relations with the police, or interactions with irate parents. In many cases, these issues required, or at least could benefit from, external assistance or intervention.

While large education bureaucracies are notoriously unresponsive to such matters, the districts we studied had worked on attending to such operational needs in a responsive and streamlined manner *as an essential means of maintaining an overall focus on teaching and learning.* The "one stop shop" principle that underlay network arrangements in New York City and Atlanta, for example, were meant to reduce the time that school staff would need to expend on solving operational and logistical matters, thereby helping to keep the focus on the instructional program. In this spirit, the districts we studied employed one or more of the following approaches:

- *Developing regular, tailored assistance relationships with school principals* designed to respond to the school leaders' operational as well as instructional needs.
- *Instituting arrangements within the central office,* to encourage coordinated, cross-functional follow-through on central office tasks, while discouraging the fragmentation of responsibility that so often slows down and dilutes the potency of central office response to school needs.
- *Establishing internal incentives and feedback systems within the central office* to encourage all units and staff to see themselves as having a direct service relationship with the schools.

More to the point, the systems and leaders we studied did not treat these matters as separate from instructional improvement, but rather intrinsically connected to it. Thus, helping school leaders deal with a leaky roof or rewire a school building in a timely way was part of maintaining an instructional program that kept teachers and their students focused on learning. Enabling prompt personnel transactions was part of getting good instructional staff in front of students who needed them, without loss of instructional days or weeks. Absent this kind of operational and crisis-management support, school administrators' working days were at risk of being consumed by matters that did not necessarily enhance the instructional improvement work of the school.

Sponsoring and Legitimatizing Learning-Focused Leadership

Finally, a different yet essential kind of support resided in the efforts by leaders, often those in positions of supervisory authority, to proactively *sponsor* and *legitimize* learning-focused leadership work. This kind of support was necessary because, for reasons discussed earlier—its newness, ambiguity, and lack of precedent or trust—learning-focused leadership can be organizationally fragile and easily abandoned, especially in the early stages of reorienting leadership towards learning improvement. Though their functions differed widely, an individual teacher leader in a school and the new members of a new project management team in the central office faced similar issues and quandaries: they needed to know what they were to do and why in their new roles, and that someone "had their back."

By championing the overall enterprise, reminding people what they were doing and why, and by normalizing new and unusual forms of leadership practice, leaders who acted as sponsors for learning-focused leadership communicated that it was a legitimate and expected part of the educational system, for both those occupying traditional and accepted positions and others in relatively new or unfamiliar roles. Sponsorship of learning-focused leadership showed up in three primary ways in our studies:

- *Normalizing teacher leaders' work in schools.* As explained more fully in Chapter 3, in many of the schools we studied in which teachers and others were assuming various "middle-ground" positions between the supervisory administrators and classroom teachers, conscious steps were taken by the school administrators to explain and legitimize the efforts of the new teacher leaders to staffs who were sometimes reluctant or resistant.
- *Guiding central office transformation efforts.* Transforming the central office in the sites we studied took relentless and explicit sponsorship not just by superintendents, but by various staff including chiefs of staff, executive directors, and others throughout the central office. Collectively, they developed and explained the *theory of action* underlying transformation efforts (see Chapter 5), both within the districts and to external constituencies, and created various opportunities for people to understand what the district was doing *and why*. It also involved strategically brokering external resources to support the ongoing effort to transform the system.
- *Shepherding the equity conversation in district-wide resource planning.* Through a process that could last years, described in Chapter 6, district leaders helped stakeholders identify the equity challenges facing a district or school and publicly built a community mission that prioritizes enhancing the equity of the educational system. Then, as specific actions were taken to enhance equity, the leaders engaged stakeholders in continuing conversation leading up to, and following, specific decisions to invest resources disproportionately, thereby trying to craft coherence and foster deeper commitment among the various parties.

These kinds of actions by educational leaders provide a kind of overall political support for learning-focused leaders' efforts. At the same time, these actions clarify the direction of improvement work and the compelling reasons for it. In this sense, educational systems recognize that leadership is likely to face resistance and engender conflict, and that leaders who pursue a learning improvement agenda need protection.

The Web of Leadership Support for Learning Improvement

The leadership practices and leadership supports discussed above were in evidence in the districts and schools we studied, though the degree to which they had been realized varied with local purposes and capacities, stage in a reform process, and commitment to central office transformation. And to the extent that they were both present and aligned with each other, they formed a mutually reinforcing web of support for the practice of learning-focused leadership, and ultimately for learning improvement itself, as signaled schematically by Figure 8.3 below.

One set of learning-focused leadership practices invited others: the daily public ownership of learning improvement goals often accompanied extensive evidence use in leadership work; using data regularly prompted new forms of leadership practice in both schools and central office; and so on. Similarly, one form of leadership support reinforced another, and the same structures and practices could be

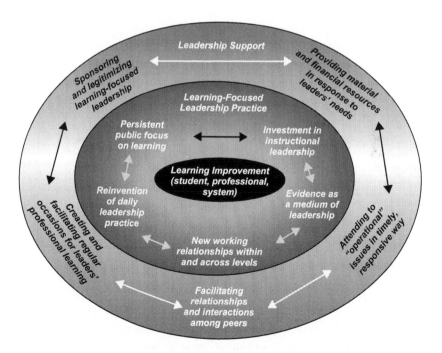

FIGURE 8.3 Web of Support for Learning Improvement

invoked in offering more than one kind of support. Network arrangements in several districts, for example, simultaneously offered school principals and other school staff intellectual, emotional, operational, and strategic support. Within the schools, principals guided and supported teacher leaders' learning and practice by offering material and financial resources, providing ideas (or access to idea sources), and legitimizing the work of teacher leaders in the eyes of staff who were not always initially receptive.

In essence, what we found were two layers of learning-focused leadership practice. The outer layer—what we are calling "leadership support"—displayed many of the same leadership practices as the inner layer. Thus, individuals guiding the professional learning of instructional leaders were simultaneously focusing effort on learning, modeling good practice, engaging educators in joint improvement work, and developing and using evidence, among other forms of learning-focused leadership practice. In this sense, support activities not only guide and assist the practice of learning-focused leadership, they also *embody* it. Leadership directed at teachers, teaching, and student learning needs support. Leadership support is itself leadership. The two are flip sides of the same coin.

Concluding Observations: Continuing Challenges and Ongoing Work

Taken together, learning-focused leadership practice and leadership support, exercised by leaders at multiple levels of the system, constitute a major potential influence on learning improvement. In the districts we studied, this leadership work accomplished its purpose by engaging the attention and talents of a variety of staff in efforts to improve teaching and learning while creating a web of support for instructional improvement and leaders' efforts to pursue it. In ways that were both overt and subtle, these actions offered a mutually reinforcing set of influences on educators' daily practice, and ultimately on student learning. Our data suggest two kinds of overall conclusions:

1. The capacity of the educational system to enhance the practices that produce student learning depends on leadership that focuses on learning improvement for both students and professional staff, and mobilizes effort to that end.
2. The power and sustainability of learning-focused leadership depends, in large measure, on the presence of a multilevel system of leadership support.

These broad conclusions come from looking carefully at schools that were making progress (by some local measures), at districts that were intentionally trying to transform their practice to support district-wide teaching and learning improvement, and at several other districts that had placed a priority on instructional improvement. Because our conclusions do not come from tracing the consequences of leadership actions all the way to student learning outcomes over time, and because we studied schools and districts that might be considered exceptional, at least not typical, two questions arise: Why should we believe that learning-focused leadership and leadership support matter for student learning? What continuing challenges would other schools and districts face in attempting to act on these ideas?

Does It Matter for Improving Student Learning?

Even though these studies did not directly assess the relationship between either leadership practices or leadership support activities and measures of student learning, there are good reasons to believe that both learning-focused leadership and leadership support are contributing to the ultimate aim of improving student learning, and consequently are likely to be affecting measures of that learning.

First of all, even though the schools and districts we studied have histories of chronic low performance, over recent years and continuing through our data collection window, measures of student performance in these systems were improving. While there is no way of demonstrating an unambiguous causal link between these trends and leadership or leadership support practices, there is nonetheless a strong likelihood that what leaders were doing and how they were supported were an important part of the story. Take, for example, the way school principals approached their responsibilities and how they were supported. Research other than our own (summarized in Leithwood & Riehl, 2005) has increasingly demonstrated strong links between student learning measures and leadership activities at the school level, among them, activities that: (1) *set direction* by articulating a vision for the school, fostering the acceptance of group goals, and creating high performance expectations; (2) *develop people* by offering intellectual stimulation, providing individualized support, and setting examples for others to follow; and (3) *redesign the organization* by strengthening school cultures, modifying organizational structures, and building collaborative processes. These are all activities that the school leaders we studied were engaged in extensively as they fashioned and pursued their respective learning improvement agendas.

What is more, evidence from the *Study of Leadership for Learning Improvement* clearly demonstrates that, through their interaction with their respective systems of leadership support, school leaders were *helped* to set (and maintain) direction, develop people, and redesign their organizations. The school leaders' visions were intimately linked to a larger vision of learning improvement projected by the district and state in which they worked (Portin et al., 2009). Interactions with others (e.g., central office staff, their peers in other schools) helped to establish and spread the high expectations (Knapp & Feldman, 2012). Through interactions with both central office staff and individuals in external reform support organizations, school principals themselves got intellectual stimulation and received individualized support, including modeling of promising practices, especially noticeable in the learning-focused partnerships between central office staff and school principals that transforming districts created (Honig, 2012). In turn, these school leaders created a variety of supports that developed the capabilities of their instructional leadership teams. They were both prompted and enabled to redesign their organizations by investment frameworks—overarching decisions about the discretion that was expected or allowed at different levels of the system, and how initiative could be exercised—that offered flexibility and some discretionary resources, especially for increasing their instructional leadership capacity (Plecki et al., 2009). And efforts to redesign organizations to facilitate learning improvement were everywhere in our data, within the central office (e.g., cross-unit project management arrangements), between the central office and schools (e.g., network team structures connecting subsets of schools with dedicated central office staff), and within schools (e.g., instructional leadership team designs of many kinds).

Our research also suggests more specific effects on instructional practice that are likely to be having a positive effect on student learning. As they engaged and responded to the expectations of the larger environments, principals and other supervisory leaders in these schools, as well as teacher leaders, were focusing teachers' efforts on particular aspects of the curriculum (especially where student performance was weak), developing a vocabulary for approaching gaps and gains in students' progress, and helping teachers differentiate their approach to students within their classrooms (Knapp & Feldman, 2012; Knapp, Feldman, & Yeh, 2013). And there is good reason to believe that focused, differentiated instruction, which is responsive to particular needs and differences among students, is helping these schools and districts improve their learning measures over time.[4]

What Challenges Will It Face in Other Schools and Districts?

Learning-focused leadership is hard work, and correspondingly, so is the work of supporting this leadership. Both are made harder by dynamics and conditions that typify educational settings that serve a diverse student population. Our analyses underscore several aspects of the effort to exercise and support leadership for learning improvement that will continue to challenge educational leaders in many schools and districts, especially under the conditions that prevail where students live in impoverished circumstances. Three broad challenges emerge from the *Study of Leadership for Learning Improvement*: assuming and maintaining a learning focus, balancing pressure and support, and working within the constraints facing large school systems.

The challenges of assuming and maintaining a learning focus. What our investigation found about learning-focused leadership practice and leadership support underscores several challenges concerning what it takes for a learning-focused practice to take root. First, participants throughout the schools and districts that wish to go this route have a steep learning curve to ascend. Second, they need to be prepared for fundamental changes in practice and the organization of their work. And third, they will need to actively search for and prepare the right people to do this leadership work.

The first continuing challenge goes without saying: There is a lot of new professional learning to do—for teacher leaders negotiating the middle ground in schools, principals figuring out how to lead instructional leadership teams successfully, central office staff engaging in learning partnerships with school principals, or others in the system. This new professional learning would be a tall order in any school or district setting, but is compounded in larger, more complex districts, given the sheer number of actors and the high proportion of struggling schools. And for all of these educators, learning to do the work described in this book is a long-term prospect under the best of circumstances.

Among other things, the new professional learning is about fundamental changes in leadership practice, and systems must assess their readiness for it. The degree of change was especially apparent for many of the teacher leaders we studied, most of whose positions didn't exist five years ago, and also for the central office staff engaged in learning partnerships with schools. Are schools and district central offices ready to take this work on? The answer can reflect various matters, among them: whether the main decision makers have been engaged in a significant period of design work or development of an appropriate theory of action, and whether the new arrangements and approaches have been tried out on a pilot basis to debug them and fine-tune the plan for contingencies particular to each local context. Not the least of the factors in the readiness equation is the willingness of key constituencies to sign on. For example, in one of the districts we studied, detailed negotiations across four years with the teachers union were necessary before a new kind of school-based instructional leadership position could be created. Urban school districts typically face tight labor markets and complicated political force fields, which may signal a lack of readiness for the fundamental change work that substantial learning improvement requires.

Among the variables in the readiness equation is the identification and availability of people to exercise leadership in the ways this report describes. Finding and preparing leaders for learning-focused leadership work remains a central challenge, especially in systems in which leadership roles are not always easily filled with well qualified candidates. What will prepare new leaders for learning-focused work and help them continue to learn productively, once they are engaged in leadership practice? While we learned a great deal about conditions that support learning-focused leadership practice, we know much less about what propels individuals through career trajectories that involve this work. The sites we studied were often engaged in growing their own leaders in a variety of ways, most visibly in district-based certification programs that set up alternative pathways to the principalship. Recent work on more comprehensive "leadership pipeline" strategies now under development in some districts are a clear step in this direction (e.g., Turnbull, Riley, Arcaira, Anderson, & MacFarlane, 2013). But these programs are just one step towards a much larger goal, which remains daunting in settings in which the incentives and rewards for assuming leadership or leadership support work are not always substantial. The continuing challenge is to both create and inform these pathways to leadership in ways that motivate participation and guide promising candidates towards new conceptions of their practice.

The challenge of balancing pressure and support. There was no mistaking the seriousness with which each of the districts we studied approach the imperative of improving both learning opportunities and learning outcomes for students. Indeed, the context of accountability insisted on such an emphasis, and the history of chronic underperformance that typified most of these districts added impetus to the effort. In such a situation, as many critics of high-stakes accountability and especially high-stakes testing have pointed out (e.g., Lipman, 2004; Orfield & Kornhaber, 2001), there is the potential for the pressures to predominate, and even to overwhelm daily practice in the schools (Amrein-Beardsley, Berliner, & Rideau, 2010). In the most extreme cases, an incentive can be established for educators to make the numbers improve, when teaching and learning are not actually improving, as evidenced in some of the test cheating scandals that have emerged over the last decade (Gabriel, 2010; Samuels, 2011), one of which was brewing in a site we studied (though unknown to us at the time of our data collection).

First of all, there seems to be no doubt that learning-focused leadership, done properly, exerts *pressure* on educators throughout a system to change practice, anchor it to performance, and hold each others' feet to the fire. Such pressures can be considerable—they are not always comfortable, and they create a kind of disequilibrium in the system, to which participants must respond. And where people don't know how to respond appropriately, have no image or vision of better practice, the pressures by themselves can be intolerable. The matter can be easily compounded by the pervasive emphasis on basing teaching and leadership practice on data, especially student test scores (Amrein-Beardsley et al., 2010). Essential as such data are, they do not tell one what to do, how to do better—only where improvement is needed.

The goal, from a learning-focused leadership perspective, seems to be twofold, and in the exemplary end of the practices we observed, it was clearly present. There, educators moved beyond simply pressuring educators to perform, by turning the leadership work itself into *teaching* and formative assistance to people on the front lines of serving young people. Second, they built and maintained the right kind of leadership support system, one that offers regular help to leaders at all levels and across the full range of their needs. In both respects the emphasis is on learning—not just learning how and where current practice is *not* meeting standards to which all aspire, but rather learning how to teach in different and more effective ways, how to support teachers' efforts to recognize and improve their practice, and how to offer leaders the kinds of support they most need. In such instances, the principle of balancing pressure and support, long established in discussions of reform policy implementation (McLaughlin, 1987), pertains in the learning-focused leadership story as well. Pressure will only produce results in proportion to the support received.

When things go awry, they seem to do so mostly where too little support is provided, while overdoing the pressure. The matter is compounded with excessive focus on a single measure such as the annual standardized tests. In such instances, too much time is devoted to punishing continued low performance on the test, urging educators and students on to better performance, and refusing to accept failure; staff evaluation communicates summative judgment at the expense of formative and growth-oriented assessment feedback. Too little energy goes into supporting continued professional learning, investment of resources, and problem solving, to get at the unanticipated impediments to better results.

One of the districts we studied (the Atlanta Public Schools) offers a case in point, but its prominence as an instance of alleged widespread test cheating (Brown & Severson, 2013) obscures much of the constructive leadership work taking place, and the insights into what it may take to make learning-focused leadership realize its ultimate goals. Accounts of cheating on the annual state assessment in this district surfaced well after the time of our data collection, in a state audit report and ongoing court cases, but a substantial amount of cheating on the annual state assessment test may have been taking place simultaneously with our study.[5] To be sure, conditions were present that might have encouraged efforts by some staff to make test scores look better than they otherwise would be: a constant focus on improving test scores, specific annual improvement targets for schools and even particular individuals within the schools, financial incentives tied to test score improvement, clear and regular insistence from school and district leaders that low performance was unacceptable, and even consequences for continued employment where improvement didn't happen (a message to principals, especially).

But concentrating on this cluster of conditions, it is easy to miss many other things going on simultaneously, also attributable to leadership practices and arrangements, such as: the affirmation of the students' capabilities and commitment to their success (yes, these students can meet high expectations, and they will) and the regular, detailed attention being paid to evidence of teaching and learning (here are some particular things that are not working in your teaching this week, and here are some ways to work on it). One might also miss the daily pattern of leadership work, in which Model Teacher Leaders, central office support staff, principals, and others worked continuously with teachers on improving their teaching. And one might fail to notice that leaders themselves were getting various forms of support—not just admonishments to do better, or else. In many ways a fairly robust leadership support system was in place in this district, and it was offering teachers, principals, coaches, and central office staff regular occasions for focusing on and improving their efforts over time.

Finally, in concentrating in this case on the dubious gains that some schools appeared to be making from reports of the state annual assessment in certain years, it is possible to forget that across a decade and more of the leadership system, the district made impressive and sustained improvement in student learning, as measured by the National Assessment of Educational Progress from 2002 to 2011 through processes that were not under the district's control (National Assessment of Educational Progress, 2011). Based on these observations, we draw the conclusion that, while all may not have been right in this case, much was. If anything, the district erred on the side of pressure, to the point that a number of educators may have given in to it, and compromised the integrity of their otherwise laudable efforts. Had greater attention been paid to the support side of the equation, the alleged serious lapses in judgment might never have happened, and the focus on learning would have been properly maintained.

The constraints facing large school systems. However educators seek to prepare themselves for learning-focused work and engage in it over time, they do so in the face of conditions that can seriously constrain learning-focused leadership. Our findings point to four such conditions. First, educational leaders are currently emerging from a major economic downturn, but with no immediate end in sight to significant resource restrictions. Second, the shortage of resources will limit leaders' capacity to address inequities, if not exacerbate the inequities themselves. Third, operational demands of schooling in such settings will persist and offer a tempting, though misleading, excuse for not prioritizing instructional improvement. And fourth, the chronic instability of top leadership in many large school systems will make it harder to maintain a persistent public focus on learning, as well as overall sponsorship of learning-focused reforms.

In the current economic climate, even with some modest recovery from the Great Recession, districts and schools continue to face bleak prospects for maintaining many aspects of the educational program that are valued, not the least of which are the investments in instructional leadership detailed in earlier chapters. That said, the schools and districts we studied had seen recent periods of retrenchment and/or declining enrollment, and notably, much of the investment in instructional leadership was achieved through the *reallocation* of existing funds rather than with additional resources. To be sure, anything not perceived as the core work of the school or district is an easy target in times of budget cutting. In this regard, investments made in the leadership support system will continue to be challenged, and school and district leaders will need to articulate how and why this aspect of the leadership system is central to the improvement of learning.

Because contests over resource allocation intensify when times are tight, the differential allocation of staffing and other resources that are needed to address equity goals in learning improvement may be at risk. Because many large school systems serve populations of concentrated poverty and other specialized learning needs, the inequities in question are likely to be substantial. As our findings and others have demonstrated, ambitious learning improvement efforts anchored to equity principles that imply differential investment of resources will generate predictable pushback from formerly advantaged interests. The sheer diversity of interests and the stark gaps between advantaged and less advantaged segments of the community, no less competing interest groups within the district workforce, set the stage for major tensions regarding differential resource investments. To manage the dynamics of differential investment, district and school leaders must exercise as much foresight as possible in laying the groundwork for equity-focused conversations, and shepherding these conversations over time.

The operational demands of running schools and large school systems—including facility, accounting, personnel, procurement, compliance reporting, and other basic management tasks—are often complex and all-consuming, tempting leaders at all levels to think of themselves as "noninstructional" managers. What is more, these demands may increase in times of acute resource shortage. This situation presents learning-focused leaders with the continuing challenge of translating operational demands into opportunities for strengthening the focus on instructional improvement, as we found most noticeably in districts seeking to transform their central offices into a support system for teaching and learning improvement. As principals or others seek help with matters that appear to have little to do with instructional improvement, or for which they are initially unable to see the instructional ramifications, learning-focused leadership support systems will need to be able to show the connections and keep the focus on teaching and learning.

Finally, learning-focused leadership and leadership support depends on continuity of leadership over time. In the sites we studied, this was especially obvious in the role that superintendents and executive-level staff performed in sustaining a transformation strategy or shepherding the development of an equity-focused learning improvement agenda. School principals who had long tenure in their buildings displayed a comparable capacity. Leaders such as these who are around for long periods of time are better able to make long-term investments and hold to them, not to mention develop and deepen work relationships. The nature of leadership support, as we have described it, depends utterly on sufficient consistency in leadership—that is, among leaders within the system who are committed to making learning improvement a centerpiece of their own and the system's work—to allow people and the system as a whole to learn over time.

A sufficiently distributed leadership support system can help to weather the disappearance of one or another key player, and we found viable efforts at leadership support continuing, despite sudden changes or disruptions. Nonetheless, the well-established pattern of instability in top leadership positions within many large educational systems, especially those in urban areas, will pose a continuing challenge to the sustainability of learning-focused leadership and leadership support system. The challenge is to develop deep, distributed leadership roots that can help the system manage top leadership turnover at the same time that the system seeks greater continuity in top leadership—a state of affairs that can become increasingly likely, the more the system succeeds at learning improvement.

Accomplishments and Unfinished Business

The schools and districts we studied have clearly made substantial progress in putting into place leadership practices and supports that go a long way towards realizing the promise of learning-focused leadership. As such, they offer instructive images of what is possible in the complex work of leading schools and school systems, and what it means to put learning-focused leadership principles into action. In that regard, it is worth highlighting the various ways in which *learning* pervades these sites.

First, these schools and districts make students' learning a paramount duty and focus of educators' work, both rhetorically and through numerous routines that put questions about, and evidence of, student learning in the foreground of deliberations, whether about system-wide policy or the next day's lessons. In most cases (though not all), the attention to student learning transcends a concern about high-stakes test scores and how to make them improve, though that is clearly a main agenda item for all. While we must acknowledge that a preoccupation with test scores can be counterproductive, and even destructive in some instances, paying close and continuing attention to specific evidence of learning—including tests—is inescapably part of any attempt to improve learning opportunities and outcomes for students.

Second, these schools and districts are sites of professional learning in many ways. Teachers are clearly learning how to teach more effectively, as are the instructional leaders working most directly with them (e.g., principals, coaches, other teacher leaders), who are learning what it takes to become effective leaders (and leadership support providers) in instructional leadership teams and other staff configurations (e.g., network teams). But just as important, other members of the leadership support cadre, one or more steps removed from direct interaction with teachers (e.g., central office staff working with principals or making system-wide resource allocation decisions) are being given regular opportunities to enhance their own learning about their practice and about those with whom they are working. In certain instances, the supports for professional learning extend throughout the central office and help *all* staff reconceive of their daily work. In many instances, these opportunities for professional learning are based in sound principles of adult learning, and as such are likely to produce sustainable changes in the way educators do their work, as well as the results they achieve.

Third, an infrastructure for collective learning about the system's performance and possibilities for improvement—including a wider range of data that are increasingly accessible, along with regular occasions for considering what these data might mean—is in place in most of the schools and districts we studied, to some degree. And, where coupled with an ethos of inquiry and the regular habit of inquiring into performance and outcomes, the system as a whole, if not subparts within it (e.g., a single school), are demonstrably "learning" about educational activities and results.

These accomplishments are possible in many schools and districts, not just those we studied, and the examples of learning-focused leadership in action we have uncovered do not exhaust the possibilities for realizing the principles set forth in this book. Nor do the analyses we have offered probe as fully as they could all the dimensions of this many-faceted approach to educational leadership. Educational leaders and scholars will need to continue the search we have undertaken here. For one thing, much more can be said and learned about the fine detail of learning-focused leadership practice, as carried out by individuals and teams in schools and district central offices. Similarly, we need to explore further the way this approach to leadership intersects with particular visions of high-quality instruction, such as those embodied in well developed and validated instructional frameworks or in work that visualizes powerful learning in particular subject areas. We need to know more about how learning-focused leadership becomes sufficiently sensitive to subject matter differences, at the same time that it instills practices and expectations that cut across subject areas. The search for equitable learning opportunities and outcomes presents a third area of further learning educational leaders and scholars will need to do. Within the broad parameters of investing in equity we have been able to describe, we need to know more specifically how learning-focused leaders can maintain a focus on equity in all aspects of their leadership work.

These and other matters of unfinished business lie ahead for educators, reformers, and scholars who take learning improvement seriously and see leadership and leadership support systems as essential avenues for attaining it. But the further learning will not end with the next demonstration, study, or local experiment. Rather, learning is and always needs to be, a continuing goal, process, and stance of all educators, and especially those who exercise and support educational leadership. As long as leaders never lose sight of that prospect, they and the systems they lead will be moving in the right direction.

Notes

1 This investment pattern may have slowed somewhat under the current tight budget constraints that many districts operate within these days. Nonetheless, the commitment to investing in instructional leadership can still be maintained, albeit at reduced levels, under fiscally adverse conditions.

2 The Instructional Leadership Directors held various actual job titles, but all shared a primary responsibility for working directly with school principals, individually and collectively, on enhancing instructional leadership work. For a more detailed discussion of

the Instructional Leadership Directors' work, see Honig, 2012 and Honig and Rainey, in press.

3 The research base for the notion of "high quality assistance relationship" is fully described in Honig (2008).

4 While there is not yet an extensive research base on the topic, converging lines of theory and empirical work suggest the potential power of appropriately differentiating instruction. For a summary of this work see Tomlinson & McTighe (2006). More recently, questions about the effects of differentiated instruction on student learning have begun to be explored experimentally, and the results suggest benefits to student learning—e.g., in reading, see Reis, McCoach, Little, Muller, & Kaniskan (2011).

5 Evidence of systematic cheating on the annual state assessment in the Atlanta Public Schools emerged first in a state-initiated special investigators' report in 2011, based on analyses of the 2009 testing year—a year after we completed our data collection—and was documented through extensive interviewing of educators across the district following that school year. The report identified possible or likely cheating in roughly half of the district's schools; only one of our case study schools was among these identified by the report. Furthermore, our focus on daily practice and ongoing arrangements for leading and supporting learning improvement paid little attention to the annual testing cycle, and instead concentrated on the various forms of diagnostic work, targeted leadership, training, and other activities that were designed to improve student learning results as well as professional competence. Our analyses thus highlighted changes in professional practice and alteration in roles and structure that brought more focused and frequent attention to instructional improvement efforts, accompanied by a great deal of assistance. In these respects, Atlanta exemplified many of the most promising aspects of learning-focused leadership.

METHODOLOGICAL APPENDIX

The *Study of Leadership for Learning Improvement* was set up as a multicomponent investigation with three primary study strands, addressing related facets of the practice of learning-focused leadership and its support in urban districts (the configuration of central offices to support teaching and learning improvement district-wide, and the investment of resources at the school and district levels to realize equitable learning improvement). Each operated, in effect, as a separate study, with a distinct research team and design; each undertook a separate line of analysis with somewhat different purposes; and the results of each have been reported separately. That said, the designs were intentionally coordinated in several ways, and shared some study sites and data collection, as well as an orientation to several overarching ideas about learning-focused leadership. What is more, all three were designed in similar ways: they were largely qualitative, multiple-case designs, featuring repeated visits across a year and a half; they triangulated findings and conclusions among interview, observational, and archival data sources; and they focused on leadership phenomena at the district and school levels, though their degree of emphasis on these levels differed.

Overlapping Study Samples

The overarching study design linked the three lines of investigation, in part, through overlapping samples. All three study strands used two sites in common, while adding one or two others that provided useful contrasts for the particular purposes of the study strand, as shown in Figure M.1.

While the specific selection criteria differed somewhat by study strand, all three samples emphasized urban districts that were proactively pursuing a learning

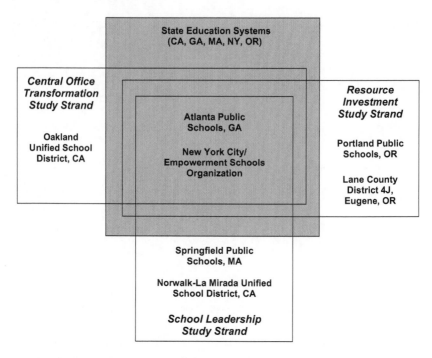

FIGURE M.1 District Samples for the Three Study Strands

improvement agenda, with special emphasis on leadership development and the improvement of leadership practice. What is more, all seven sites displayed evidence, at the time of site selection, of improvement on measures of student learning, though the actual measures and timeframes for evidence differed by site, and so they cannot be compared in any strictly comparable way; that said, comparable measures were available for the two common sites—Atlanta Public Schools and NYC/Department of Education—through the National Assessment of Educational Progress (NAEP) Trial Urban District Assessment, and this source revealed clear evidence of progress from 2003 to 2007, in 4th and 8th grade mathematics and reading (NAEP, 2010). We also sought sites that had a prior relationship with The Wallace Foundation and had received grant support for pursuing leadership-related improvement work; four of the seven districts and all but one of the five states in which these districts sat also had received leadership-related grants from The Foundation.

Within these districts, three to five schools were selected for intensive study, chiefly for the school-level analyses that were a focus of the School Leadership and Resource Investment study strands (for a total of 21 intensive case schools across the two studies). Across all sites, other schools, visited less frequently, added depth to the data collection for purposes of that study strand, as in the Central Office Transformation investigation, in which central office administrators were sometimes followed to school sites to develop observational evidence of their school-based work. The 21 intensively studied schools were selected to demonstrate: (1) progress on improving student learning for the full range of a diverse student population (on whatever local measures were taken as the most important indicator of school performance), (2) reconfigured leadership arrangements within the school designed to share the leadership work and maximize leaders' attention to teaching and learning, and (3) experimentation with the allocation of staffing resources to maximize attention to the equitable improvement of student learning. The resulting set of schools was at all levels: elementary (11), middle and high (10)—and varied in other important respects: longevity of the principal, school size (from several hundred students to well over two thousand), neighborhood versus district-wide attendance area, and school of choice versus district-assigned student population.

Similarities in Data Collection and Analytic Design

The three investigations pursue their research through parallel, nested, multiple case designs (Merriam, 1998; Yin, 2003) that relied heavily on qualitative data sources collected through iterative site visits across a year and half (the 2007–08 school year and the first half of the following school year). Each site was visited approximately four times (e.g., autumn, winter, and spring of one school year, and autumn of the following year), though depending on site proximity to the study team home base, and the precise purposes of the study strand, some were visited more often. Our rationale for such an intensive study was that in order to capture relative subtle leadership events and processes, we needed to focus in greater depth on a smaller number of settings and to do so in way that could follow leadership events and processes over time. The cycle of repeated visits allowed us to develop relationships with key informants, as well as to allow periods of analytic work between visits to help focus further site visiting efforts.

Our analytic work in each of the three investigations also followed a relatively common pattern, with iterative cycles of coding, theme generation, and memoing, using NVivo software to organize the many items of data (hundreds of interviews for each investigation, as well a large number of observations, especially for the central office transformation study). That said, there were distinct differences in analytic approach noted below that reflected the specific purposes of each investigation.

Chief Differences in Design and Analytic Approach

Despite their considerable similarities, the three investigations differed in several important respects, summarized below (readers may find further detail in a lengthy technical appendix in each of the three study reports).

School Leadership Study strand. This investigation (Portin et al., 2009) concentrated effort on school-level events, including a limited amount of classroom observation, and various observations of the interaction between school-level leaders and other staff. The study relied heavily on repeated interviews with a range of educators cutting across the school staff (principal and assistant principals, teacher leaders, coaches, staff developers, data specialists and assessment coordinators, classroom teachers, and other support staff), supplemented by some interview data from outsiders (e.g., district staff who worked with the school, staff from reform support organizations). Various forms of archival evidence (e.g., school improvement plans, curriculum and other design documents, planning tools, memos to staff from school leaders) rounded out the data sources for our analytic work. In particular, we paid attention to organizational representations of the school and its work (e.g., Web-based or paper descriptions of its mission, programs, or recent events), strategic planning documents, leadership communications, rosters of staff and descriptions of their roles, and information about how resources were distributed in the school. We also collected documents sent to the school by the district central office.

Analyses followed a two-stage process, reflecting an adapted form of "grounded theory" analysis (Strauss & Corbin, 1994, 1998), situated in two waves of analytic work that took advantage of the situated "within-site" meanings of the data from each case school, while enabling "cross-site" claims to be developed and substantiated (Miles & Huberman, 1994). The first wave, interspersed with and immediately following field visits, carried out within-site analyses of leadership arrangements and practice in each case study school. Here, data from each school were coded with a broad set of analytic study codes mapped on to a conceptualization of school-based learning-focused leadership, and then used to generate lengthy analytic memos about each school. The second wave, drawing on the results of the first, developed cross-site insights and patterns based on the common patterns and divergences between the within-site patterns. Across all, we treated the school as the primary unit of analysis, and within that organizational unit, leadership practice (e.g., of principals, teacher leaders) as a frequent analytic unit.

Though less focused on systematic category identification and elaboration, nonetheless, as in classical grounded theory, the analytic design utilized a largely inductive frame and without firm commitments to an *a priori* conceptual framework, preferring to evolve and refine analytic categories and relationships in the course of the analysis process. The resulting "theory" offered "local empirical models surrounding the phenomenon under study" (Hughes & Jones, 2003) drawing on various conceptual ideas about the nature of learning-focused leadership and the conditions and action surrounding it that might influence it, rooted in our assessment of relevant literature at the outset of the study (Portin, Knapp, Plecki, & Copland, 2008).

Central Office Transformation Study strand. This investigation (Honig et al., 2010) captured the dynamics and contours of efforts by study districts to fundamentally reform the work practices, organization, and working culture within the central office, while altering the working relationships between school and central office, so that the district focused more singularly and effectively on the improvement of teaching and learning. The design placed a greater emphasis on a detailed conceptual framework, reflecting sociocultural and organizational learning theories (see Honig, 2008), which offered a reference point for both data collection and subsequent analysis.

With interview protocols and observation guides based in this framework, this study strand team concentrated on interviewing a wide range of central office staff, but with a special focus on those who worked most directly and continuously with school principals; each of these central office staff were interviewed four times across the study. These data sources were coupled with an extensive observational record of meetings and other leadership activities (e.g., central office staff visits to schools, which the research team shadowed) in which central office staff participated; these sources yielded a continuous record across the year of central office leadership practice for particular categories of staff on which the study was concentrating (within a specific realm of their work, which afforded a window on other realms, as meeting participants often brought their other experiences into meeting discussion). Various documents helped us understand the design of the central office transformation effort at each site, communication and other dimensions of the relationships between central office administrators and school principals, and how central office administrators worked with school principals to improve their instructional leadership practice (e.g., tools used by central office staff in their work with schools, documents that described the overall central office transformation process and its underlying rationale).

Using NVivo 8 software over 16 months, the study team went through several rounds of coding and interpretive work, starting with an initial set of broad and relatively low-inference codes derived from our conceptual framework. This analysis created broad categories to separate out how other central office administrators participated in implementation. This phase also identified data that related to the outcomes of the central office transformation process, using simple categories to distinguish outcomes for principals, schools, and the district overall. In the second, "recoding" phase, the team went back into the data, this time through the codes used in the first phase, and further scrutinized whether or not the data coded in the first phase actually fit the constructs, and we recoded those data using codes at a higher level of inference. In a third phase, the team took another pass through the data set to collapse redundant categories or eliminate those whose points could not be substantiated with at least three different data sources (either a combination of interviews, observations, and documents, or self-reports of at least three different respondents). This phase identified five main dimensions of central office transformation that were subsequently used to organize findings. During this phase, we also linked particular central office work practices with outcomes when those associations could be justified with at least three different data sources.

Resource Investment Study strand. Unlike the other two, this investigation connected qualitative investigations with quantitative analyses of resource investment patterns, while de-emphasizing the observation of leadership practice and events (Plecki et al., 2009). To this end, the investigation employed an embedded, concurrent mixed-methods design (Creswell & Plano Clark, 2001; Johnson & Christensen, 2008), that emphasized qualitative data, while using quantitative sources to pinpoint and elaborate resource distribution patterns. Overall, the investigation paid most attention to staffing resources, and the decisions made at all levels to allocate or reallocate these resources. The qualitative data came primarily from interviews of district and school staff members who were in a position to make or influence decisions about the distributions of the resources (dollars, staff FTE, or time) that might figure prominently in learning improvement initiatives. Quantitative data came from budget documents, staff rosters, personnel databases, planning documents of various kinds, and other sources that offered insight into what resources were directed where and how they were used. In addition to fiscal and staffing data, the study team also examined district and school trend data about student demographics and achievement. Gathered across a year and a half, these data allowed the team to watch one full cycle of budgeting or other resource decision and to see how (and whether) they were enacted the following year.

Documentary sources also offered some qualitative evidence of resource allocation rationales, the nature of leadership position descriptions, or contextual conditions that affected the observed resource patterns. This evidence came from a wide range of documents, such as district strategic plans, letters to the community from district and school leaders, policies governing school attendance boundaries and staff assignment and transfers, district memoranda to school staff, human resource policies and procedures, district and school improvement plans, school board meeting minutes, and the like. Information gleaned from these sources served as additional points of triangulation with data collected from interviews and analysis of fiscal and staffing data.

District and school-level resource profiles were prepared as a preliminary step leading towards the cross-case analyses that underlay the study strand's main conclusions. Our overall approach to data analysis involved the triangulation and integration of data from the qualitative and quantitative sources through multiple methods appropriate to each type of data collected (Johnson & Christensen, 2008). Quantitative data were verified and cross-checked before converting the data to variables that could be compared across districts and schools (e.g., student–staff ratios, expenditures as a percent of the total budget, instructional support staff as a percent of total certificated staff). The bulk of the analytic work involved a systematic cross-case comparison of schools and districts, in relation to an inductively derived analytic template. The qualitative analysis process followed a "grounded theory" approach similar to that described above for the school leadership study strand.

REFERENCES

Adams, J. (2008). National working group on funding student success: Final report. Paper presented at the annual meeting of the American Education Finance Association, April 10–12, Denver, CO.

Adamson, F., & Darling-Hammond, L. (2012). Funding disparities and the inequitable distribution of teachers: Evaluating sources and solutions. *Education Policy Analysis Archives*, *20*, 37.

Amrein-Beardsley, A., Berliner, D.C., & Rideau, S. (2010). Cheating in the first, second, and third degree: Educators' responses to high-stakes testing. *Education Policy Analysis Archives, 18*, 1–36.

Archibald, S., & Odden, A. (2000, March). *A case study of resource allocation to implement a whole school reform model and boost student achievement: Parnell Elementary School*. Madison, WI: Consortium for Policy Research in Education.

Argyris, C., & Schön, D. (1974). *Organizational learning*. Reading, PA: Addison-Wesley.

Argyris, C., & Schön, D. (1996). *Organizational learning II: Theory, method, practice*. Reading, PA: Addison-Wesley.

Bach, D. (2005, February 16). Budget shortfall forces tough choices at Seattle Public Schools. *Seattle Post-Intelligencer*. Retrieved August 1, 2008, from http://seattlepi.nwsource.com/local/212232_ schools16.html

Baker, B., & Green, P. (2008). Conceptions of equity and adequacy in school finance. In H. Ladd & E. Fiske (Eds.), *Handbook of research in education finance and policy* (pp. 203–221). New York: Routledge.

Baker, B.D., & Corcoran, S.P. (2012). *The stealth inequities of school funding: How state and local school finance systems perpetuate inequitable student spending*. Washington DC: Center for American Progress.

Bass, B.M., & Avolio, B.J. (1990). The implications of transactional and transformational leadership for individual, team, and organizational development. *Research in Organizational Change and Development, 4*, 231–272.

Beck, L., & Murphy, J. (1998). Site-based management and school success: Untangling the variables. *School Effectiveness and School Improvement, 9*(4), 358–385.

Becker, B., & Huselid, M. (2006, December). Strategic human resource management: Where do we go from here? *Journal of Management, 32*(6), 898–925.

Bellamy, G.T., Fulmer, C.L., Murphy, M.J., & Muth, R. (2007). *Principal accomplishments: How school leaders succeed.* New York: Teachers College Press.

Berends, M., Bodilly, S.J., & Kirby, S.M. (2002). The future of whole school designs: Conclusions, observations, and policy implications. In M. Berends, S.J. Bodilly, & S.M. Kirby (Eds.), *Facing the challenges of whole school reform: New American Schools after a decade* (pp. 142–154). Santa Monica, CA: RAND Corporation.

Berne, R., & Stiefel, L. (1999). Concepts of school finance equity: 1970 to the present. In H. Ladd, R. Chalk, & J. Hansen (Eds.), *Equity and adequacy in education: Issues and perspectives.* Washington, DC: National Research Council Committee on Education Finance.

Blachowicz, C.L.Z., Obrochta, C., & Fogelberg. E. (2005). Literacy coaching for change. *Educational Leadership, 62*(6), 55–58.

Blanchard, K., Zigarmi, P., & Zigarmi, D. (1985). *Leadership and the one-minute manager.* New York: William Morrow.

Blase, J., & Blase, J. (1997). The micro-political orientation of facilitative school principals and its effects on teachers' sense of empowerment. *Journal of Educational Administration, 35*(2), 138–164.

Boghossian, N. (2005, July 21). LAUSD fails its special students. *Daily News of Los Angeles,* p. N1. Seattle, WA: Center for Educational Leadership.

Borman, G., & Dowling, M. (2008). Teacher attrition and retention: A meta analytic and narrative review of the research. *American Educational Research Association 78*(3), 367–409.

Boyd, D., Grossman, P., Ing, M., Lankford, H., Loeb, S., & Wyckoff, J. (2011). The influence of school administrators on teacher retention decisions. *American Educational Research Journal, 48*(2), 303–333.

Boyd, D., Lankford, H., & Wyckoff, J. (2008). Increasing the effectiveness of teachers in low-performing schools. In H. Ladd & E. Fiske (Eds.), *Handbook of research in education finance and policy* (pp. 535–550). New York: Routledge.

Brantlinger, E. (2003). *Dividing classes: How the middle class negotiates and rationalizes school advantage.* New York, NY: Routledge.

Bredeson, P., & Kelley, C. (Eds.) (2013). Distributed instructional leadership as a reform strategy: Activating teacher leadership to improve student learning in urban high schools. [Special issue] *Journal of School Leadership, 23*(2), 214-219.

Breidenstein, A., Fahey, K., Glickman, C., & Hensley, F. (2012). *Leading for powerful learning: A guide for instructional leaders.* New York: Teachers College Press.

Brown, D., & Saks, D. (1987). The microeconomics of the allocation of teacher's time and student learning. *Economics of Education Review, 6*(4), 319–332.

Brown, K.M., & Wynn, S.R. (2009). Finding, supporting, and keeping: The role of the principal in teacher retention issues. *Leadership and Policy in Schools, 8*(1), 37–63.

Brown, R., & Severson, K. (2013, March 29). Former Atlanta schools chief is charged in testing scandal. *New York Times.* Retrieved March 30, 2013, from www.nytimes.com/2013/03/30/

Bryk, A.S., & Schneider, B. (2002). *Trust in schools: A core resource for improvement.* New York, NY: Russell Sage Foundation.

Bryk, A.S., Sebring, P.B., Allensworth, E., Luppescu, S., & Easton, J.Q. (2010). *Organizing schools for improvement: Lessons from Chicago.* Chicago: University of Chicago Press.

Bryk, A.S., Sebring, P.B., Kerbow, D., Rollow, S., & Easton, J.Q. (1998). *Charting Chicago school reform: Democratic localism as a lever for change.* Boulder, CO: Westview Press.

Bulkley, K.E. (2013). Conceptions of equity: How influential actors view a contested concept. *Peabody Journal of Education, 88*(1), 10–21.

Calvo, N., & Miles, K.H. (2012). Turning crisis into opportunity. *Educational Leadership, 69*(4), 19–20.

Campbell, C., DeArmond, M., & Schumwinger, A. (2004). *From bystander to ally: Transforming the district human resources department.* Seattle, WA: Center on Reinventing Public Education, University of Washington.

Cascio, W., & Boudreau, J. (2008). *Investing in people: Financial impact of human resource initiatives.* Upper Saddle River, NJ: Pearson Education.

Chambers, J., Shambaugh, L., Levin, J., Muraki, M., & Poland, L. (2008). *A tale of two districts: A comparative study of student-based funding and school-based decision making in San Francisco and Oakland Unified School Districts.* Washington, DC: American Institutes for Research.

Chambers, J.G., Levin, J.D., & Shambaugh, L. (2010). Exploring weighted student formulas as a policy for improving equity for distributing resources to schools: A case study of two California school districts. *Economics of Education Review, 29*(2), 283–300.

Chubb, J.E., & Moe, T.M. (1990). *Politics, markets, and America's schools.* Washington, DC: The Brookings Institution.

Chute, E. (2007). Schools' racial balancing rejected. *Pittsburgh Post-Gazette.* Retrieved August 1, 2008, from www.post-gazette.com/pg/07180/798069–84.stm

City, E.A. (2010). *Resourceful leadership: Tradeoffs and tough decisions on the road to school improvement.* Cambridge, MA: Harvard Education Press.

City, E.A., Elmore, R.F., Fiarman, S.E., & Teitel, L. (2009). *Instructional rounds in education.* Cambridge, MA: Harvard Education Press.

Clotfelter, C.T., Ladd, H.F., & Vigdor, J.L. (2006). Teacher-student matching and the assessment of teacher effectiveness. *Journal of Human Resources, 41,* 778–820

Clotfelter, C., Vigdor, J., & Ladd, H. (2010). Teacher credentials and student achievement in high school: A cross-subject analysis with student fixed effects. *Journal of Human Resources, 45*(3), 655–681.

Clune, W. (1994). The shift from equity to adequacy in school finance. *Educational Policy, 8*(4), 376–394.

Coggins, C., Stoddard, P., & Cutler, E. (2003). Improving instructional capacity through field-based reform coaches. Paper presented at the annual meeting of the American Educational Research Association, April 21–25, Chicago, IL.

Copland, M. (2003). Leadership of inquiry: Building and sustaining capacity for school improvement. *Educational Evaluation and Policy Analysis, 25*(4), 375–396.

Copland, M.A., & Knapp, M.S. (2006). *Connecting leadership with learning: A framework for reflection, planning, and action.* Alexandria, VA: Association for Supervision & Curriculum Development.

Corbett, H.D., Wilson, B., & Williams, B. (2002). *Effort and excellence in urban classrooms: Expecting—and getting—success with all students.* New York: Teachers College Press.

Corcoran, S., & Evans, W. (2008). Equity, adequacy and the evolving state role in education finance. In H. Ladd & E. Fiske (Eds.), *Handbook of research in education finance and policy* (pp. 332–356). New York: Routledge.

Corcoran, T., Fuhrman, S.H., & Belcher, C.L. (2001). The district role in instructional improvement. *Phi Delta Kappan, 83*(1), 78–84.

Cremin, L.A. (1982). *American education: The national experience, 1783–1876.* New York: Harper and Row.

Creswell, J.W., & Plano Clark, V.L. (2010). *Designing and conducting mixed methods research* (2nd ed.). Thousand Oaks CA: SAGE.

Cuban, L. (1984). *How teachers taught.* New York: Longman.

Danzig, A.B., Borman, K.M., Jones, B.A., & Wright, W.F. (Eds.) (2009). *Learner-centered leadership.* Mahway NJ: Lawrence Erlbaum.

Darling-Hammond, L., Hightower, A., Husbands, J., Lafors, J., Young, V., & Christopher, C. (2005). *Instructional leadership for systemic change: The story of San Diego's reform.* Lanham, MD: Rowan and Littlefield Education.

Davis, M. (2008). Financial crisis now striking home for school districts. *Education Week.* Retrieved March 21, 2010, from www.edweek.org/ew/articles/2008/10/15/08credit. h28.html

Donaldson, G.A., Jr. (2006). *Cultivating leadership in schools.* New York: Teachers College Press.

Donaldson, G.A., Jr. (2008). *How leaders learn: Cultivating capacities for school improvement.* New York: Teachers College Press.

Downes, T., & Shay, M. (2006). The effect of school finance reforms on the level and growth of per-pupil expenditures. *Peabody Journal of Education, 81*(3), 1–38.

Downes, T., & Stiefel, L. (2008). Measuring equity and adequacy in school finance. In H.F. Ladd & H.B. Fiske (Eds.), *Handbook of research on education finance and policy* (pp. 222–237). New York: Routledge.

Drago-Severson, E. (2009). *Leading adult learning: Supporting adult development in our schools— A joint publication with the National Staff Development Council.* Thousand Oaks, CA: Corwin Press.

DuFour, R. (2002, May). The learning-centered principal. *Educational Leadership, (59)*8, 12–15.

DuFour, R., & Marzano, R.J. (2011). *Leaders of learning: How district, school, and classroom leaders improve student achievement.* Bloomington IN: Solution Tree Press.

Earl, L. & Katz, S. (2006). *Leading in a data rich world: Harnessing data for school improvement.* Thousand Oaks, CA: Corwin.

Elmore, R., & Burney, D. (1999). Investing in teacher learning: Staff development and instructional improvement. In L. Darling-Hammond & G. Sykes (Eds.), *Teaching as the learning profession: Handbook of policy and practice* (pp. 263–291). San Francisco: Jossey-Bass.

Erlichson, B., & Goertz, M. (2002). Whole school reform and school-based budgeting in New Jersey: Three years of implementation. In C. Roellke & J. Rice (Eds.), *Fiscal policy in urban education: A volume in research in education fiscal policy and practice.* Greenwich, CT: Information Age Publishing.

Evans, R. (1996). *The human side of school change: Reform, resistance, and the real-life problems of innovation.* San Francisco: Jossey-Bass.

Farkas, S., Johnson, J., Duffett, A., Syat, B., & Vine, J. (2003). *Rolling up their sleeves: Super-intendents and principals talk about what's needed to fix public schools.* New York: Public Agenda. Retrieved February 9, 2009, from www.publicagenda.org/files/pdf/rolling_ up_their_sleeves.pdf

Farrell, C., Wohlstetter, P., & Smith, J. (2012). Charter management organizations an emerging approach to scaling up what works. *Educational Policy, 26*(4), 499–532.

Feng, L. (2010). Hire today, gone tomorrow: New teacher classroom assignments and teacher mobility. *Education Finance & Policy, 5,* 278–316.

Fink, E., & Resnick, L. (2001). Developing principals as instructional leaders. *Phi Delta Kappan, 82*(8), 598–610.

Fink, S., & Markholt, A. (2011). *Leading for instructional improvement.* San Francisco: Jossey-Bass.

Finnigan, K., (2007). Charter school autonomy: The mismatch between theory and practice. *Educational Policy, 21,* 503–526.

Firestone, W.A., & Martinez, M.C. (2007). Districts, teacher leaders, and distributed leadership: Changing instructional practice. *Leadership and Policy in Schools, 6*(1), 3–35.

Flessa, J. (2009). Educational micropolitics and distributed leadership. *Peabody Journal of Education, 84*(3), 331–349.

Ford, B.L. (2011). *Experiencing racial conflict in leadership interactions: The case of white principals who lead for social justice and the success of students of color* (Unpublished doctoral dissertation). University of Washington, Seattle, WA.

Fruchter, N. (2007). *Urban schools, public will: Making education work for all our children.* New York: Teachers College Press.

Fullan, M. (1994). Coordinating top-down and bottom-up strategies for educational reform. In R. Elmore & S. Fuhrman (Eds.), *The governance of curriculum* (pp. 186–202). Alexandria, VA: Association for Supervision and Curriculum Development.

Gabriel, T. (2010, June 10). Under pressure, teachers tamper with tests. *New York Times.*

Gallucci, C. (2008). District-wide instructional reform: Using sociocultural theory to link professional learning to organizational support. *American Journal of Education, 114*(4), 541–581.

Gallucci, C., Van Lare, M.D., Yoon, I.H., & Boatright, B. (2010). Instructional coaching: Building theory about the role and organizational support for professional learning. *American Educational Research Journal, 47*(4), 919–963.

Garber, A. (2008, November 30). Gregoire looking at massive state budget cuts. *The Seattle Times.* Retrieved July 3, 2009, from http://seattletimes.nwsource.com/html/politics/2008451090_budgetcuts30m.html

Gibson, S. (2006). Lesson observation and feedback: The practice of an expert reading coach. *Reading Research and Instruction, 45*(4), 295–318.

Ginsberg, M., Knapp, M.S., & Farrington, C. (2012). Using transformative experiences to prepare doctoral-level instructional leaders. Presented at the annual meeting of the American Educational Research Association, April 13–17, Vancouver, BC, Canada.

Glickman, C. (2002), *Leadership for learning: How to help teachers succeed.* Alexandria VA: Association for Supervision and Curriculum Development.

Goertz, M., & Duffy, M. (2003). Mapping the landscape of high-stakes testing and accountability programs. *Theory into Practice, 42*(1), 4–11.

Goleman, D., Boyatzis, R., & McKee, A. (2002). *The new leaders: Transforming the art of leadership into the science of results.* London: Little Brown.

González, N., Moll, L.C., & Amanti, C. (Eds.) (2013). *Funds of knowledge: Theorizing practices in households, communities, and classrooms.* New York, NY: Routledge.

Grubb, N. (2009). *The money myth: School resources, outcomes, and equity.* New York: Russell Sage Foundation.

Guarino, C.M., Santibanez, L., & Daley, G.A. (2006). Teacher recruitment and retention: A review of the recent empirical literature. *Review of Educational Research, 76,* 173–208.

Hallinger, P. (2005). Instructional leadership and the school principal: A passing fancy that refuses to fade away. *Leadership & Policy in Schools, 4(3),* 221–239.

Hallinger, P. (2011). Leadership for learning: Lessons from 40 years of empirical research. *Journal of Educational Administration, 49*(2), 125–142.

Hallinger, P., & Heck, R. (1996). Reassessing the principal's role in school effectiveness: A review of empirical evidence. *Educational Administration Quarterly, 32*(1), 5–44.

Hallinger, P., & Heck, R. (2009). Leadership effects on school improvement: Testing unidirectional and reciprocal effects models. Paper presented at the annual meeting of the American Educational Research Association, April 13–17, San Diego, CA.

Hallinger, P., & Heck, R. (2010). Collaborative leadership and school improvement: Understanding the impact on school capacity and student learning. *School Leadership & Management, 30*(2), 95–110.

Hallinger, P., & Murphy, J. (1985). Assessing the instructional leadership behavior of principals. *Elementary School Journal, 86*(2), 217–248.

Halverson, R., & Clifford, M. (2013). Distributed instructional leadership in high schools. *Journal of School Leadership, 23*(2), 389–419.

Halverson, R., Grigg, J., Prichett, R., & Thomas, C. (2007). The new instructional leadership: Creating data-driven instructional systems in school. *Journal of School Leadership, 17*(2), 159–194.

Hanushek, E. (2011). The economic value of higher teacher quality. *Economics of Education Review 30*(3), 466–479.

Hanushek, E., & Lindseth, A. (2009). *Schoolhouses, courthouses, and statehouses: Solving the funding-achievement puzzle in America's public schools.* Princeton, NJ: Princeton University Press.

Hargreaves, A., & Fullan, M. (2012). Professional capital: Transforming teaching in every school. New York, NY: Teachers College Press.

Harris, D. (2008). Educational outcomes of disadvantaged students: From desegregation to accountability. In H. Ladd & E. Fiske (Eds.), *Handbook of research in education finance and policy* (pp. 551–570). New York: Routledge.

Harris, D., & Sass, T. (2011). Teacher training, teacher quality, and student achievement. *Journal of Public Economics 95*(7–8), 798–812.

Hartman, W. (1999). *School district budgeting.* Reston, VA: Association of School Business Officials International.

Haynes, V.D. (2007, December 13). Special education to boost services; D.C. officials seek to comply with 2006 court order. *Washington Post.*

Henry, G.T., Fortner, C.K., & Thompson, C.L. (2010). Targeted funding for educationally disadvantaged students: A regression discontinuity estimate of the impact on high school student achievement. *Educational Evaluation & Policy Analysis, 32*(2), 183–204.

Hightower, A.M., Knapp, M.S., Marsh, J.A., & McLaughlin, M.W. (Eds.) (2002). *School districts and instructional renewal.* New York, NY: Teachers College Press.

Hill, P.T., Campbell, C., & Gross, B. (2013). *Strife and progress: Portfolio strategies for managing urban schools.* Washington DC: Brookings Institution Press.

Hill, S.E.K. (2006). Team leadership. In Northouse, P.G., *Leadership: Theory and practice, 4th edition* (pp. 207–236). Thousand Oaks, CA: SAGE.

Honig, M.I. (2003). Building policy from practice: District central office administrators' roles and capacity for implementing collaborative education policy. *Educational Administration Quarterly, 39*(3), 292–338.

Honig, M.I. (2004a). District central office-community partnerships: From contracts to collaboration to control. In W. Hoy & C. Miskel (Eds.), *Educational administration, policy, and reform: Research and measurement* (pp. 59–90). Greenwich, CT: Information Age Publishing.

Honig, M.I. (2004b).The new middle management: Intermediary organizations in educa-tion policy. *Educational Evaluation and Policy Analysis, 26*(1), 65–87.

Honig, M.I. (2008). District central offices as learning organizations: How sociocultural and organizational learning theories elaborate district central office administrators' par-ticipation in teaching and learning improvement efforts. *American Journal of Education, 114*(4), 627–644.

Honig, M.I. (2009). No small thing: School district central office bureaucracies and the implementation of new small autonomous schools initiatives. *American Educational Research Journal, 46*(2), 387–422.

Honig, M.I. (2012). District central office leadership as teaching: How central office admin-istrators support principals' development as instructional leaders. *Education Administra-tion Quarterly, 48*(4), 733–774.

Honig, M.I. (2013). *From tinkering to transformation: Strengthening school district central office performance—Education Outlook, 4 (June).* Washington DC: American Enterprise Insti-tute for Public Policy Research.

Honig, M.I., & Coburn, C.E. (2008). Evidence-based decision-making in school district central offices: Toward a research agenda. *Educational Policy, 22*(4), 578–608.

Honig, M.I., & Copland, M.A. (2008). *Reinventing district central offices to expand stu-dent learning.* Washington DC: The Center for Comprehensive School Reform and Improvement.

Honig, M.I., Copland, M.A., Rainey, L., Lorton, J.A., & Newton, M. (2010). *Central office transformation for district-wide teaching and learning improvement.* Seattle WA: Center for the Study of Teaching & Policy, University of Washington.

Honig, M.I., & DeArmond, M. (2010). Where's the "management" in portfolio manage-ment: Conceptualizing the role of school district central offices in implementation. In K. Bulkley, J. Henig, & H. Levin (Eds.), *Portfolio management reform* (pp. 195–216). Cam-bridge, MA: Harvard Education Press.

Honig, M.I., Lorton, J.S., & Copland, M.A. (2009). The promises and pitfalls of the "new localism" for urban school district central offices. In R. Crowson & E. Goldring (Eds.), *The new localism in American education: Re-examining issues of neighborhood and commu-nity in public education, 105th Yearbook of the National Society for the Study of Education* (pp. 21–40). Chicago, IL: University of Chicago Press.

Honig, M.I., & Rainey, L. (2011). Autonomy and school improvement: What do we know and where do we go from here? *Educational Policy, 26*(3) 465–495.

Honig, M.I., & Rainey, L.R. (in press). Central office leadership in principal professional learning communities: The practice beneath the policy. *Teachers College Record.*

Hubbard, L., Mehan, H., & Stein, M.K. (2006). *Reform as learning: When school reform collides with school culture and community politics.* New York, NY: Routledge.

Hughes, J., & Jones, S. (2003). Reflections on the use of grounded theory in interpretive information systems research. *Proceedings of the European Conference on Information Sys-tems (ECIS),* Naples, Italy.

Ingersoll, R. (2004). *Why do high-poverty schools have difficulty staffing their schools with qualified teachers?* Washington DC: Center for American Progress.

Jackson, B.L., & Kelley, C. (2002). Exceptional and innovative programs in educational leadership. *Educational Administration Quarterly, 38*(2), 192–212.

Jimenez-Castellanos, O., & Topper, A.M. (2012). The cost of providing an adequate edu-cation to English language learners: A review of the literature. *Review of Educational Research, 82*(2), 179–232.

Johnson, B., & Christensen, L. (2008). *Quantitative, qualitative, and mixed approaches*. Thousand Oaks, CA: SAGE Publications.

Jordan, W.J. (2010). Defining equity: Multiple perspectives to analyzing the performance of diverse learners. *Review of Research in Education, 34*(1), 142–178.

Katz, A. (2003). State takeover appears certain. *Oakland Tribune*. Retrieved August 1, 2008, from http://findarticles.com/p/articles/mi_qn4176/is_20030410/ain14549730/pg_1?tag=artBody;col1

Kalogrides, D., Loeb, S., & Beteille, T. (2011). Power play? Teacher characteristics and class assignments. CALDER Working Paper No. 59. Retrieved from www.urban.org/uploadedpdf/1001530-Teacher-Characteristics-and-Class-Assignments.pdf

Kelley, C., & Salisbury, J. (2013). Defining and activating the role of department chair as instructional leader. *Journal of School Leadership, 23*(2), 287–232.

Kilgore, S.B., & Jones, J.D. (2003). Leadership in comprehensive school reform initiatives: The case of the Modern Red School House. In J. Murphy & A. Datnow (Eds.), *Leadership for school reform: Lessons from comprehensive school reform designs* (pp. 52–84). Thousand Oaks, CA: Corwin Press.

Kimball, S., Milanowski, A., & Heneman, H. (2010). *Principal as human capital manager: Evidence from two large districts*. Madison, WI: University of Wisconsin-Madison Consortium for Policy Research in Education.

King, R., Swanson, A., & Sweetland, S. (2005). Designing school finance structures to satisfy equity and adequacy goals. *Educational Policy Analysis Archives, 13*(15), 37–62. Retrieved February 24, 2009, from http://epaa.asu.edu/epaa/v13n15/

Klar, H.W. (2013). Principals fostering the instructional leadership capacities of department chairs: A strategy for urban high school reform. *Journal of School Leadership, 23*(2), 324–361.

Knapp, M.S., Copland, M.A., Honig, M.I., Plecki, M.L., & Portin, B.S. (2010). *Learning-focused leadership and leadership support: Meaning and practice in urban systems*. Seattle, WA: Center for the Study of Teaching and Policy, University of Washington.

Knapp, M.S., Copland, M.A., Plecki, M.L., & Portin, B.S. (2006). *Leading, learning, and leadership support*. Seattle, WA: Center for the Study of Teaching and Policy, University of Washington.

Knapp, M.S., Copland, M.A., & Swinnerton, J.A. (2007). Understanding the promise and dynamics of data-informed leadership. In P.A. Moss (Ed.), *Evidence and decision making*, 107th Volume of the National Society for the Study of Education (1) (pp. 74–104). New York: Teachers College Record.

Knapp, M.S., Copland, M.A., & Talbert, J.E. (2003). *Leading for learning: Reflective tools for school and district leaders*. Seattle, WA: Center for the Study of Teaching & Policy, University of Washington.

Knapp, M.S., & Feldman, S. (2012). Managing the intersection of external and internal accountability: Challenge for urban school leadership in the United States. *Journal of Educational Administration, 50*(5), 666–694.

Knapp, M.S., Feldman, S., & Yeh, T.L. (2013). Learning-focused leadership in urban high schools: Response to demanding environments. *Journal of School Leadership, 23*(2), 253–286.

Knapp, M.S., Mkhwanazi, S., & Portin, B.S. (2012). School-based instructional leadership in demanding environments: New challenges, new practices. In B.G. Barnett, A.R. Shoho, & A. T. Cypres (Eds.), *The changing nature of instructional leadership in the 21st century* (pp. 185–212). Charlotte NC: Information Age Publishing.

Knight, J. (2006). Instructional coaching. *The School Administrator, 63*(4), 36–40.

Knight, J. (2007). *Instructional coaching: A partnership approach to improving instruction.* Thousand Oaks, CA: Corwin Press.

Knight, J. (2009). Coaching. *Journal of Staff Development, 30*(1), 18–22.

Kozol, J. (1991). *Savage inequalities.* New York: Crown Publishers.

Ladd, H.F. (2008). Reflections on equity, adequacy, and weighted student funding. *Education Finance and Policy, 3*(2), 402–423.

Ladd, H.F. (2012). Education and poverty: Confronting the evidence. *Journal of Policy Analysis and Management, 31*(2), 203–227.

Ladson-Billings, G. (1999). Preparing teachers for diverse populations: A critical race theory perspective. *Review of Research in Education, 24,* 211–247.

Ladson-Billings, G. (2006). From the achievement gap to the education debt: Understanding achievement in U.S. schools. *Educational Researcher, 35*(7), 3–12.

Lambert, L. (2006). Lasting leadership: A study of high leadership capacity schools. *The Educational Forum, 70*(3), 238–254

Larson, C., & LaFasto, F.M.J. (1989). *Teamwork: What must go right, what can go wrong.* Thousand Oaks, CA: SAGE Publications.

Lawler, E.L. (2008). *Strategic talent management: Lessons from the corporate world.* Madison, WI: Consortium for Policy Research in Education.

Leander, K.M., & Osborne, M.D. (2008). Complex positioning: Teachers as agents of curricular and pedagogical reform. *Journal of Curriculum Studies, 40*(1), 23–46.

Lee, J., & Wong, K.K. (2004). The impact of accountability on racial and socioeconomic equity: Considering both school resources and achievement outcomes. *American Educational Research Journal, 41*(4), 797–832.

Leithwood, K., & Duke, D.L. (1999). A century's quest to understand school leadership. In J. Murphy & K.S. Louis (Eds.), *Handbook of research on educational administration* (pp. 45–72). San Francisco: Jossey-Bass.

Leithwood, K., & Louis, K.S. (2012). *Linking leadership to student learning.* San Francisco: Jossey-Bass.

Leithwood, K., Louis, K.S., Anderson, S., & Wahlstrom, K. (2004). *How leadership influences student learning.* New York: The Wallace Foundation.

Leithwood, K., Mascall, B., & Strauss, T. (2009). What we have learned and where we go from here. In Leithwood, K., Mascall, B., & Strauss, T. (Eds.), *Distributed leadership according to the evidence* (pp. 269–282). New York and London: Routledge.

Leithwood, K., Patten, S., & Jantzi, D. (2010). Testing a conception of how school leadership influences student learning. *Educational Administration Quarterly, 46*(5), 671–706.

Leithwood, K., & Riehl, C. (2005). What we already know about successful school leadership. In W.A. Firestone & C. Riehl (Eds.), *A new agenda: Directions for research on educational leadership* (pp. 12–27). New York: Teachers College Press.

Levine, A. (2005). *Educating school leaders.* Washington DC: Education Schools Project.

Levine, D.U., & Lezotte, L.W. (1990). *Unusually effective schools: A review and analysis of research and practice.* Madison, WI: National Center for Effective Schools Research and Practice.

Lezotte, L.W. (1994). The nexus of instructional leadership and effective schools. *The School Administrator, 51*(6), 20–23.

Lieberman, A., & Friedrich, L.D. (2010). *How teachers become leaders: Learning from practice and research.* New York: Teachers College Press.

Lieberman, A., & Miller, L. (2004). *Teacher leadership.* San Francisco: Jossey-Bass.

Lipman, P. (2004). *High stakes education: Inequality, globalization, and urban school reform.* New York: RoutledgeFalmer.

Lochmiller, C. (2012). Leading with less: Principal leadership in austere times. In B.G. Barnett, A.R. Shoho, & A.T. Cypres (Eds.), *The changing nature of instructional leadership in the 21st century* (pp. 185–212). Charlotte NC: Information Age Publishing.

Loeb, S., Kalogrides, D., & Horng, E.L. (2010). Principal preferences and the uneven distribution of principals across schools. *Educational Evaluation and Policy Analysis, 32*(2), 205–229.

Lortie, D.C. (1975). *Schoolteacher.* Chicago: University of Chicago Press.

Lowenhaupt, R., & McKinney, S. (2007). Coaching in context: The role of relationships in the work of three literacy coaches. Paper presented at the Annual Meeting of the American Educational Research Association, April, San Francisco, CA.

Lucas, T. (Ed.) (2011). *Teacher preparation for linguistically diverse classrooms: A resource for teacher educators.* New York: Taylor & Francis.

MacBeath, J., & Cheng, Y.C. (Eds.) (2008). *Leadership for learning: International perspectives.* Rotterdam, The Netherlands: Sense Publishers.

MacBeath, J., & Dempster, N. (Eds.) (2009). *Connecting leadership and learning: Principles for practice.* London and New York: Routledge.

Malen, B., & Cochran, M.V. (2008). Beyond pluralistic patterns of power: Research on the micropolitics of schools. In B. Cooper, J. Cibulka, & L. Fusarelli (Eds.), *Handbook of education politics and policy* (pp. 148–178). New York: Routledge.

Malen, B., Ogawa, R.T., & Kranz, J. (1990). What do we know about school-based management? A case study of the literature—A call for research. In W.H. Clune & J.F. White (Eds.), *Choice and control in American schools* (pp. 289–342). Philadelphia: Falmer.

Mangin, M.M. (2009). Literacy coach role implementation: How district context influences reform efforts. *Educational Administration Quarterly, 45*(5), 759–792.

Mangin, M.M., & Stoelinga, S.R. (Eds.) (2008). *Effective teacher leadership: Using research to inform and reform.* New York: Teachers College Press.

Marks, H.M., & Printy, S.M. (2003). Principal leadership and school performance: An integration of transformational and instructional leadership. *Education Administration Quarterly, 39*(3), 370–397.

Marshall, C., & Ward, M. (2004). " Yes, but . . .": Education leaders discuss social justice. *Journal of School Leadership, 14*(5), 530–563.

Marshall, K. (2003). A principal looks back: Standards matter. *Phi Delta Kappan, 85,* 104–113.

Marzano, R., Waters, T., & McNulty, B.A. (2003). Balanced leadership: What 30 years of research tells us about the effects of school leadership on student achievement. Denver, CO: Mid-Continent Research For Education and Learning.

Marzano, R., Waters, T., & McNulty, B.A. (2005). *School leadership that works: From research to results.* Alexandria, VA: Association for Supervision & Curriculum Development.

Mayer, A.P., Donaldson, M.L., Le Chasseur, K., Welton, A.D., & Cobb, C.D. (2013). Negotiating site-based management and expanded teacher decision making: A case study of six urban schools. *Educational Administration Quarterly, 49*(5), 695–731.

Mayrowetz, D., Murphy, J., Louis, K.S., & Smylie, M. (2007). Distributed leadership as work redesign: Retrofitting the job characteristics model. *Leadership and Policy in Schools, 6*(1), 69–101.

Mayrowetz, D., Murphy, J., Louis, K.S., Smylie, M. (2009). Conceptualizing distributed leadership as a school reform: Revisiting job redesign theory. In K. Leithwood,

B. Mascall, & T. Strauss (Eds.), *Distributed leadership according to the evidence* (pp. 167–196). New York and London: Routledge.

McLaughlin, M.W. (1987). Learning from experience: Lessons from policy implementation. *Educational Evaluation & Policy Analysis, 9*(2), 171–178.

McLaughlin, M.W., & Talbert, J.E. (2002). Reforming districts: How districts support school reform. In A.M. Hightower, M.S. Knapp, J.A. Marsh, & M.W. McLaughlin (Eds.), *School districts and instructional renewal* (pp. 173–192). New York, NY: Teachers College Press.

Merriam, S. (1998). *Qualitative research and case study applications in education* (2nd ed.). San Francisco: Jossey-Bass.

Michelson, J. (2013). *Instructional coach learning through problems of practice.* (Unpublished doctoral dissertation). University of Washington, Seattle, WA.

Miles, K.H. (1995). Freeing resources for improving schools: A case study of teacher allocation in Boston Public Schools. *Educational Evaluation and Policy Analysis, 17*(4), 476–493.

Miles, K.H. (2001). *District issues brief: Rethinking school resources.* Arlington, VA: New American Schools. Retrieved July 30, 2008, from www.educationresourcestrategies.org/documents/rethinking-resources.pdf

Miles, K.H., & Frank, S. (2008). *The strategic school: Making the most of people, time, and money.* Thousand Oaks, CA: Corwin.

Miles, M., & Huberman, M. (1994). *Qualitative data analysis: A sourcebook.* Thousand Oaks, CA: SAGE Publications.

Mirel, J.E. (1990). Progressive school reform in comparative perspective. In D. Plank & R. Ginsberg (Eds.), *Southern cities, southern schools: Public education in the urban south* (pp. 151–174). New York: Greenwood Press.

Moll, L., Velez-Ibanez, C., & Greenberg, J. (1990). Community knowledge and classroom practice: Combining resources for literacy instruction. *Handbook for Teachers and Planners—Innovative Approaches Research Project.* Arlington, VA: Development Associates, Inc.

Monk, D. (1987). School district enrollment and inequality in the supply of classes. *Economics of Education Review, 6*(4), 365–377.

Monk, D. (1994). Resource allocation in schools and school systems. In T. Husen & T.N. Postlethwaite (Eds.), *The international encyclopedia of education* (pp. 5061–5066). Oxford, UK: Pergamon Press.

Murnane, R., City, E., & Singleton, K. (2008). Using data to inform decision making in urban school districts: Progress and new challenges. *Voices in Urban Education: Using Data for Decisions, 18*, 5–13.

Murphy, J. (2005). *Connecting teacher leadership and school improvement.* Thousand Oaks, CA: Corwin Press.

Murphy, J., & Datnow, A. (2003). Leadership lessons from comprehensive school reform designs. In J. Murphy & A. Datnow (Eds.), *Leadership for school reform: Lessons from comprehensive school reform designs* (pp. 263–278). Thousand Oaks, CA: Corwin Press.

Murphy, J., Elliott, S.N., Goldring, E., & Porter, A.C. (2006). *Learning-centered leadership: A conceptual foundation.* New York: The Wallace Foundation.

Murphy, J., & Hallinger, P. (1988). Characteristics of instructionally effective school districts. *Journal of Educational Research, 81*(3), 175–181.

Murray, J. (2013). Critical issues facing school leaders concerning data-informed decision-making. *School Leadership and Management, 33*(2), 169–177.

National Assessment of Educational Progress (2010). *The nation's report card.* Washington DC: Author. Accessed July 25, 2010. http://nces.ed.gov/nationsreportcard/

National Center for Education Statistics (2013). *Common core of data, national public education financial survey fiscal year 2009, version 1a.* Washington, DC: Author.

National Clearinghouse for English Language Acquisition. (2011). The growing number of limited English proficient students 1998–96/2008–09. Washington, DC: Author. Available at: www.ncela.gwu.edu/files/uploads/9/growingLEP_0809.pdf

National Research Council. (1999). Making money matter: Financing America's schools. In H.F. Ladd & J.S. Hansen (Eds.), *Committee on Education Finance, Commission on Behavioral and Social Sciences in Education.* Washington, DC: National Academy Press.

Neumerski, C.M. (2013). Rethinking instructional leadership: What do we know about principal, teacher, and coach instructional leadership, and where should we go from here? *Educational Administration Quarterly, 49*(2), 310–347.

Nordengren, C. (2012). Collective leadership models in educational research: Toward a focus on theories of action. Paper presented at the annual conference of the University Council on Educational Administration, November 15–18, Denver, CO.

Northouse, P. G (2006). *Leadership theory & practice* (4th ed.). Thousand Oaks, CA: SAGE Publications.

Oakes, J. (2005). *Keeping track: How schools structure inequality* (2nd ed.). New Haven, CT: Yale University Press.

Oakes, J. (2008). Keeping track: Structuring equality and inequality in an era of accountability. *The Teachers College Record, 110*(3), 700–712.

Odden, A. (2003). Equity and adequacy in school finance today. *Phi Delta Kappan, 85*(2), 120–125.

Odden, A.R. (2011). *Strategic management of human capital in education: Improving instructional practice and student learning in schools.* London: Taylor & Francis.

Odden, A., & Archibald, S. (2001). *Reallocating resources: How to boost student achievement without asking for more.* Thousand Oaks, CA: Corwin Press.

Odden, A., & Kelly, J. (2008). *Strategic management of human capital in education.* Madison, WI: Consortium for Policy Research in Education. Retrieved November 18, 2008, from www.smhc-cpre.org/

Odden, A., & Picus, L. (2011). Improving teaching and learning when budgets are tight. *Phi Delta Kappan, 93*(1): 42–48.

O'Donoghue, T., & Clarke, S.W. (2010). *Leading learning: Process, themes, and issues in international contexts.* London and New York: Routledge.

Orfield, G., & Kornhaber, M. (2001). *Raising standards or raising barriers? Inequality and high-stakes testing in public education.* New York City: Century Foundation.

Organisation for Economic Co-operation and Development. (2007). *No more failures: Ten steps to equity in education.* Proceedings from the Fairness and Inclusion Conference, June, Trondheim, Norway.

Orr, M.T., Byrne-Jimenez, M., McFarlane, P., & Brown, B. (2005). Leading out from low-performing schools: The urban principal experience. *Leadership and Policy Studies in Schools, 4*(1), 23–54.

Payne, C.M. (2008). *So much reform, so little change: The persistence of failure in urban schools.* Cambridge, MA: Harvard Education Press.

Pfeffer, J. (1998). *The human equation: Building profits by putting people first.* Boston: Harvard Business School Press.

Plecki, M., Alejano, C., Lochmiller, C., & Knapp, M. (2006). *Allocating resources and creating incentives to improve teaching and learning.* Seattle, WA: Center for the Study of Teaching & Policy, University of Washington.

Plecki, M., Knapp, M.S., Castañeda, T., Halverson, T., LaSota, R., & Lochmiller, C. (2009). *How leaders invest staffing resources for learning improvement.* Seattle WA: Center for the Study of Teaching & Policy, University of Washington.

Portin, B.S., DeArmond, M., Gundlach, L., & Schneider, P. (2003). *Making sense of leading schools: A national study of the principalship.* Seattle: Center on Reinventing Public Education, University of Washington.

Portin, B.S., & Knapp, M.S. (2011). Expanding learning-focused leadership in US urban schools. In T. Townsend & J. MacBeath (Eds.), *International handbook of leadership for learning* (pp. 501–525). Dordrecht, The Netherlands: Springer Publications.

Portin, B.S., Knapp, M.S., Dareff, S., Feldman, S., Russell, F.A., Samuelson, C., & Yeh, T.L. (2009). *Leadership for learning improvement in urban schools.* Seattle, WA: Center for the Study of Teaching & Policy, University of Washington.

Portin, B.S., Knapp, M. S, Plecki, M.L., & Copland, M.A. (2008). Supporting and guiding learning-focused leadership in US Schools. In J. MacBeath & Y.C. Cheng (Eds.), *Leadership for learning: International perspectives* (pp. 189–203). Rotterdam, The Netherlands: Sense Publishers.

Portin, B.S., Russell, F., Samuelson, C., & Knapp, M.S. (2013). Leading learning-focused teacher leadership in urban high schools. *Journal of School Leadership, 23*(2), 220–252.

Printy, S., Marks, H., & Bowers, A. (2009). Integrated leadership: How principals and teachers share transformational and instructional influence. *Journal of School Leadership, 19*(5), 504–532.

Purkey, S.C., & Smith, M.S. (1985). School reform: The district policy implications of the effective schools literature. *The Elementary School Journal, 85*(3), 353–389.

Ravitch, D., & Viteritti, J.P. (1997). *New schools for a new century: The redesign of urban education.* New Haven, CT: Yale University Press.

Raywid, M. (1996). *Taking stock: The movement to create mini-schools, schools-within-schools, and other small schools.* New York: ERIC Clearinghouse on Urban Education.

Reardon, S., & Robinson, J. (2008). Patterns and trends in racial/ethnic and socioeconomic academic achievement gaps. In H.F. Ladd & E.B. Fiske (Eds.), *Handbook of research in education finance and policy* (pp. 497–516). New York: Routledge.

Reeves, D.B. (2006). *The learning leader: How to focus school improvement for better results.* Alexandria, VA: Association for Supervision & Curriculum Development.

Reis, S.M., McCoach, D.B., Little, C.A., Muller, L.M., & Kaniskan, R.B. (2011). The effects of differentiated instruction and enrichment pedagogy on achievement in five elementary schools. *American Education Research Journal, 48*(2), 462–501.

Resnick, L., & Glennan, T. (2002). Leadership for learning: A theory of action for urban school districts. In A. Hightower, M.S. Knapp, J. Marsh, & M.W. McLaughlin (Eds.), *School districts and instructional renewal* (pp. 160–172). New York: Teachers College Press.

Rice, J. (2003). Investing in teacher quality: A framework of estimating the cost of teacher professional development. In W. Hoy & C. Miskel (Eds.), *Theory and research in educational administration, Volume 2* (pp. 209–233). Greenwich, CT: Information Age Publishing, Inc.

Rice, J., & Schwartz, A. (2008). Toward an understanding of productivity in education. In H. Ladd & E. Fiske (Eds.), *Handbook of research in education finance and policy* (pp. 131–145). New York: Routledge.

Robertson, J., & Timperley, H. (Eds.) (2012). *Leadership and learning.* Thousand Oaks, CA, and London: SAGE Publications.

Robinson, V.M. (2010). From instructional leadership to leadership capabilities: Empirical findings and methodological challenges. *Leadership and Policy in Schools, 9*(1), 1–26.

Robinson, V.M. (2011). *Student-centered leadership.* San Francisco: Jossey-Bass.

Robinson, V.M.J., Lloyd, C.A., & Rowe, K.J. (2008). The impact of student leadership on student outcomes: An analysis of the differential effects of leadership types. *Educational Administration Quarterly, 44,* 635–674.

Rockoff, J.E. (2004). The impact of individual teachers on student achievement: Evidence from panel data. *American Economic Review, 94*(2), 247–252.

Rodriguez, G.M. (2004). Vertical equity in school finance and the potential for increasing school responsiveness to student and staff needs. *Peabody Journal of Education, 79*(3), 7–30.

Ronfeldt, M., Lankford, H., Loeb, S., & Wyckoff, J. (2013). How teacher turnover harms student achievement. *American Educational Research Journal 50*(1), 4–36.

Rothstein, R. (2004). *Class and schools: Using social, economic, and educational reform to close the black-white achievement gap.* New York: Teachers College Press.

Rubenstein, R., Schwartz, A.E., Stiefel, L., & Amor, H. (2007). From districts to schools: The distribution of resources across schools in big city school districts. *Economics of Education Review, 26*(5), 532–545.

Samuels, C. (2011). Cheating scandals intensify focus on test pressure. *Education Week, 30*(37).

Scheurich, J., & Skrla, L. (2003). *Leadership for equity and excellence: Creating high-achievement classrooms, schools, and districts.* Thousand Oaks, CA: Corwin Press.

Schlechty, P. (2009). *Leading for learning: How to transform schools into learning organizations.* San Francisco: Jossey-Bass.

Schwartz, A., Rubenstein, R., & Stiefel, L. (2009). *Why do some schools get more and others less? An examination of school-level funding in New York City.* New York City: Institute of Education and Social Policy, New York University.

Smith, W.F., & Andrews, R.L. (1989). *Instructional leadership: How principals make a difference.* Alexandria, VA: Association for Supervision and Curriculum Development.

Smylie, M. (2010). *Continuous school improvement.* Thousand Oaks, CA: Corwin Press.

Smylie, M., & Wenzel, S. (2006). *Promoting instructional improvement: A strategic human resource management perspective.* Chicago: University of Chicago Press.

Song, J. (2009, June 23). L.A. School board approves huge budget cuts. *The Los Angeles Times.* Retrieved July 3, 2009, from http://latimesblogs.latimes.com/lanow/2009/06/la-school-board-approves-huge-budgetcuts.html

Sorenson, R., & Goldsmith, L. (2013). *The principal's guide to school budgeting.* Thousand Oaks, CA: Corwin Press.

Southern Regional Education Board. (2006). *Good principals aren't born–they're mentored: Are we investing enough to get the school leaders we need?* Atlanta, GA: Author.

Spillane, J.P. (1998). State policy and the non-monolithic nature of the local school district: Organizational and professional considerations. *American Educational Research Journal, 35*(1), 33–63.

Spillane, J.P. (2000). Cognition and policy implementation: District policymakers and the reform of mathematics education. *Cognition and Instruction, 18*(2), 141–179.

Spillane, J. (2006). *Distributed leadership.* San Francisco: Jossey-Bass.

Spillane, J.P., & Thompson, C.L. (1997). Reconstructing conceptions of local capacity: The local education agency's capacity for ambitious instructional reform. *Educational Evaluation & Policy Analysis, 19*(2), 185–203.

Springer, M., Houck, E., & Guthrie, J. (2008). History and scholarship. In H. Ladd & E. Fiske (Eds.), *Handbook of research in education finance and policy* (pp. 3–22). New York: Routledge.

Steffes. T.L., (2008). Solving the "rural school problem": New state aid, standards, and supervision of local schools, 1900–1933. *History of Education Quarterly, 48*(2), 181–220.

Stein, M.K., & Nelson, B. (2003). Leadership content knowledge. *Educational Evaluation and Policy Analysis, 25*(4), 423–448.

Stoelinga, S.R., & Mangin, M.M. (2008). Drawing conclusions about instructional teacher leadership. In M.M. Mangin & S.R. Stoelinga (Eds.), *Effective teacher leadership: Using research to inform and reform* (pp. 183–192). New York: Teachers College Press.

Stoll, L., Fink, D., & Earl, L. (2002). *It's about learning [and it's about time]: What's in it for schools?* London and New York: RoutledgeFalmer.

Strauss, A., & Corbin, J. (1998). *Basics of qualitative research: Techniques and procedures for developing grounded theory.* Thousand Oaks, CA: SAGE Publications.

Strunk, K.O., & Grissom, J.A. (2010). Do strong unions shape district policies? Collective bargaining, teacher contract restrictiveness, and the political power of teachers' unions. *Educational Evaluation & Policy Analysis, 32*(3), 389–406.

Supovitz, J.A. (2002). Developing communities of instructional practice. *Teachers College Record, 104*(8), 1591–1626.

Supovitz, J. (2006). *The case for district-based reform.* Cambridge, MA: Harvard Education Press.

Supovitz, J., & Klein, V. (2003). *Mapping a course for improved student learning: How innovative schools use student performance data to guide improvement.* Philadelphia: Consortium for Policy Research in Education.

Supovitz, J., Sirinides, P., & May, H. (2010). How principals and peers influence teaching and learning. *Educational Administration Quarterly, 46*(1), 31–56.

Swaffield, S., & MacBeath, J. (2009). Leadership for learning. In J. Macbeath & N. Dempster (Eds.), *Connecting leadership and learning: Principles for practice* (pp. 32–52). London and New York: Routledge.

Swinnerton, J.A. (2006). *Learning to lead what you "don't (yet) know": District leaders engaged in instructional reform* (Unpublished doctoral dissertation). University of Washington, Seattle, WA.

Swinnerton, J. (2007). Brokers and boundary crossers in an urban school district: Understanding central office coaches as instructional leaders. *Journal of School Leadership, 17*(2), 195–221.

Talbert, J.E. (2011). Collaborative inquiry to expand student achievement in New York City Schools. In J. O'Day, C. Bitter, & L. Gomez, L. (Eds.), *Education reform in New York City: Ambitious change in the nation's most complex school system* (pp. 131–155). Cambridge, MA: Harvard Education Press.

Taylor, J.E. (2008). Instructional coaching. In M.M. Mangin, & S.R. Stoelinga (Eds.), *Effective teacher leadership: Using research to inform and reform* (pp. 10–35). New York: Teachers College Press.

Thacker, T., Bell, J.S., & Schargel, F.P. (2009). *Creating school cultures that embrace learning: What successful leaders do.* Larchmont, NY: Eye on Education.

Theoharis, G. (2007). Social justice educational leaders and resistance: Toward a theory of social justice leadership. *Educational Administration Quarterly, 43*(2), 221–258.

Thompson, C.L., & Zeuli, J.S. (1999). The frame and the tapestry: Standards-based reform and professional development. In L. Darling-Hammond & G. Sykes (Eds.), *Teaching as the learning profession: Handbook of policy & practice* (pp. 341–375). San Francisco: Jossey-Bass.

Thompson, D., Crampton, F., & Wood, C. (2012). *Money and schools.* Larchmont, NY: Eye on Education.

Tichy, N., (2002). *The cycle of leadership: How great leaders teach their companies to win.* New York: Harper Business.

Tomlinson, C.A., & McTighe, J. (2006). *Integrating differentiated instruction and understanding by design: Connecting content and kids* (pp. 179–184). Alexandria VA: Association for Supervision and Curriculum Development.

Townsend, T., & MacBeath, J. (2011). *International handbook of leadership for learning.* Dordrecht, The Netherlands: Springer.

Tschannen-Moran, M. (2004). *Trust matters: Leadership for successful schools.* San Francisco: Jossey-Bass.

Turnbull, B., Riley, D.L., Arcaira, E.R., Anderson, K.L., & MacFarlane, J. (2013). *Forging a stronger principalship: Six districts begin the principal pipeline initiative.* New York City: The Wallace Foundation.

Underwood, J. (1994). School finance as vertical equity. *University of Michigan Journal of Law Reform, 28,* 493.

Usher, A. (2011, December). *AYP results for 2010–11.* Washington, DC: Center on Education Policy.

Valli, L., & Buese, D. (2007). The changing roles of teachers in an era of high-stakes accountability. *American Educational Research Journal, 44*(3), 519–558.

The Wallace Foundation. (2007, March). *Getting principal mentoring right: Lessons from the field.* New York: Author.

Wayman, J.C., Midgley, S., & Stringfield, S. (2007). Leadership for data-based decision-making: Collaborative educator teams. In A.B. Danzig, K.M. Borman, B.A. Jones, & W.F. Wright (Eds.), *Learner-centered leadership: Research, policy, & practice* (pp. 189–206). Mahwah, NJ: Lawrence Erlbaum Associates.

Woodworth, K., David, J. L, Guha, R., Wang, H., & Lopez Torkos, A., (2008*). San Francisco Bay area KIPP schools, a study of early implementation and achievement: Final report.* Menlo Park, CA: SRI, International.

Yamasaki, J., & Goes, L. (2009). *The distribution of highly qualified, experienced teachers: Challenges and opportunities—A research and policy brief.* Washington DC: National Comprehensive Center for Teacher Quality.

Yin, R. (2003). *Case study research: Design and methods* (3rd edition). Thousand Oaks, CA: SAGE.

Ylimaki, R. (2007). Instructional leadership in challenging U.S. Schools. *International Studies in Educational Administration, 35*(3), 11–19.

York-Barr, J., & Duke, K. (2004). What do we know about teacher leadership? Findings from two decades of scholarship. *Review of Educational Research, 74*(3), 255–316.

Zohar, A., Degani, A., & Vaaknin, E. (2001). Teachers' beliefs about low-achieving students and higher-order thinking. *Teaching and Teacher Education, 17,* 469–485.

INDEX

Riehl, C. 127, 201
Riley, D. L. 204
Robertson, J., & Timperley, H. 9
Robinson, V. M. J. 4, 58, 135
Robinson, V. M. J., et al. 10, 31, 42, 60
Rockoff, J. E. 129
Rodriguez, G. M. 158
Ronfeldt, M., et al. 129
Rothstein, R. 157
Rubenstein, R. 125, 162

Samuels, C. 204
Scheurich, J. & Skrla, L. 153
Schlechty, P. 9, 20
school improvement or change processes 56
School Reform Team 69, 72, 97, 108,
   112–13, 137–8, 189
School Support Organization (SSO) 20;
   see also New York City/Empowerment
   Schools Organization
Schwartz, A. E., et al. 125–6, 162
Senior Achievement Facilitators 147
"silo'ing" of central office functions 93,
   95, 105
Smith, W. F., & Andrews, R. L. 59
Smylie, M. 98
Smylie, M., & Wenzel, S. 135
Song, J. 86
Sorenson, R. & Goldsmith, L. 127
Southern Regional Education Board 56
Spillane, J. P. 10
Spillane, J. P., & Thompson, C. L. 83, 85, 102
Springer, M., et al. 157
Springfield MA Public Schools 6, 21, 36,
   43, 65, 70, 71, 73, 77, 152, 212
staffing: challenges in demanding contexts
   128–30; cultivating supply related to
   learning improvement 130; current and
   potential sources of 134; reallocating and
   repurposing 130; resource investments,
   types of 130–3; strengthening capacity
   of 129, 130
stakeholder resistance see political
   dynamics of learning-focused leadership
Steffes, T. L. 84
Stein, M. K., & Nelson, B. 57, 64, 83–5
Stoelinga, S. R., & Mangin, M. M. 11
Stoll, L., et al. 4
Strauss, A., & Corbin, J. 214
Strunk, K. O., & Grissom, J. A. 154
Student Achievement Coordinator see
   leadership roles

student learning 7, 9–11, 13, 15–16, 18,
   26–7, 36, 47, 51, 60, 69, 94, 102, 121,
   124, 136, 147, 183–4, 200–01; belief
   in capabilities for 31–2; influence of
   learning-focused leadership on 10,
   201–2; as paramount duty and focus of
   leadership 208
study design, 211–16
Study of Leadership for Learning
   Improvement 4, 5–7, 21, 24–5, 54–55,
   181, 201
study strands: investment of resources for
   equitable learning improvement (strand
   3) 6, 121–2, 153; leadership for learning
   improvement in the school (strand 1)
   5, 21–2, 54–5; transformation of the
   district central office's leadership for
   learning improvement (strand 2) 6,
   79–80
supervisory leaders, leadership: engaging
   teachers 40–2; informal dimensions
   of 41; shift in roles of 39, 41; see also
   leadership roles and positions
Supovitz, J. A. 24, 146
Supovitz, J. A., & Klein, V. 47
Supovitz, J. A., et al. 10, 130
support for leaders' professional learning
   see professional learning
Swaffield, S., & MacBeath, J. 4
Swinnerton, J. A. 56, 85, 146

Talbert, J. E. ix, 12, 35, 136, 143
Taylor, J. E. 11, 27, 56
teacher leadership 5, 10, 22, 38–9, 62, 66,
   138, 140; clarifying role ambiguity 11,
   62–3; normalizing, in schools 62, 198;
   role 43, 54
Teacher on Special Assignment (TOSA)
   136
team-based instructional leadership in
   schools 187–8; challenges and prospects
   facing 50–1; creating "space" for 36–7;
   resources for 50; team cohesion 38; see
   also instructional leadership teams
team leadership 29, 38–40; dynamics
   of teams in schools 28–9; engaging
   diversity 45; to foster team dialogue
   about teaching and learning 38–9; as a
   teaching role 39
team-oriented school culture: cultural
   challenges facing 34; fostering, building
   24, 33–4, 40, 72

Printed in Great Britain
by Amazon